"The radio bug bit Rob Quicke as a student. After discovering the magic of audio media, he went on to successfully apply for a radio license. Here's a truth: Rob's passion, belief and determination have been as important in his success story as his broadcasting skills and training and his gift as an educator. Rob's new book, *Finding Your Voice in Radio, Audio, and Podcast Production* offers a 'journey of self-discovery' approach to audio. Breaking it into easily accessible practical pieces, you'll learn the stages: Discoverer, Developer, Deliverer, Decoder. Under these, he drills down offering methods to teach and help you find your authentic voice. Become the communicator you've dreamed of becoming. Buy the book. Benefit from this wisdom and experience."

– **Valerie Geller,** *international broadcast consultant and author of* Creating Powerful Radio: A Communicator's Handbook for News, Talk, Information and Personality *and* Beyond Powerful Radio: A Communicator's Guide to the Internet Age – News, Talk, Information and Personality for Broadcasting, Podcasting, Satellite and Internet

"Rob Quicke lays out a philosophy of what it takes to create great audio content, with an emphasis on the role of personal awareness and discovery. He reminds us that broadcast radio and the wider world of digital audio platforms all offer the power to inform, entertain and awe."

– **Paul McLane,** *Editor in Chief,* Radio World

"A fantastic academic, practical and exploratory work that asks the question, 'What promotes you to first press the record button?' and much more when it comes to a passion for radio throughout one's life."

– **Barry Rooke,** *Executive Director, National Campus and Community Radio Association (Canada)*

"This book is a practical guide to creating audio content. It's not just about learning; it's about doing, growing, and ultimately expressing your ideas with confidence. The blend of theory and hands-on exercises though makes this more than just a book; it's a roadmap to finding your voice. For anyone interested in audio content creation, this book is an essential read. It culminates in R.E.A.L. communication – creating content that is Relatable, Engaging, Authentic, and Liberating."

– **Bradley C. Freeman,** *Ph.D. Associate Dean (Education) and Professor of Mass Communication, School of Arts, Sunway University, Malaysia*

FINDING YOUR VOICE IN RADIO, AUDIO, AND PODCAST PRODUCTION

This book provides a unique identity-centered approach to radio, audio, and podcast production which encourages readers to build their confidence and create audio content that matters to them.

Written for those just starting out in audio production and focusing on the process of their self-development, readers will learn how to use sound to express themselves in a variety of ways and to create powerful stories in the process – all with the tools already available to them. At the center of this approach is the author's R.E.A.L. method, referring to the creation of audio that is relatable, engaging, authentic, and liberating. Students will learn to apply this concept to each step of the production process, from planning and writing through to interviewing, broadcasting, and responding to feedback. By the end of this book readers will have developed a working knowledge of podcast, audio, and radio production alongside their own means of self-expression.

Supported by exercises and interviews with audio practitioners throughout, *Finding Your Voice in Radio, Audio, and Podcast Production* is a key resource for anyone approaching radio, audio, or podcasting for the first time.

A supporting companion website with Instructor and Student Resources is available at www.robquicke.com.

Rob Quicke is director and professor at the W. Page Pitt School of Journalism and Mass Communications at Marshall University, USA.

FINDING YOUR VOICE IN RADIO, AUDIO, AND PODCAST PRODUCTION

Rob Quicke

Routledge
Taylor & Francis Group

NEW YORK AND LONDON

Designed cover image: © Erubbey Cantoral / Getty Images

First published 2024
by Routledge
605 Third Avenue, New York, NY 10158

and by Routledge
4 Park Square, Milton Park, Abingdon, Oxon, OX14 4RN

Routledge is an imprint of the Taylor & Francis Group, an informa business

© 2024 Rob Quicke

Library of Congress Cataloging-in-Publication Data
Names: Quicke, Robert, author.
Title: Finding your voice in radio, audio, and podcast production / Rob Quicke.
Description: New York, NY : Routledge, 2024. | Includes bibliographical references and index.
Identifiers: LCCN 2023037822 (print) | LCCN 2023037823 (ebook) | ISBN 9781032204789 (hardback) | ISBN 9781032204765 (paperback) | ISBN 9781003263739 (ebook)
Subjects: LCSH: Radio authorship. | Podcasting. | Self-actualization (Psychology) | Expression (Philosophy)
Classification: LCC PN1991.7 .Q53 2024 (print) | LCC PN1991.7 (ebook) | DDC 791.4402/32--dc23/eng/20231006
LC record available at https://lccn.loc.gov/2023037822
LC ebook record available at https://lccn.loc.gov/2023037823

ISBN: 978-1-032-20478-9 (hbk)
ISBN: 978-1-032-20476-5 (pbk)
ISBN: 978-1-003-26373-9 (ebk)

DOI: 10.4324/9781003263739

Typeset in Galliard
by MPS Limited, Dehradun

Access the Instructor and Student Resources: www.robquicke.com

*Dedicated to my Mother and Father (Carol & Michael)
who have always encouraged me to find my voice*

CONTENTS

ACKNOWLEDGMENTS

I am most grateful for the following people who helped me get to the finish line:

First and foremost, my deep thanks to my father for the inspiration, encouragement, and extraordinary support in the writing of this book!

My incredibly supportive family: Lori, Elliot, and Sophie (and Captain the immortal cat).

My ever encouraging Mum & Dad (Michael & Carol Quicke – the Cambridge family).

Diane & Dwayne Claasen (with loving remembrance for Dwayne).

Russ, Chandelle, Dellen, and Sam (the Kansas family).

Simon, Dara, Milo, Luca, and Anton (the London family).

Dr. Matthew Crick for excellent advice along the way and calming strategies in stressful moments.

Dr. Nick Hirshon for superb support, guidance, and witty quips!

Dr. Diana Peck for kind encouragement and spiritual wisdom!

Dr. Joann Lee for always believing in me and being a great mentor long after we have both left WPUNJ.

Greg Mattison for great feedback on technical equipment and specifically on Chapters 6 and 7.

Nick Sciortino for detailed feedback on Chapter 8.

Dr. Tim Craig for herculean efforts in copyediting my first draft and going above and beyond as a friend and good bloke!

Peter Kreten, my Chi-Town brother from WXAV 88.3 FM – Saint Xavier University, Chicago.

R. Todd Richards from WBWC 88.3 The Sting, Hello Cleveland!

Dr. Charles Bailey and WMUL at Marshall University for inspiration.

Robert Taylor and Lance Liguez for good feedback advice.

Professor Elizabeth Birge for carrying the torch for the Dead Podcasters Society.

Dave & Yolanda Kozuha – we can because we coffee!

Greg Buck for building inspiration.

The Dead Podcasters Society (first chapter): Marc Agustin, El Barba, Jonny Buffa, Jess Carfello, Vincent Civetta, Ryan Cormier, Daniel Cruz, Eric Garza, Nahum Jukes, Gavin McKeown, Rob Meyer, Justin Reynoso-Dume, Steffany Rios, Nick Sciortino, and Jenna Vergara.

Aakif Khan for assistance with citations and references.

The superb team at Routledge – Hannah McKeating and Elizabeth Cox.

Everyone who was interviewed for this book and generously gave their time and insights.

INTRODUCTION

Introduction

I was 60 seconds away from creating a moment of radio history. In one minute, my friend Damian and I, both of us students, were about to go live on the first ever FM student radio station in the United Kingdom. It was an unprecedented moment for us. I was terrified and wondered whether I would either faint, throw up, or be rendered speechless when the mics went live in 60 seconds. I felt anxiety from unadulterated adrenaline coursing through my veins, very little sleep the night before, and the feeling that we were about to do something that really *mattered*.

Over the previous three years I had been involved in strenuous efforts to establish and launch the first ever student radio station in the UK, formed by students at Oxford University. We had been told repeatedly that it would never happen. The prospect of a group of students being awarded an FM license from the Radio Authority in the UK was remote if not impossible. At least, that's what had been communicated to us. Our attempt to change the Authority's mind required an all-out effort. My primary residence became the radio station studios rather than the lecture halls or library, much to the chagrin of my professors. My passion for radio became all-consuming, even if I had little idea what I was doing. To say that we were raw and unpolished would be an understatement. But we were committed and enthusiastic.

DOI: 10.4324/9781003263739-1

Against the odds, we won the FM license, in part because of our audacious programming commitment to create radio that reflected the voices, views and needs of the students and residents of Oxford. This was a first for the radio audiences of the UK and a surprise for those working in the radio industry. It caught some off-guard. Nationally renowned BBC Radio One DJ at the time Kevin Greening said, "To be honest, I never thought it would happen. I wish them well" (Allen, 1997, pp. 39–42). The two students who came up with the idea, Nick Molden and Philip Weiss, were invited to Buckingham Palace and recognized by the Queen for their remarkable accomplishment. We generated a flurry of national publicity, as British newspapers such as *The Times, The Guardian,* and *The Independent* wrote stories about us. My favorite quote was from *The Sunday Telegraph's* Peter Elson, who wrote, "Big-time university radio, more synonymous with North American campus cool than Oxford fogeyism, has finally hit Britain at the nation's oldest university" (Elson, 1995, p. 17). We were legit, and now we were about to take to the airwaves.

All that led up to this exciting moment. Perhaps a pressure to meet expectations contributed to the heaviness I was now feeling, with just a few seconds to go before we were live on air. Damian and I just looked at each other. We had no prior professional radio experience between us. *Ten seconds to go.* I already had a dry mouth, and I scanned the studio for a bottle of water. *Five seconds.* I looked at my show scripts and copious notes and found it difficult to focus on my scrawled handwriting surrounding lists of bullet points.

I hope the audience realizes that we are just students doing this, I thought. What did *we* have to say that people needed to hear? Could we communicate to the audience something they would not hear anywhere else? Would people take us seriously?

3... 2 ... 1 ... The mics opened. *We were live.*

—

That moment was over twenty-five years ago! Now, after years of working in radio, audio, and podcasting, I strongly believe that students can produce truly remarkable content. Sometimes they can produce audio that can compete with, and even surpass, those who work in audio and radio professionally. They can produce podcasts and audio pieces that are astonishingly powerful. I have witnessed several occasions when everyone in the room recognizes that they are hearing something special, something memorable. Those moments are rare but possible.

By the way, and this is important, when I use the word *student* in this book I am not just thinking of younger people in college. Obviously my own student experiences, and a lifetime of teaching university students since, colors some of this book's feel. After all, that's why I have such a passion for audio. But, please realize that I use the word *student* (as in the next paragraphs) for people of all ages, not just for "formal" students. Indeed, it's for anyone who would like to develop their audio production experience and catch the passion, for learners in all kinds of situations.

All my experiences have led me to believe that compelling and powerful audio can be produced by students, even shortly after embarking upon a course that teaches audio and radio production. It does not always have to be the *end product* of a specific course, of college graduation, or being exclusively attainable by those who go on to work in radio or audio professionally. Indeed, I believe that sometimes a student and non-professional can have an advantage when it comes to producing unique content. In short, students can create audio and radio genuinely different from the professionals.

This book defines audio as *including* radio content, podcasts, and audio more generally, which may include items such as personal recordings like diaries, travelogs and even ambient and experimental sound art recordings. I also do not assume that audio must always be created to be heard by another person. Indeed, there is a good reason why you should *not share some audio you create*, and this book explores the benefits of doing that.

Admittedly, student-produced audio may have a poor reputation because, from a technical standpoint, it is perceived as raw, unpolished and perhaps poorly edited and mixed. You might think such weaknesses disqualify and nullify its audience appeal. However, I argue that these characteristics distinguish student-produced audio as being authentic, unfiltered, and emotionally potent. Technically poorly produced content must never be prematurely discarded. Its ideas and raw emotional power capture authentic expression. Even though we'll cover how to use technology to create audio content, this book does not consider technical expertise as being a barrier to start creating meaningful audio.

Rather, I have developed a hands-on, practical approach to the business of creating audio content. Recognizing that a student starts from a point of lacking the technical skills to produce polished, well-edited audio, the objective is to develop their working knowledge of audio production, making the most of their personality and expressiveness. The goal is to encourage students' passion and creativity in the learning process.

To this end, I present a four-stage journey, from *discoverer* to *decoder*, which results in R.E.A.L. communication.

The R.E.A.L. journey

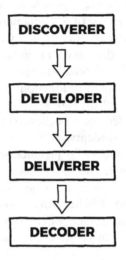

FIGURE I.1 The R.E.A.L. Journey.

Beginning the journey as *a discoverer* involves important work on two aspects. It introduces you to the wonders of audio, its qualities and potential. And more importantly, it encourages you to find out more about yourself as a thinker and communicator. Many will find that learning *who you are* in the context of audio production is a fresh exercise, which will stretch and (hopefully) invigorate you as you find your own voice and discern what particular interests and concerns really matter to you. Working with yourself at first, positive *discovery* will enrich you as a person even as you are preparing to create audio. It's one of the great by-products of the learning process. Rather than plunging into the technical nuts and bolts of audio production, we delve first into *who we are* as potential communicators. We all have so much to learn about ourselves. Self-awareness is the communicator's great strength and asset, and yet so many people are happy to talk without having any.

Having gained greater self-awareness and direction, you can move onto the *developer* stage of the journey. Here there are more practicalities of audio production, facing key questions about the kind of audio you intend to produce and the mechanics involved. By now you should be aware of your own strengths, and how you would create content to meet what's required.

The third stage in the journey is being *a deliverer*, when you share with the world the finished audio content you have created. Whether it's live broadcasting on radio or livestream or an edited audio piece, you are delivering content that is carefully planned and produced for an audience to hear.

The final stage in the journey is the *decoder*. Once an audio piece has been completed, it's rarely returned to. Yet, if a piece is successful, can we learn exactly what made it so? Can we also seek to understand why something did *not* work, or did not achieve its full potential? Perhaps even more useful is returning to some work after a long period of time and realizing what could be improved that you did not realize at the time. The *decoder* phase explores the usefulness of feedback, both from yourself, and from others. It's a part of the journey when you break things down and understand how your audio works. The process allows you to decode other people's audio, too, and learn from them.

From my experience of teaching audio, I am convinced that this process of moving from *discoverer* to *decoder* is fundamental to successful audio production. Miss out on any part of the journey and a student is likely to struggle in finding purpose and confidence. This is especially true for a student who fails to do the necessary introspective work at the beginning. Even if they end up in their dream audio job, they can still feel imposter syndrome because they never did the important work of understanding themselves first. Understanding yourself is how you *find your voice*.

Vitally, this journey is accompanied by the acronym R.E.A.L., which describes the distinguishing hallmarks of what audio sounds like from someone *who has gone through this journey of self-discovery*, from *discoverer* to *decoder*.

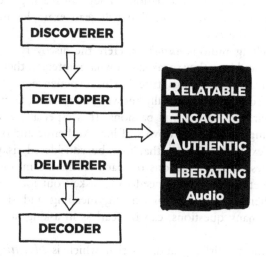

FIGURE I.2 R.E.A.L. audio.

First, audio needs to be *relatable*. Relatable audio brings listeners *into* the story by carefully leaving room for them to *feel* that they can identify with its content. Sometimes its content will be unfamiliar to listeners, but careful consideration of their place within its story, allowing them to absorb its details and emotions, moves them toward identification. You encourage them to relate to something that may be new and challenging by inviting them to enter its dynamics. At the end of this book I give a powerful example of how Ukrainian students created audio in their awful wartorn circumstances, which enabled listeners back in the safe USA to feel their emotion and visualize their situation. Genuinely relatable audio takes audiences into identifying with the speakers and their situation! Have you ever listened to something in your car which is so gripping that you cannot stop listening even after you have arrived at your destination? Such stories with rich use of sounds, music, and dialogue can take listeners to another place. It can move an audience to feel comfort, or horror, or amusement, or even bewilderment.

Engaging audio captures a listener's attention and interest. Each listener passes through a range of life experiences, of highs and lows in a wide range of situations, and engaging audio connects with them where they are. Unafraid to express the full range of human emotions, including vulnerability, its creators share themselves with listeners empathizing in return. It shares in the human search that seeks to find deeper meaning in their circumstances. A podcast about losing a loved one, or celebrating an important achievement, will readily find an audience that can identify with the range of emotions. I have found, working with younger students, that their unrestrained emotions, not yet molded into acceptable norms of adult emotional behavior, can really connect with listeners in their situations. They can reach places that professionally produced audio may not. You will read examples in some of the interviews later in the book.

Third, compelling audio is *authentic*. Here the discovery stage bears fruit. Who is speaking and how they speak about what matters to them comes across genuinely to hearers. It "rings true." This experience of "ringing true" depends on the communicators really knowing themselves, their strengths and weaknesses, their own stories and passions. It is especially evident in storytelling, navigating the ups and downs of life. Authentic audio also describes how someone exploring a topic that may be considered risky, obscure, or brave, recognizes their reservations or fears. Authentic means holding very little back. Sometimes questions need to be asked out loud. Students especially, who inherit a world of preexisting meaning and signification and inevitably have many questions, can be fearless in asking about what really matters.

Finally, the most satisfying audio is that which is *liberating*. Its content invites listeners to become freer or less oppressed through fresh understanding. Again, as you will see in some of the interviews later in this book, such audio is arguably life-changing. Communicators, who ask big questions, challenge conventional wisdom and understanding, are liberators actively engaged with freeing themselves and their audiences from concepts, thoughts and structures (both physical and abstract) that can confine. It is a bold claim, but liberating content can encourage understanding of fresh possibilities and even a sense of purpose.

Of course, I am focusing on the positive side of R.E.A.L., in its relatability, engagement, authenticity, and liberation. We are all too aware that there is a dark side to audio's power when these characteristics are allied to content that conveys hate speech and outright untruths. Communicators with passion about – for example – conspiracy theories, can equally develop these qualities in unhappily negative ways. We should not become more effective communicators only to use our influence to persuade others of misinformation or to advance divisive ideologies.

In this book I seek to be positive. You will likely make mistakes along the way, but that's progress too. By learning what does not work, you understand what does. Dotted throughout this book are a variety of exercises and guidelines that ask you to try something that you might not normally consider. You'll also read stories from people just like you, who have experienced remarkable moments on their audio production journeys. It's important for me that this book encourages you to discover more of who you are, and where you are.

The French fashion icon Coco Chanel (1883–1971) famously said, "The most courageous act is still to think for yourself. Aloud" (Eisen, 1992, p. 39). What Coco Chanel did not make explicit is that thinking out loud can still be a private experience. No one has to hear your courageous thoughts until you are ready to share them. The R.E.A.L. approach encourages today's students to express their own thoughts; to be on their own journey of expression.

My convictions about the power of audio led me to found College Radio Day, which morphed into World College Radio Day. Over the last decade it has grown to involve over 1,000 college radio stations in fifty-seven countries around the world. Listening in, I am often unable to understand the language, yet I can grasp the essential meaning of their communication. It's emotionally powerful to tune into students in Thailand, France, Mexico, Ghana, Israel, and other countries as they broadcast with pride and excitement. As cultural ambassadors, they play music and content that proudly reflects their country and story. They are R.E.A.L. communicators!

I know, from my experience of managing college radio stations in the USA, that only a small number of students will end up in the professional audio industry. Similarly, most students who produce podcasts will not do that for a living. For the minority who seek a path into the audio and radio industry, I hope this book will help facilitate your entry into getting such a job.

However, I believe that there are principles, concepts, and strategies in this book that apply to a great variety of careers. The audio journey helps all readers develop skills, methods, and practices to communicate your ideas and thoughts.

How this book works

The following chapters are divided into four parts according to the four D's of the journey. Critical to the effectiveness of this book are the exercises in each chapter. I encourage you to treat all these exercises with a high degree of intentionality and seriousness. Also I encourage you to retain your exercise answers and responses in one place, digitally or physically. Review them later when you have gained more experience, and you are likely to be surprised to realize just how much you have developed and progressed since you started. As you progress through the book, you will, at the midpoint, be asked to create a particular in-depth exercise that will offer you an opportunity to create something spectacular, a piece of work of which you can be proud.

It is my hope that this book will encourage, inspire, and equip you with the lifelong tools and methods you will need to succeed in life. From firsthand experience, I have seen students grow in confidence and ability, building upon their audio and radio experiences to become more fully realized in their self-identity. That's what happens when you find your voice. You realize *who you are* and *what you want to say.* A graduating student once said to me, "I hate to leave, I really enjoyed bringing my ideas to life! It's a shame it has to end." *End?* Not at all. This is merely the beginning of a lifetime of authentic communication. I am asking you to be brave and take this journey. *Let's start.*

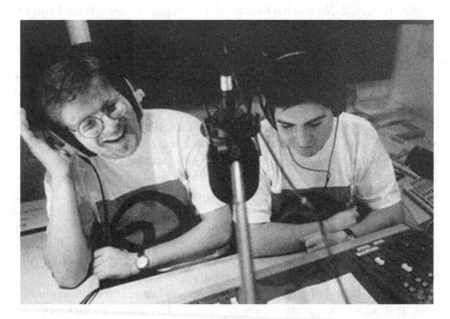

FIGURE I.3 Rob Quicke (left) and Damian Radcliffe launching Oxygen Student Radio in 1997 (Photo credit: Rob Quicke archives).

References

Allen, L. (1997, September). Making student radio history. *High Fliers*, pp. 39–42.

Eisen, A. (1992). *Believing in ourselves: The wisdom of women*. Andrews and McMeel.

Elson, P. (1995, November 19). Oxford students take to airwaves on Oxygen radio. *The Sunday Telegraph*, 17.

PART I

Discoverer

You begin with an audience of one: *You*. That is the safest and most creative way to start the journey of finding your voice. As a *discoverer* you shouldn't worry about mistakes and flaws – feeling comfortable in front of a microphone is your goal. Next comes the question of what you will say into the microphone. As you explore your self-identity, you will experience growth in self-confidence and the vital realization that you have something unique to say.

DOI: 10.4324/9781003263739-2

1

WELCOME DISCOVERER

Creating audio within reach

First thoughts: *The story of Nervous Steve:* **How creating radio transformed a student's life and placed him on a pathway to success**

Picture this: The inside of a college radio station studio, with peeling paint and torn music posters on the wall. Standing next to the mic, all alone, is a male student, a freshman, with blood on his hands. Blood is on his script as well. He's having a nosebleed while being on the air. He looks terrified.

The student is Stephan Bisaha and it was his first time live on the radio on his own. He remembers: "I got a nosebleed! That's how nervous I was, in the middle of this on-air live broadcasting, blood dripping from my nose onto this sheet of paper that I was reading," From that first day, his anxiety about going on the air would create a reputation and he was soon called "Nervous Steve" by the other students at the station. Even though the students used it affectionately. Stephan sighs "there was part of me that was disappointed to get the name of Nervous Steve. But it was an accurate one."

The reason for his anxiety was that he wanted to perform well, especially after the professor of his freshman seminar class had given all the students a cold dose of reality. "I remember, the professor had talked about all these professionals, all these former students of hers, that were working at NBC and other places, who were doing well. And I raised my hand, and I said, 'Those are your best students, because you're using them as an example, but what happens to the average communication student?' And she said, 'Well, *they don't make it.*' And that was a very sharp early wakeup call! My nervousness stemmed completely from the idea of not being one of the ones that made it!"

But Stephan was passionately committed to college radio and continued to put many hours in his time at the station. "Anxiety is a good thing. It keeps

DOI: 10.4324/9781003263739-3

you focused. But what was so great about college radio was that it gave me the time to work through that. It gave me the time to get the hours on the mic, to really get a certain level of comfort that I wouldn't have had otherwise. It was very important to just get those reps in."

Did it help him find his "voice"? In a way it did. "Maybe it helped me realize that was *not* what my radio voice was. Because I was very much doing the morning-zoo-style-DJ, with this crazy inflection up and down. That is not what I loved when I listened to the radio. I very much fell in love with NPR at the time and public radio. So, I didn't develop what I consider my voice now on the radio there. But I developed the confidence to find that voice later on … it allowed me to eventually have comfort with my voice down the line."

What had given Stephan the desire to persevere with radio? He explains the memorable moment came when he was listening to an episode of WNYC's *Radiolab* and was "astonished by the empathy that episode elicited, the raw emotion in someone's voice. The production value of everything was incredible, but really it was how well connected I felt to the people with the stories I was hearing. I remember I grabbed my new laptop, I sprinted into my best friend's dorm, and I was like, '*I need to show you this!*'" In the excitement of the moment, the laptop was fumbled and dropped, falling on the floor. Picking it up, Stephan saw that his new laptop now had a massive dent in it. He reflected on this new imperfection. "Yes, I nearly broke this new laptop, but for the rest of the four years I was at university, I had this laptop with a giant dent in the corner that made me think, *I want to create stories good enough and with enough emotion and empathy, that it causes someone to get so excited that they dent their new laptop!*" Stephan's love of radio was clearly growing.

During his remaining time at university, Stephan rose through the ranks and eventually became Program Director for the radio station, the highest student position available. After graduating from William Paterson University with a BA in Communication, he was accepted to do an MA in Journalism at Columbia University and thereafter applied to be a prestigious Ray Kroc fellow at NPR. He was one of just three graduates accepted for this fellowship in the entire country. These days he's the Wealth and Poverty Reporter in the Gulf States Newsroom, which is a collaboration between NPR, WBHM in Alabama, WWNO in New Orleans, and Mississippi Public Broadcasting. His radio stories are played across the country, and millions of people hear his voice.

So, how does he feel about his Nervous Steve days now? He smiles. "It is rather shocking how far I have come as far as the craft, and how I was just stumbling on that mic and nose bleeding on the air, just being absolutely terrible at the job and so darn nervous. And now here I am."

Stephan pauses before offering his concluding thoughts. "It almost feels like looking back on a different person." But would he, if he had been around

FIGURE 1.1 Stephen Bisaha (Photo Credit: Kacy Meinecke).

at the time, tell that student to be less anxious and nervous? Stephan gives an emphatic *no*. "I would not go back and tell that college student to relax, because I think that nervousness was *incredibly useful*. I think that fear was definitely helpful."

Stephan recognizes that his experiences, all the highs and the lows, have led him to where he is today, and he would not change anything about his journey so far (See Figure 1.1).

Your journey begins

This book begins differently. Many audio production books begin with instructions about meeting certain technical standards of the medium, presuming that a level of technical proficiency must be achieved before you can say anything worthwhile and start producing audio. It's almost as though anyone learning about audio has first to understand what makes for best production practice, found in professional audio and radio environments. Of course, the end result if you are producing content professionally does require high technical competence. But I am convinced that before you start *developing* and *delivering* content, a *discoverer* stage is needed. This first stage enables a wider range of students, including the majority for whom it will not be their long-term profession, to have as accessible an entrance as possible into the world of audio. This book is also different because it asks that you first seek within yourself to discover who you are and what you would like to say before you create audio for an audience.

It might not seem like it, but what you are holding right now is a kind of ticket. A ticket for a journey through four stages: *discoverer, developer, deliverer,* and *decoder.* It's a journey I have traveled. You will see in the various interviews through this book how contrasting these journeys are. I began when I was sixteen and volunteered during my school breaks to work for the radio station at the large Addenbrooke's Hospital in Cambridge, UK. Of course it was a simple beginning and, as a brash teenager, I had little apprehension like Nervous Steve. One of my jobs involved visiting the hospital wards to gain music requests from patients. But three things happened to me.

First, I fell under the spell of radio. I discovered what an extraordinary medium it is, able to communicate so intimately and directly. I was captivated by its unique qualities, by the sheer wonder of radio. From that moment its potential captured my interest and I began my lifelong journey.

Second, something happened that was more subtle and more important. I found working with radio helped me discover truths about myself. I needed to find my own voice, and I discovered this involved much more than the mechanics for using my voice well (which do matter). Finding my voice launched me into deeper issues of learning who I was and what mattered in my own story. It exposed me to a demanding journey to becoming a true self-discoverer.

Third, I had my first chance to grapple with audio equipment and learn some of the basics of having an audio toolbox that I could use to create audio content. I happily experimented with my equipment to produce content that was both good and bad! But, through hands-on experience, I learned how to get the best out of my equipment. We shall examine this in chapter 2.

So, I do not want anyone to miss out any part of this audio journey. Sadly, many students learning about audio production elsewhere can miss two important stages of this book's R.E.A.L. journey. They skip the *discoverer* and *decoder* stage, as they go straight into the pressures of the *developer* and *deliverer* stages. I believe that without doing the necessary self-reflection of both the *discoverer* and *decoder* stages, especially *discoverer* at the beginning, students are thrust into a far from ideal environment, without learning who they are and what they have to say. They're working to satisfy an audience from almost the very start. Those are tough conditions for anyone to find their voice (See Figure 1.2).

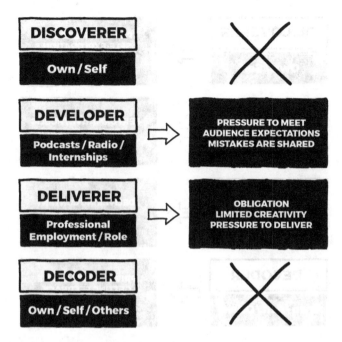

FIGURE 1.2 Omit these stages at your peril.

That's also a recipe for creative burnout. Students will find themselves learning as they go, but their mistakes could be made in public. That pressure only increases if they then go into a role (paid or unpaid) at a radio station or audio production environment. This brings heavy obligations with continuous pressure to deliver. I do not believe that going straight into such an environment is the best start. Rather, I want you to find your own voice and that can only come from the time spent as a *discoverer*, on your own, exploring your identity. Similarly, time spent as *decoder*, after you have created audio, receiving valuable feedback, is crucial to understand how your and others' audio pieces *work*.

Starting as a *discoverer* is never wasted time or energy. I promise you that you will learn things on your own that will make massive positive ripples throughout your work. Plus, you will develop a strong sense of your own voice, and that's what this book is all about. You'll be creating audio that's *relatable, engaging, authentic,* and *liberating!* (See Figure 1.3)

Anyone can go on this journey. You will be surprised just how few barriers there are to even start trying. You may be reading this as a textbook assigned to your class, or because you are just interested in audio production. Maybe, you are now at a college or community radio station and someone recommended this book as a starting point. For all these reasons, and more, what you hold in your hands is a ticket for a full positive experience. It's a journey

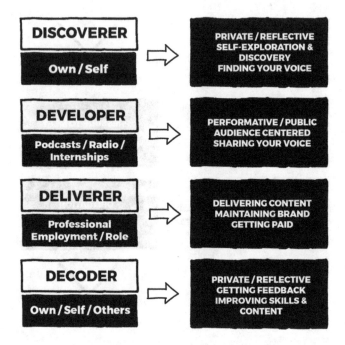

FIGURE 1.3 The full *Finding Your Voice* positive experience.

to discover more about yourself, about the medium of audio, as well as learning how to create it (whether that's radio, podcasts, or other forms of audio content). Along the way, it can change and develop your own life skills and outlook.

Now, I admit that in certain places there are different opinions about the continuing role of radio itself. It is no surprise when you read how I began my story that I remain a fully signed up fan of radio. But some claim that radio is now well past its sell-by-date, even seeing it as a dying medium. Yes, we can agree that radio has been around for a long, long time, but that longevity should not be mistaken for declining influence. When I visited and broadcast from the very birthplace of wireless radio in Italy, invented by Guillermo Marconi over 125 years ago, I marveled how the original technology remains essentially the same today, yet the medium has endured and continues to impact millions of people around the world. It still changes lives. It should continue to be taken seriously.

Many of my students begin their journey working within more traditional radio, and I shall sometimes assume this approach in this book. Traditional radio, typically FM radio, continues to have an important role. Like an old boxer who somehow survives for yet another round, radio has developed a reputation for sticking around and surviving, even if it has sometimes been battered along the way. But we must also take seriously the more recent digitization of media with the rise and explosive popularity of social media platforms. Now people can listen to audio and radio on different devices, in different environments. It is now audio *on demand* (Knopper, 2009). We can listen to what we want, when we feel like it. Today, the medium of audio encompasses a vast number of forms, including traditional radio broadcasting, podcasts, live streaming, new phone apps that emerge all the time, audio-books, music and drama productions, and even CB (Citizens Band) and "ham" amateur radio.

While some of these have primarily a non-visual audio/sound format, other forms of media such as film, television, and live theater, marry visual image with sound. But, clearly verbal speech remains the most likely way for humans to communicate. Radio has never been more accessible, especially when you consider that podcasts are essentially radio on demand. In the last decade, podcasts have become massively successful as a media format because of their accessibility. Undeniably, podcasting has a very bright future.

So, this book is your ticket for a journey. On the way you will not only explore the audio media available to you but receive practical help to *create* content. My hope is that you develop vital understanding and skills so that ultimately you will become an enthusiast like me. That by gaining increasing proficiency you will be inspired and develop fresh confidence in new ways. I recognize that some readers have no audio or radio experience at all. You will have many questions, and I aim to answer them as we go along. From basic queries like "How do I begin?" to more advanced questions like "How do I produce a radio program or podcast?", the answers are all in the journey ahead.

The wonder of audio

The first thing that grabbed me as a sixteen-year-old was the unique power of audio. Especially in a small hospital radio station, I saw how audiences cherished its intimacy. Later on I learned to describe this as its power of *immersive presence*. While other forms of visual/audio media reveal exactly what you are to see and feel at any given moment, radio steps back and allows the *theater of the imagination* to react and respond to what it is hearing. Audio does not control imagery. It gives latitude to imagine things in your own mind and space, to paint your own mental pictures. Listeners can imagine a scene, a place, a picture, an environment, or a moment in time, furnishing the details from their own experiences. That's its power.

Audio does not patronize listeners. It engages life stories individually. Those who create find their own life story and experiences inevitably shape the content too. Every person's voice, like their own fingerprints, is unique and contributes emotional potency. No one will ever be able to tell your life's story, or talk of the things you have experienced and seen, as you can. Audio captures and communicates that.

R.E.A.L. Moment

As I have already shared, my very first radio experience was at Radio Addenbrooke's, a radio station in Cambridge, England, that played to the wards and patients in the hospital. Despite the fact that no one else could hear the radio station outside of the hospital, I experienced firsthand how special it could be for a patient to request a song and then hear it played by their bedside. One day, a patient requested some music and after I played the song, the patient's reaction stayed with me. Beaming broadly he said to me, "That really cheered me up, son!" Many of the patients were elderly and alone. So any relief or enjoyment I could bring to them proved to me the power of radio and its ability to bring hope in the direst of times, to be a bedside companion in the darkness.

Entering a long tradition

When Guglielmo Marconi (1874–1937) invented the medium of wireless radio, he understood its power as a communication tool from the beginning. Delivering more than the contemporary Morse code, he foresaw the radio revolution communicating ideas, thoughts, entertainment, music, and speech.

In the age before television, radio held a matchless place. Its "Golden Age", as it would be called, occurred in the 1920s and 1930s, with American audiences enthralled by episodic radio entertainment such as *The Green Hornet*, *The Lone Ranger*, and the *Amos and Andy Show*. Early radio sets were behemoths of ornate wood treated as focal furniture. In the USA, old photographs show families huddled around their radio sets, listening with awe and wonder. Successive radio shows captivated audiences throughout the USA and cemented radio as the primary technology of mass communication. It reached across the country, touching people in ways that newspapers could not. In those early days the experience of radio was like witnessing some powerful alchemy at work.

At some point in any audio and radio production textbook, Orson Welles usually crops up. Welles's production of *The War of the Worlds* in 1938 famously illustrated the power of radio. Its story of an alien invasion seemed so terrifyingly believable that it is claimed some listeners panicked, assuming that they were listening to real events. The moment stands out as an early example of the power of story on radio.

In the 1960s and through today, radio continues as a musical tastemaker and influencer, playing music that dominates culture and conversation. The Beatles invaded America in 1964, Oasis and Blur took over the airwaves in the UK with 1990s Britpop, and vibrant independent music stations emerged throughout India in the 2000s. Radio has enjoyed a wide reputation for making waves. Its history contains fascinating stories such as the all-important life-saving broadcasts from the sinking Titanic.

Over the past twenty years I have also regularly taught radio in India, and I never cease to be amazed by the continuing popularity of radio there. I was told that some Indians cannot afford a television and cannot read a newspaper, so that has left radio as the only medium truly accessible to the poor. They value its affordability and portability. I once drove past a village in remote southern India, and I saw a group of villagers huddled around a radio listening with concentration. Radio is still a lifeline for many people around the world.

This long tradition has now burgeoned into other forms of media, especially podcasting, which many consider to be more popular than radio as a media format today. The rise in popularity of many audio formats, audiobooks, streaming music services, and social media apps, owes everything to the invention that started it all: radio.

Audio: Ideal for storytelling

We are naturally storytelling beings. We all recognize the enthralling power of a well-told story unfolding before us. We are predisposed to want to know what happens *next* in a story because human empathy and imagination draw us into others' experiences and give stories amazing power. We tell stories because we seek understanding of our lives and to grasp a greater sense of purpose. We are "meaning-seeking creatures" (Armstrong, 2005, p. 1) that seek order in the chaos of the universe around us. Experiencing a story "shows us how to look into our own hearts and to see our world from a perspective that goes beyond our own self-interest," according to Karen Armstrong (Armstrong, 2005, p. 149). Stories have always played a major role in our lives.

One of audio's greatest strengths is how it can be used to tell stories. It traces its roots back to preliterate oral culture when speaking and listening was primary. Speaking and listening was the only way by which such cultures passed on history and knowledge from person to person, generation to generation, telling stories around blazing campfires by vivid oral culture. Storytelling is therefore an essential human activity traceable to our earliest ancestors, and listening to audio creates a sense of primordial intimacy. It can feel as though you are being transported back in time to those oral cultures of preliterate days. Later, literate cultures diminished the primary role of hearing as writing enabled telling stories to future generations.

Today, visual communication in Western culture appears to reign supreme with its powerful storytelling. Our visual culture enjoys binge-watching hours of television, films, and entertainment streaming. Phone screens keep us glued to them for hours everyday. Unsurprisingly, fueling visual culture costs billions of dollars every year, feeding an escalating appetite for adventure and excitement. It grows ever more sophisticated with computer-generated imagery (CGI) beefing up visual effects.

Yet, I find that often the most compelling and effective stories that stay in my consciousness long afterwards are *spoken stories* based on *real life experiences*. Their authenticity is transparent. No clutter distracts you. We are back with our ancestors around the campfire, with imagination given freedom to roam, being emotionally touched, person to person. Audio works by its intimate storytelling, its personal connectedness.

Turn off the lights

When I teach audio production and listen to students' work, I sometimes close the window blinds and turn off the lights, plunging the classroom into darkness. Startled students ask, *why did you do that?* I respond that it allows us to listen better. In the darkness, the absence of one sense accentuates the others. With no visual distractions, we can concentrate better. Often, by the end of the semester students have become enthusiasts for listening in darkness also, so much so that when I enter the classroom the students are already prepared and are sitting in darkness, ready to listen!

Considered the grandfather of mass communication by many, Marshall McLuhan, in his groundbreaking 1967 book, *The Medium is the Massage,* wrote that "the ear favors no particular 'point of view.' We are enveloped by sound. It forms a seamless web around us. We never say, 'Music shall fill a particular segment of the air.' We hear sounds from everywhere, without ever having to focus" (Mcluhan & Fiore, 1967/2005, p. 112). Audio can be immersive in ways that other media cannot.

Turning off the lights helps the brain focus on sound and draw on personal experiences. We see pictures and feel emotions such as love, fear, anger, hatred, sacrifice, pain, and suffering. Our imaginations fill in the details as we personalize and interpret what we hear. We do our best to ensure we understand and engage with the audio.

So far I have concentrated on words, but we are walking libraries of additional sounds which have personal meanings, especially music. Later we shall need to consider other sounds and how they can add to or detract from our words.

Finding your voice

On my own journey, beginning as a low-level teenage volunteer with hospital radio, I made a second discovery that proved to be vitally important. As this book's title puts it, it was a discovery about *finding your own voice*. Before you start your journey in earnest, it's important to take stock of where *you* are starting from. This simple exercise will help you determine your starting point.

Finding your voice: Starting self-assessment

In the table that follows, assess your own interest in exploring each of these areas on a scale of 1 to 10, where 1 means you have the *least* interest, and 10 means you have the *most*. It's important that you assess each area individually, not thinking of the whole when you write your number on the line for each area.

Becoming a more effective communicator	Developing self-confidence	Recognizing what makes me unique	Accepting myself as I am, including imperfections	Identifying my unique perspectives, values, and beliefs
_____	_____	_____	_____	_____
Developing my speaking voice	Identifying my strengths and weaknesses as a communicator	Improving as a storyteller	Becoming an effective interviewer	Learning editing skills
_____	_____	_____	_____	_____
Learning audio production skills	Creating content for radio	Creating content for podcasts	Learning from other people's audio experiences	Deciding my future path
_____	_____	_____	_____	_____

After you have completed this exercise, look at the numbers you have written for each area. Circle the top three or four highest numbers. You have now identified your strongest areas of interest, and what you'd like to explore and develop the most. This will help you to focus on what you specifically want to get out of this book as you go on the *finding your voice* journey.

The challenge of finding your voice is a challenge of taking initially small risks so that you can more fully understand who you are and grow in your comfort level. You are seeking to engage in activities that invite you to express yourself with authenticity as you learn new skills. You must also practice self-acceptance by embracing your imperfections. It's a journey that also takes time, so patience is required too!

It all starts with taking a look at the main focus of this book's title: *your voice.*

Your two voices

First hearing their own voice when it's recorded can often make a person feel very uncomfortable. Do we really *sound* like that? Some students find this experience anxiety-inducing (Jacquay, 2019), and for a few students, hearing themselves has been so uncomfortable they have left the room! Such discomfort is an entirely natural reaction. The reason for our discomfort lies in the basic fact that our voices heard outside our heads sound so differently to our ears. That's why they may be almost unrecognizable at first. We protest: *No, that's not me!* But it *is*, because that's your *outside* voice.

Berry (2003) explains how the voice you are hearing is simply not the same that you hear in your head:

> You hear your own voice via the bone conduction in your own head, and this gives it a different resonance: you are therefore not hearing it as other people do. This accounts for the shock when you hear your recorded voice for the first time: it often seems unrecognizable ... because you are hearing it via the outside waves and your outer ear, you are hearing it as someone else. (p. 8)

Our *physiology* explains, to a certain extent, why our voices sound like they do. Put simply, the sound of your voice is produced when your vocal cords vibrate. Located inside your neck, in the larynx a few inches beneath your jaw, your vocal cords (or vocal folds) are like elastic bands that move and adjust as you use them. When you are silent they remain open, to allow you to breathe. But when you speak, they vibrate as they open and close (See Figure 1.4).

Energy to make the vocal cords audibly vibrate comes from air, rushing up from your lungs, after you have taken a breath. Normal breathing requires breaths in and out every two or three seconds. Speaking needs more energy, more air. So when we speak, breathing changes with quick breaths, which are then exhaled over several seconds.

How much air our lungs can hold, how large the size of our nasal cavities, and the diameter of our throat – all of these affect the sound and tone of our voices. Just as our bodies are unique, so are our physical voices. By our distinctive outside voices people know and recognize us, although to us they may seem almost like a stranger's voice when we first hear ourselves.

Changes in breathing (as with much else) obviously involves your brain, which works in conjunction with the muscles of your vocal cords and co-ordinates their vibrations by regulating the air passing through them. Audible words result! Have you ever noticed that you cannot talk when you are breathing in? Talking and breathing is a careful balancing act that the brain manages for you, mercifully without requiring conscious thought.

The Respiratory System

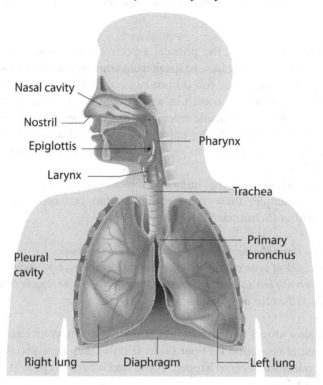

Nasal cavity

Nostril

Epiglottis — Pharynx

Larynx

Trachea

Primary bronchus

Pleural cavity

Right lung — Diaphragm — Left lung

FIGURE 1.4 The Human Body and Breathing (Photo: Alila Medical Media/ Shutterstock.com).

While every voice is unique with distinctive voice prints, you can train your voice. For example, deep sea divers, swimmers, and singers can develop longer times between breaths by expanding lung capacity. Other factors also affect how you speak, including your posture, health, and age, but especially how well you use your diaphragm.

Fia Fasbender, CEO of the Moxie Institute, explains the diaphragm's importance. "You would think that everyone knows how to breathe, right? Or, at least, everyone thinks they do. But, in reality, most people are taking shallow breaths instead of using their diaphragms" (Fasbinder, 2017, para. 1). She explains further:

> The diaphragm is a muscle, and just like any other muscle in your body, it can be strengthened. To beef it up, use the 'low and slow' method. Pretend you have a balloon in your belly. Breathe in deeply to inflate the balloon, pulling the air down into your navel. Don't rush – take it in slow, you don't

want that balloon to fill up too quickly, after all ... . Once your diaphragm is full of breath, exhale slowly and completely (Activate Those Benefits section).

Discovering more about the physical aspects of breathing is worth your time. In particular, learning how to speak from your diaphragm gives a kind of secret power. It ensures that you do not run out of breath and can maintain the pace and speed of your speech as well as regulating volume. Also, when you begin recording your outside voice, many of us experience anxiety, which inevitably affects us physically by tightening our muscles. We breathe more rapidly and possibly hyperventilate, too, because shallow breathing means we are inhaling less oxygen.

Breathing exercises can be immeasurably helpful in developing breath control. For example, these steps recommended by voice coach Lucille Schutmaat-Rubin (Schutmaat-Rubin, n.d.):

1 *Breathe in through your mouth when preparing to speak.*
2 *Relax the back of your tongue on inhalation to avoid a gaspy, noisy air intake.*
3 *Trace the breath low in your body sensing your belly rise as the air floats in and your belly fall as the air flows out.*

When you slow down your breathing, you slow down your heart rate and induce a state of relaxation for your body. It only takes a few seconds for this remarkable transformation to happen. If you find it hard sleeping at night, this can help you fall asleep!

This book is about finding your own outside voice and learning to use it well. Go easy on yourself when you start to speak. As Houseman says, "To work on your voice you need to start by getting to know it: approaching it with curiosity and respect rather than judgment and demand" (Houseman, 2002, p. xiv). Perhaps when you listen to the exercises you will soon undertake you will be tempted to rush to judgment about your speaking ability. Maybe you do not believe that you have a "good voice." But there is every reason to believe that you are mistaken.

While I have emphasized the physiology of your outside voice, I must stress the vital importance of recognizing how your *outside* voice relates to your *inside* voice. This is critical. Why? Because our inside voice expresses our emotions and thoughts before we speak them aloud.

In a 2018 speech before his students at Lawrence University called "Voice, the Muscle of the Soul: Finding Yourself Through Finding Your Voice," Professor Kenneth Bozeman explained the important connection:

The first thing a baby does is to take a breath. Often the second thing the baby does is to apply that breath to its vocal folds to express how it feels about what just happened and its new situation. It is a completely primal, visceral response. You express feelings through various kinds of movement, but you are hardwired to communicate feelings to others through your voice. It is your primary means of inducing empathy and inviting compassion from others – at first in your caregivers and siblings, and later in the other people that populate your extended community (Bozeman, 2018, para. 4).

The voice is a powerful tool, used to connect emotionally with others. It's an outlet of pure emotion. As we get older and develop our vocabulary, we speak with increased erudition, but the voice's function remains the same. We may refine the words that we use, but the emotions we convey are strongly personal.

Our voices also express our thoughts. Ethan Kross, author of *Chatter: The Voice in Our Head, Why It Matters, and How to Harness It,* explains this idea further:

The bottom line is that we all have a voice in our head in some shape or form. The flow of words is so inextricable from our inner lives that it persists even in the face of vocal impairments. Some people who stutter, for example, report talking more fluently in their minds than they do out loud. Deaf people who use sign language talk to themselves too, though they have their own form of signing to themselves, similar to how people who can hear use words to talk to themselves privately (Kross, 2021, p. xxi).

Accepting that our inner voice expresses emotions and words from our inner lives, pushes us to discover more about ourselves. Indeed, the last part of this chapter focuses on key questions such as: *Who am I? Where do I come from? What do I believe?* Answering these questions takes us to the heart of the *discoverer stage.* The only way to create R.E.A.L. audio requires you to gain a genuine understanding of what influences your inside voice as it relates to your outside voice.

Who am I?

Everyone's life story is different. From our day of birth, some argue even before, we are shaped by the experiences of living with others. We can never presume that others share similar experiences, outlook on the world, and sense of self-identity. People may come from the same geographic area and same city and even street within it, but they are still likely to have markedly differing experiences. Some who suffered unhappy, deeply difficult childhoods can live alongside others who have experienced the opposite. So, you are unique as a person, as is your story, *as is your voice.*

I have learned how important it is for students to recognize their uniqueness. They all start with very different life experiences which will inevitably affect how they will create audio content. It is vital that they answer questions like these:

How do I describe myself to others?
What are my strengths and weaknesses?
What are my beliefs?
Who did I learn the most from?
Who inspires me?

Of course, answers to these questions can change over the course of a lifetime. Self-identity is ever malleable and flexible. Aristotle (384-322 BC) once suggested that "Knowing yourself is the beginning of all wisdom" (Plato, 2011). We will keep that goal in mind with our first exercise.

Chapter 1, R.E.A.L. Exercise #1: Who am I?

This is not an audio exercise, but you will need a notepad or a blank document on your computer. It's for your eyes only. Find a private space and take time to read, think, and respond to the following four questions:

1 **Who has shaped or influenced you most in your life?**

2 **What relationships are the most important to you?**

3 **What are your most important beliefs or values?**

4 **Who inspires you the most?**

These questions explore key aspects of your life so far. Typically thirty minutes is enough to write down your answers. Once completed, wait at least twenty-four hours before returning to read your words. You may find that, even after such a short period of time, you may have further reflections. Looking at it with fresh eyes, you may want to change some details. Hopefully, it ends up as an honest reflection which will serve as a bedrock for the journey ahead. "There's no fate but what we make for ourselves" (Cameron, 2003), as a character says in *Terminator 2: Judgment Day* (1991). Aristotle would probably agree.

Congratulations, you have now taken the first major step of your journey!

Where do I come from? Be a Pickles!

Your answers in exercise #1 reveal so much about you and what has shaped your life so far, but answering where you come from opens up another dimension. Because we are concerned with finding your voice, it's at this point that we recognize how much our voices disclose our background. As Love and Frazier (2016) comment, "We absorb the information packed into a voice almost intuitively" (p. 4). Hearing someone, we can jump to conclusions about their education level, where they live, their age, health, politics, personality, and much else. In particular, the place of our upbringing usually affects the way we talk. Unconsciously, we are quick to make judgments about how people sound when they talk, especially if they speak with an accent.

Vocal coach Denise Woods encourages: "Where you come from does not have to be a source of embarrassment, and a regional accent is not something to be erased. Your *isms* and the rhythm of your speech are a part of what makes you *you*" (Woods, 2022, pp. 192–3). The good news is that increasingly we live in a time where accents are more readily accepted in the media. That was not always the case, as in UK broadcasting, for example. Prior to the 1990s, the British Broadcasting Corporation had only allowed the distinct, upper class English accent or *Received Pronunciation* to be heard, which was "commonly known as the Queen's English and was considered to be the language of elites, power and royalty" (Hogenboom, 2018). The BBC voices obviously did not represent the millions of citizens who spoke very differently.

I love the story of Wilfred Pickles, who should be better known in the history of radio. He spoke with a strikingly broad Yorkshire accent, from the north of England. Joining the BBC in 1941, he stuck out like a sore thumb. What a furor he caused when he read the news! Many were outraged. "It was even said that some listeners were less inclined to believe the news when Pickles was reading it" (Eschner, 2017, para. 4). Yet, his inclusion on the airwaves was deliberate. It was a time when the Nazis were creating fake propaganda radio broadcasts to demoralize the British public. Pickles had an accent that could not be easily impersonated. Apparently, it simply bamboozled the Nazis.

Eventually, by the 1990s the BBC "veered away from its strict ways, embracing not only all forms of English heard in Britain, but those heard in the United States as well" (MacLeod, 1996, para. 2). Indeed, "the BBC now allows all sorts of regional accents on its broadcasts – and even encourages it, aiming to both represent the diverse audience the BBC has and to draw new people in" (Hogenboom, 2018, para. 2). Wilfred Pickles broke through a barrier. All voices from all over the spectrum are welcome.

We should take ownership, without apology or reservation, of our own voice. The wonder of today's audio and radio is that it is a medium for *everyone*. In the past, it was sometimes considered a place of privilege, giving access only to a certain kind of person. More than ever, people can freely express themselves through audio.

What do I believe?

Exercise #1, question 3, asked: "*What are your most important beliefs and values?*" I wonder how easily you wrote down your answer? At first sight, you might think that your beliefs seem irrelevant for creating audio. Indeed, when we are faced with expressing something out loud, we can often feel that we have nothing interesting to say. I have witnessed students who seem to say, *I haven't really experienced anything in life, so what do I have to say that's of value?* Realize that you have as much a right to be heard as anyone else. You may still be young and inexperienced but, nevertheless, you can share things you care about. Of course, it's also easier to communicate when you are with people you know, of the same generation, and in the same place. That's why I believe that a great starting environment to learn and grow is at a college or student radio station, which will be discussed later.

But, however inexperienced you may feel, you must ask yourself *why* you are interested in creating audio content. What is your goal? What do you want to talk about or bring to the attention of others? What stories, news, topics, or opinions strike you as important? At this *discoverer* stage, identifying what really matters to you, what motivates you, is a vital part of personal development. What prompts you to first press the record button? The WHY provides the initial motivation to generate content, and makes the crucial difference in seeing an idea through to reality.

Consider what former USA Secretary of State, Madeleine Albright, once said, "It took me quite a long time to develop a voice, and now that I have it, I am not going to be silent" (Schnal, 2017, para. 1). Searching for your voice can result in finding a spark of passion that grows into a roaring fire. Will you share that fire with others?

For this second exercise, we move into basic recording of yourself. Chapter 2 deals with our audio equipment in detail, but I hope you have some simple way to be able to record yourself on your cell/mobile phone or your computer. If you at least have a smartphone (iOS or Android, for example) then you may be surprised how capable it can be as a recording device. At this point do not be concerned about sound quality, though try to be clear. Find a private space, and take the time to read and reflect on these questions before recording your answers.

Chapter 1, R.E.A.L. Exercise #2: "What do I believe?"

For this exercise, your spoken answers may come more easily to you than in the previous exercise. Reflect on your beliefs and values, and then talk out loud as you answer these questions.

1 Who or what shaped the values and beliefs you have right now?

2 So far in life, what has been the hardest challenge you have had to overcome?

3 How do you decide what is right and what is wrong?

4 Name an issue or topic that you feel strongly about and explain why.

5 What is worth fighting for?

These questions probe at your worldview, how certain issues and topics resonate with you. I often hear students respond positively to the last question. Often they are strident in support of equality and justice for all people. Some students, however, confess they have never considered the question before. Its seriousness challenges them to think of a response.

R.E.A.L. Moment

The Australian podcast "Seen" by Yumi Stynes (Stynes, 2023-2023) is an extraordinary listen. Yumi describes herself as "a half-Japanese, half-white Australian woman who grew up four hours away from the nearest capital city." She says that, "Flicking between the two TV channels when I was a kid in regional Victoria, I never saw anyone who looked like me." The focus of "Seen" is on interviewing successful leaders, people who have done remarkable things, while facing racial prejudice and blatant discrimination. "When I started, you were kidding yourself if you thought you could do this work and not be white." Yumi draws upon her own life story to be a brilliant interviewer and to draw out remarkable stories from her guests. She says her mission is "speaking to other people who, in spite of being told they don't belong, have carved out space, found a voice and are creating pathways for those who follow!" Yumi is a powerfully authentic communicator who creates R.E.A.L. audio content that inspires.

Welcome to your voice

These last three sections should have strengthened your self-understanding. This process of seeking self-knowledge is not an invitation to become narcissistic and inward-focused but rather is an essential journey of understanding yourself better. Socrates once declared that "the unexamined life is not worth living for a human being" (Plato, 1966). Hopefully, you have taken enough time to recognize how you possess qualities, abilities, as well as limitations which contribute to your unique personality with distinctive gift-mixes. Our personal experiences of joys, hurts, fears, and our interests all contribute greatly to our communication. These questions find out who we are, where we come from, and what we believe. American philosopher William James (1842–1910) once wrote, "Believe that life is worth living and your belief will help create the fact" (James, 1895, p. 24). We can adjust his words: "Believe that you have something worth saying and your belief will help create the fact." It will help you discover *your* voice.

One of my key objectives is to encourage you to be comfortable with your voice, knowing that most people feel, in the beginning, uncomfortable about how their voice sounds. You should push through discomfort and believe that your voice *already* has authenticity. It really is 100% naturally you. The developer stage later provides (from chapter 5 onwards) help in crafting your voice, but it's vital you recognize that your voice *is good enough already to make an authentic start.* There is no such thing as a perfect voice. Everyone's voice is as valid as anyone else's.

As this chapter's final exercise I have set another spoken exercise to help you become more practiced at hearing your own voice.

Chapter 1, R.E.A.L. Exercise #3: Welcome to your voice
Again you will need a private, quiet space to think over your answers to these five questions, which should take only about fifteen minutes to complete.

1 **What is your full name and where were you born?**

2 **What is your earliest childhood memory?**

3 **Briefly describe the place you grew up and the place you now live today.**

4 **How would you describe yourself to another person?**

5 **Name one piece of advice that was given to you that you live by.**

These questions should unlock some easy sharing and maybe some passion when you answer question 5! Having recorded your voice now you need to take time to hear yourself as other people hear you. So, take a breath and listen to yourself without judgment. Do not be critical of what you sound like but rather take note of how you say certain words, how you breathe when you talk, and other aspects of your voice that perhaps you have not previously given much thought. By taking an objective stance "outside" ourselves we can become aware of verbal habits such as slurring, pacing, and diction.

Remember my earlier comments about the strangeness of listening to your outside voice, which should, because of our work in this chapter, be true to your inner voice. Do you notice what role your voice has in communicating your views? Is your voice full of energy and passion? Do you speak quickly with short breaths? Do you emphasize certain words over others? I hope you grasp the connection between subject matter and the way that you talk about it. A key principle is *understanding just how many options there are for using your voice to communicate powerfully and effectively.* You'll need to experiment before you can discover and recognize the most comfortable vocal style and delivery for you.

I have seen students transformed when, finding their voice and realizing they have something to say, are then placed in front of a microphone. Nervous Steve's story is a stellar example. Once nervousness is faced and the initial fear of filling the silence of dead air is overcome, students can be unleashed in front of a microphone. They can develop into completely different people – for the better. With honesty and passion, they can speak truth to power!

These exercises are important because they are the first step towards you creating R.E.A.L. audio. The *R* stands for *relatable* audio that draws people into stories, enabling them to identify with the speakers' situation, which may be far removed from their own. *E* is for *engaging* and is all about sharing experiences and life stories that grab your audiences' attention. Because you have spent time thinking about who you are, your own story, and your beliefs, you can more easily create audio that shares real human life experiences. People listen more closely to what you have to say. They feel the emotional highs and lows of your stories because they have experienced at least some part of your story. *A* at its best is the *authenticity* we yearn for. Even though listeners may have no firsthand experience of some of these stories, they continue to listen. They all want to know how a story ends, and they also like to imagine how they might respond to its challenge. All this adds up to audio that takes audiences to new places, or exposes them to truths in their own lives. *L* stands for *liberating* audio. That's when an audience hears something that encourages them to make brave decisions, to think and feel emotions that they might not normally feel able to.

I know that you will be eager to start creating content such as news stories, sports podcasts, entertainment features, comedy skits, and a myriad of other topics. But before you can create content you need the self-awareness that comes from the "examined life" of necessary self-reflection. In my experience, when students fail to do this, they sabotage their hopes of sustaining commitment and interest in audio. Too quickly energy dissipates, ideas dry up, and there is silence. They do not know what to say if they have not thought about who they are.

Finally, let's step back and take stock of what we propose to do. When you begin creating audio it's easy to feel inadequate, for we live in a world where other people's stories dominate. "As a culture we are encouraged to consume the stories of others – in films and books, on TV and in the tabloids – few ordinary people find opportunities for producing their own stories" (LaChapelle, 2008, p. 10).

Others' stories may seem to crowd us out, intimidate us. Indeed, they may create a sense of competition.

Put the thought of competing with others out of your mind. Your journey of self-discovery is not in competition with anyone else. What you have to say is unique, and important. Your personality and your communication style is yours alone. By definition, authenticity is not false, nor copied, nor pretended. When it comes to producing audio content, your mission is to be comfortable with hearing your outside voice and what it has to say. No one else can be you.

Professor Tim Crook, my former mentor at Goldsmiths College, University of London, describes what it's like when someone communicates authentically:

> It's an overall euphony, an effective and successful sum total of all the parts; that fusion of inner confidence with skills performance that is present in programs which people will stop other things to listen to, find memorable and thought-provoking and want to talk about. It's a clicking and sonic charisma of humanitarian communication and understanding (T. Crook, Personal communication, July 29, 2022).

Doesn't that sound great?

Final thoughts: *Radio is with me forever:* **How radio was so important to one student, it made a permanent mark on her life. Literally**

Picture this: Inside a tattoo parlor in Los Angeles. A 28-year-old brunette woman is lying face down, with her arms by her side as a tattoo artist works on an intricate tattoo of a microphone on her arm. She must lie very still as the tattoo is permanently inked into her skin. A riot is about to break out.

Dana Schaeffer is at a defining moment. It is the culmination of a journey in radio that started as a student, becoming involved in college radio in New Jersey before taking her across the country to live and work in Los Angeles. She recalls what happened. "It was 2018, and I was living in LA, and I moved there for radio." Because of her love for radio and also baking, she decided she would get tattooed with "a baking whisk on one arm and a radio mic on the other, for my two favorite passions and my two jobs."

Dana chose an antique microphone design, which "took a long time because it's very detailed. I'm lying on my stomach, and I have my arms facing the tattoo artist, so I'm basically trapped; I can't move." She became aware of two people arguing outside the shop with increasing vehemency. What's happening? "My tattoo artist is like, nope, we're not stopping. We're keeping going."

But then suddenly all hell breaks loose. "A guy comes in and starts fighting with someone … a few more people come in, and they all start to fight." Stuck in position Dana is alarmed. "They just started brawling outside … and then they were coming in, and running inside the tattoo shop, fist fighting."

Dana was pretty sure that the tattoo artist should stop. "I was like, *are you sure you don't want to take a break?* Because we can. I don't want you to mess up on this." But the tattoo artist insisted on continuing, "He's like, no, I'm in the mode, we're gonna keep going!" Now about six people are openly fighting each other, just a few feet from where Dana is lying.

Finally, the police arrive and enter the fray which has turned into a riot. "One of the guys then knocked someone out. And then the ambulance came. Meanwhile, I'm still getting tattooed, so I can't really turn back and look. I hear all this commotion, but I can't see what's going on." Arrests are made, the injured are stretchered out, and "everything calmed down by the time my tattoo was done," says Dana. Was the experience of getting her microphone tattoo worth it? "It actually came out perfect," says Dana. "And I always joke that if I ever forget what I do for a living, I have my resume tattooed on me!"

Actually, getting a tattoo was a declaration that radio was life-changing for Dana. Early on as a student, Dana was drawn to radio, becoming involved in the college radio station on campus. "I really loved it because it was theater of the mind. And I think you must work a little harder sometimes in radio, because you don't have that visual aspect. So, you have to write the stories for people to imagine in their own mind. And I find that fascinating,"

Convincing her parents that her passion for radio should be taken seriously took some time. "I think they didn't believe I was doing that at first because I was young. I was saying, yeah, I'm going to stay over at the college radio station. They're like, she's probably partying or something like that! And really, I wasn't, I was at the station! And I remember sleeping on two chairs in the middle of the night in the studio when we were doing College Radio Day. So, I have the pictures to prove it. I wasn't out partying!"

After graduating from college, Dana's radio career would take her to places such as WPLJ, CBS Radio, and 1010 WINS in New York City, KISS FM and KFI AM in Los Angeles, iHeartRadio Countdown, to where she is today at ABC News Radio in New York City. With such experiences Dana's parents soon realized this *was* a lifetime calling for their daughter. "I think at first, they didn't get it. But, at a certain time, I think they realized, okay, well, she's obviously going to keep doing this no matter what. And we've just got to let her go."

A recent highlight for Dana was being selected by the *Mentoring & Inspiring Women in Radio* group as just one of four mentees inducted for their 2020 mentoring program. Dana was partnered with the legendary radio author and leader Valerie Geller. "I actually got paired up with her when I was selected for this mentorship, which was amazing, because I couldn't ask for anyone better," says Dana. Her relationship with Geller taught her that she needed to discover her own voice. "I always tried to mimic someone else. And I didn't feel right doing that. So, she kind of gave me my voice. It's been so helpful. And she's just a joy to work with. I love every minute of it." Then, in December 2022, Dana was named as one of *Radio Ink's 30 and Under Superstars* in the US radio industry.

FIGURE 1.5   Dana Schaeffer (Photo credit: Dana Schaeffer).

For Dana, the power of radio enables you to communicate your authentic self. "You can't be someone else, you have to be yourself," she says. "If I have a story I want to tell, it has to be meaningful to me. And if it's meaningful to me, there's going to be people out there that are going to believe it's meaningful for them too, because we all have different perspectives and hobbies where we can relate and I think it's important to voice your own opinions, or to tell your story. Because someone out there might be too afraid to do it. And if they hear yours, that might help them or just let them know that they're not alone."

Dana is confident about the future of radio. "Obviously, radio is constantly changing, and evolving to the point where people have told me, 'your tattoo might outlast radio.' Some people may believe that, but I don't. I always reply: 'As long as I have this tattoo, and I'm still alive, radio will be alive'" (See Figure 1.5).

References

Armstrong, K. (2005). *A short history of myth*. Canongate.
Berry, C. (2003). *Your voice and how to use it* (2nd Rev. ed.). Virgin Books.

Bozeman, K. (2018, May 22). *Voice, the muscle of the soul: Finding yourself through finding your voice* [Speech]. Lawrence University. Honors Convocation, Appleton, WI. https://lux.lawrence.edu/convocations/9

Cameron, J. (Director). (2003). *Terminator 2: Judgment Day* [Film]. Artisan Home Entertainment.

Eschner, K. (2017, November 17). How a new accent overturned BBC tradition and messed with the NAZIs. *Smithsonian Magazine.* https://www.smithsonianmag.com/smart-news/how-north-england-voice-overturned-bbc-tradition-180967208/

Fasbinder, F. (2017, October 2). *The secret to confident speaking? You're already doing it.* https://www.inc.com/fia-fasbinder/key-to-confident-communication-is-something-that-most-speakers-never-do.html

Hogenboom, M. (2018, March 9). *What does your accent say about you?* BBC Future. https://www.bbc.com/future/article/20180307-what-does-your-accent-say-about-you

Houseman, B. (with Branagh, K.). (2002). *Finding your voice: A step-by-step guide for actors.* Routledge.

Jacquay, G. (2019). *Is this thing on? The learning possibilities for participants at a college radio station* [Doctoral dissertation, California State University, Stanislaus]. http://hdl.handle.net/10211.3/214425

James, W. (1895). Is life worth living? *The International Journal of Ethics, 6*(1), 1–24. 10.1086/intejethi.6.1.2375619

Knopper, S. (2009). *Appetite for self-destruction: The spectacular crash of the record industry in the digital age.* Catapult.

Kross, E. (2021). *Chatter: The voice in our head, why it matters, and how to harness it.* Crown.

LaChapelle, C. (2008). *Finding your voice, telling your stories: 167 ways to tell your life stories.* Marion Street Press.

Love, R., & Frazier, D. (2016). *Set your voice free: How to get the singing or speaking voice you want.* Little Brown and Company.

MacLeod, A. (1996, September 4). Once-fussy BBC begins to speak with Scottish, Irish, even American accents. *The Christian Science Monitor.* https://www.csmonitor.com/1996/0904/090496.intl.global.2.html

Mcluhan, M., & Fiore, Q. (2005). The medium is the massage. In J. Agel (Ed.). Gingko Press. (Original work published 1967).

Plato. (with Lamb, W. R. M.). (1966). *Plato: Euthyphro. Apology. Crito. Phaedo. Phaedrus.* H. N. Fowler (Trans.) (Vol. 1). Harvard University Press.

Plato. (2011). *Plato: Phaedrus.* H. Yunis (Ed.) (Rev. ed.). Cambridge University Press. 10.1017/CBO9780511977237

Schnal, M. (2017, December 6). *Madeleine Albright: An exclusive interview.* Huffpost. https://www.huffpost.com/entry/madeleine-albright-an-exc_b_604418

Schutmaat-Rubin, L. (n.d.). *Breathe & speak with ease professionally speaking tips.* Retrieved June 22, 2023, from https://voicefoundation.org/articles/breathe-and-speak-with-ease/

Stynes, Y. (2023, February 21–2023, May 16). *Seen* [Audio podcast]. Special Broadcasting Service. https://www.sbs.com.au/audio/podcast/seen

Woods, D. (with Ali, M.). (2022). *The power of voice: A guide to making yourself heard.* HarperCollins.

2

THE DISCOVERER'S TOOLKIT

What you'll need to get going

First thoughts: *When the pandemic came, we knew what to do:* **How one student advisor was ready for radio in all circumstances because of his open-minded approach**

Picture this: March 16, 2020. Inside a meeting room at Neumann University in Pennsylvania, USA, a group of university leaders are holding a crisis meeting about the COVID-19 pandemic. Sweeping across the country, it is shutting everything down. Uncertainty rules. Yet one person in that room senses an idea beginning to develop. The Director of Neumann Media is not sure about the specifics, but a plan is forming. His name is Sean McDonald.

"I began thinking about what I needed to do next. I was like everyone else … concerned, but I didn't fully grasp what was going on." Part of his role oversees the WNUW radio and television station, and he saw immediate changes were going to be needed. "I figured that if we had to go online, I already knew that I had built an infrastructure that could get students on the air." But there was an atmosphere of panic. "There was a lot of uncertainty for the students. No one, at their age, had lived through something like this. So, it was stressful. They didn't know what was safe, what wasn't safe. You could begin to see them kind of not wanting to get close to each other. But they wanted to continue working."

Sean was determined the students could find a way to continue to create radio content. "I began to tell them, even if you go home, even if we're online, there's a way to do this. And I had to put my own fears and thoughts aside, because my role at that moment was not to be a radio person, it was to be a mentor to the students. So, I had to focus my energy on keeping them calm. Even if *I* wasn't calm!" Sean started thinking about what tools the

DOI: 10.4324/9781003263739-4

students could use to get back on the air, and to create content for the radio station. "As long as I have a console, a computer attached to a console, I can get anybody on the air. So, I was confident that I already had one solution, and then I was probably going to be able to make a lot more pretty quickly," says Sean. His prior experience as a remote broadcast engineer for Greater Media Philadelphia kicked in. Solutions were required, and Sean was trained to be a problem solver.

Yet, some students were fixed in their understanding about how to create radio. "They had to overcome it in their heads that radio is getting a signal to listeners. I had to take it back to the basics. It's making them realize that I'm still on the radio, even if I'm at my house. It was basically teaching them about remote broadcasting. They were used to taking a remote broadcasting device called a Comrex Access and broadcasting from the campus. They understood that concept of going out with a device, what they didn't understand was, that's the same thing that we're now going to do. You're going to be remote broadcasting from home. So, it was rewiring them to understand, 'Oh, this is still radio, even if I'm not in the studio.'"

Before the lockdown came, Sean purchased as many webcams and microphones as possible and began shipping them to his students' homes as soon as he could get his hands on them. He anticipated what the rest of the world was going to develop. "I also made sure that they had some sort of a headphone. I taught them the best way to find a quiet space where it's not going to sound too echoey if you have a USB mic, making sure they don't have a fan on nearby, things like that." Then the lockdown came.

When the email from the university said all classes would be online for the rest of the semester, Sean organized a Zoom session for his students. "I brought them all in and just said, 'Let it out. Let everything that you are worried about, that you're upset about, let it all out.' And then at the end of it, I asked, 'Do you feel better? Because tomorrow we start working again, and we're going *to create something great!*'"

They started using apps like Discord, Microsoft Teams and Slack to communicate with each other and to record and create live audio on the air. Even though they were at home, the quality was impressive. "If they had a good USB mic, and they were recording on Discord, it sounded like they were in the studio!" says Sean. The students had found a way to create and share audio.

Yet, to begin with, the students perhaps struggled with the transition from working in a studio on campus to being at home. "At first, I think they felt weird and awkward that their family was home, they could hear them doing it in their room or screwing up if they were trying to do a prerecorded piece. It was awkward for them. The place where they did their homework, or they slept, or they went to after they had a fight with their family, was also their workspace now. It was a little awkward for them to get over it. But they did it."

The idea that was to become great would be called *Coronacasts*. Originally suggested by a faculty member, Dr. Chakars, who taught Communications and Digital Media at the university, it involved creating podcasts that would capture the experiences of the students and those in the university who were enduring the COVID-19 pandemic. Providing a historic record expressing the hopes and fears was an emotionally powerful collection of audio stories that proved to be powerful listening. People outside of the university were also invited to submit their own audio to be included in the *Coronocasts*.

It took off. "We started getting audio pieces from all over the world. I think there were over 150 of them that came in and some were in different languages! One was a poem from an autistic nonverbal child. Writing it in his head, I voiced it. Incredibly powerful words. And you heard from people in Spain where they were not allowed to leave their houses for three weeks, and they ventured out for the first time, and they recorded it while they were doing it."

One day, Sean received a Google Alert that startled him. Neumann University was apparently in the *New York Times*. Sean could not believe it. "I just kind of sat there. What in the world is this? Our little idea was mentioned in the *New York Times*?! It was mind blowing." The students also could not believe it. "They were shocked when I told them. Arguably the most well-known publication in the world had written something about the work they were doing. They just stared. They were like, *we didn't think it would matter*. And clearly it did. What was originally an assignment to them became a life-changing piece of history. We can use our voices, and we can make a difference."

From their own bedrooms, attics, basements, and kitchen tables, the students created content that was powerful because it was authentic. It was audio that mattered, that resonated with audiences who could relate to it. Despite not being in a radio studio, the students made content that had value. "We had to be resilient, we had to use what we had," says Sean of that time. "The technical quality is not the point. Quality to me is a high priority. But the content is where we start," says Sean emphatically.

But in such a difficult time as the pandemic, even the production of radio content was secondary to something far more important in Sean's opinion. "I would argue to you that I was not focusing on content, I was focusing on their well-being, and content was what was going to help them mentally get through it. If I'm being completely honest, I didn't care what they did to get on the air, I cared that they were okay, that they had an outlet to let things out. You know, to be themselves." When it comes down to it, Sean believes that you do not need a studio or lots of equipment to create audio that can change lives. Even if all you have is a phone, that's enough. "*What it takes is the courage to hit record, and to open your mouth*" (See Figure 2.1).

FIGURE 2.1   Sean McDonald (Photo provided by Neumann University).

Equipment check: The tools you will really need, and the ones you will not

I believe audio production does not require expensive equipment. Indeed, courtesy of the digital revolution over the last twenty-five years, you probably have enough of what you need to begin with right now. The convergence of different technologies into single electronic devices gives us more access than ever in choosing tools to create audio content. Already, two early exercises presumed you had such basic equipment to record your own voice.

The main thrust of this book is to help you find your voice and discover how you can use it to create audio content. Before you can do this, you need knowledge of how to best use whatever technology is available to you. This chapter will focus on that technology; however, if you wish to start creating audio content as quickly as possible with just your smartphone, then read about entry level audio essentials and go straight to exercise #1, on page 55.

Several times I have seen enthusiasts purchasing expensive equipment that they simply did not need. Expensive gadgets not only run away with money but also have technical capabilities beyond beginners' own needs and understanding. I recommend a more incremental approach to acquiring equipment. The emphasis here is on discovering what we want to communicate first before how we do so. In all, I shall outline three levels: *Entry, mid-level, and advanced.*

The good news is that audio production equipment is affordable, especially compared to other forms of media. "Done on the cheap, TV looks terrible ... unwatched except by friends and family. Radio can't be done except on the cheap, and with a $150 microphone ... anyone can make it sound just fine" (McKibben, 2000). It does not take much to create some audio magic.

Three principles should be kept in mind:

1 First, *the type of content always determines the tools needed for its creation.* At the early stage, you will be creating basic audio content that is relatively simple to produce and listen to, without the need for editing. Such audio content therefore does not need expensive equipment. Only when you progress in creating increasingly complex content, is more expensive equipment required.
2 Second, *recording the highest quality audio possible should always be your goal whatever level of equipment you use.* Your mission should be to record high-quality audio from the very start, so you do not waste time and energy trying to clean up or fix poor audio quality. Obviously, quality improves as you move through the three levels of equipment options. The more resources, the more options for editing and creating audio. As you begin you should be thinking about how to "keep it simple, focus on producing high-quality content with what you have, and worry about advancing different parts of the process later on" (Larson, 2020, p. 55).
3 Third, *no amount of equipment can save badly recorded audio or substitute for a bad idea.* A certain amount of editing wizardry might still work wonders to save poorly recorded audio, but no amount of resources can salvage content that has been badly thought out. Before you record anything, plan carefully and thoughtfully.

Bearing in mind these key principles to creating audio content, here are the three levels of equipment in terms of affordability.

Entry level audio essentials (with little or no budget)

Those only interested in creating basic content probably want to spend as little as possible, or nothing at all, on audio equipment. At this level there are essentially two options: smartphone or computer.

If you at least have a smartphone (iOS or Android for example) then you will be surprised how capable it can be as a recording device. No other cost need be involved. *This book assumes that some readers will only have a smartphone to work with, and that's OK!* The smartphone's big advantages are its portability and its capability to record *spontaneously*. More complicated technical setups lose this flexibility, and although they are likely to record material at a higher quality, they can miss the action. If you have a tablet like an iPad, that could also be used in much the same way as a smartphone.

For *in-the-moment* recording, a phone is the way to go. Even if you have the resources for a mid or advanced level setup, knowing how to record audio effectively and quickly with your smartphone can be incredibly handy when you need to capture something instantly.

Should a smartphone be your only recording device, it is crucial to know its full capabilities and limitations. You need to maximize the highest quality recorded audio with it. Knowing the location of your phone's microphone is essential so you can point the microphone toward what you are recording. Avoid accidentally smothering or obstructing sound by your hand or a phone case. Keeping its input clean and free from dust and grime ensures the cleanest quality audio possible. Grime can accumulate around your phone inputs, and occasional cleaning sessions are rarely wasted time.

Phone placement for recording needs careful consideration. Good microphone placement ensures that any audio is recorded at the right volume level (not too low, or too loud) and that you are recording the sound that you want, and not the sound that you do not.

Recording inside, I suggest a *coffee mug* can be a useful piece of equipment. It must be empty – spilled liquid is never good news. Since microphone stands are expensive, a mug can provide an ideal stand several inches above the table or other flat surface. That few inches of height gives the phone a far better range for recording sound. Think of its recording range as an invisible balloon, and by lifting it from a surface, you inflate the range. Admittedly not a glamorous solution, but an effective one, especially when recording your own voice and reading from a script. You will be able to use both hands to hold your script as you speak into the phone that is now closer to your mouth than if it was lying on the table. There are phone tripods you can buy that do the same thing, but you cannot beat a mug as a free solution (See Figure 2.2).

Recording in outside environments needs extra care. Here mugs are not ideal! Wind and rain obviously require protection of the microphone by strategic shielding or angling. But that is sometimes where the spontaneous action is. The strategic use of an umbrella can make all the difference in situations like these! Finding shelter can also provide a safe and dry location to record. Always be aware of the weather, noise and other people that can affect your recording when you are outside. You will have to be especially aware of how to use your microphone effectively, perhaps holding it closer than usual to the speaker if there is outside noise. Also be especially alert for your own safety in whatever surroundings you are in.

FIGURE 2.2 A mug and a smartphone: all you need to get going (Photo: Rob Quicke).

Your **smartphone** or **tablet** should have some good free options that will provide easy recording, and even some editing tools. For iOS, you can use the inbuilt *Voice Memos* recorder, but plenty of other options exist. For example, you could use *Voice recorder: Audio editor, Voice Recorder Pro, Voice Recorder Lite, Recorder Plus,* and *SoundLab Audio Editor.* Checking the Apple App Store will provide you with the latest version of these apps, as well as other suggestions.

For Android, you could use *Voice Pro, WaveEditor, MusicEditor, Voice Recorder, Smart Recorder, Dolby On, Recorder by Google,* to name a few. Often there will be a free version of the app you can use, with upgraded options unlocked for a fee. You will need to check the terms and conditions when you install and use it. Always experiment with an app first, to make sure it works for you, before paying for any upgrades or unlocked features. Inevitably, editing is less easy on a smartphone as the screen is smaller, but with patience, it can be done successfully.

The second option of recording on a **computer** clearly lacks the advantages of portability and spontaneity that a phone or tablet has. If you are using a desktop computer, your location will be fixed, whereas using a laptop computer does offer some portability, as much as the battery charge allows. Recording is again built into their use, but obviously, using a computer keyboard and mouse (or mousepad) gives advantages when using audio software over the small screens of phones and tablets. For MacOS, Windows, or Linux PC, the most widely adopted completely free audio editing software is *Audacity* (https://www.audacityteam.org), which has enough options and online supporting materials to handle almost any audio editing project. If you are ever stuck for help, many Audacity training videos on YouTube can assist. Other apps like *Ocenaudio* (https://www.ocenaudio.com), *AudioTool* (https://www.audiotool.com), and *Acoustica* (https://acondigital.com/products/acoustica) are also options that you can explore.

One more valuable piece of equipment that you likely already possess is a set of **headphones** or **earbuds**. These are essential for isolating your audio from surrounding noise. Only by listening with headphones to our recording can we tell if volume level is set right, or if other noises like traffic or air conditioning threaten to overwhelm. Ensuring clarity and crispness at an appropriate volume is central to recording good audio.

If this is your equipment situation, and you know what recording app you will use, you may now go to page 55 and begin exercise #1.

Mid-level audio equipment (with a recommended budget)

Having money allows options. These next two sections are for students who want to progress beyond using the basics of smartphones, tablets, and computers (and a mug of course!).

Fortunately, we live in a time with multiple options available for purchasing audio equipment. New equipment can be obtained from specialized vendors that serve the media industry. They typically offer discounts when buying in bulk. So be warned – that's fine for any media purchases such as blank CDs, SD cards, batteries, and other consumables, but perhaps not best for single item purchases. Even Amazon now sells audio equipment that will suit your needs and is competitively priced for single item purchases. Always check that the equipment you are purchasing has a decent warranty, certainly better than a ninety-day one, and has legitimate positive reviews. The saying holds true that *if you buy cheap, you'll buy twice*, so be careful in purchasing something that seems too good to be true.

If buying new is not an option, second-hand markets such as eBay, Facebook Marketplace, and their equivalents can offer used equipment at affordable prices, though obviously you must be careful not to purchase something that might be damaged. Always check that there is an option to return your purchase if you find it is defective. Or sometimes you can inspect the item before you make the purchase. Beware the mistake I mentioned earlier of buying equipment with functions and features that you may never use.

I suggest a simple audio checklist that you can use:

- *Recording device*
- *Microphone*
- *Mic stand or mic arm*
- *Headphones*
- *Editing software*

First, a *recording device*. Remember the principle that the type of content determines required equipment? When recording moves from an inside environment (such as your home) to outside (what we call "in the field"), questions of portability emerge. We noted earlier that recording directly into a laptop with a USB microphone allows a degree of portability. But a laptop's battery life may be considerably shorter than using a handheld recording device that may record for several hours on one set of batteries. Such handheld recorders have the great advantage that they can be used for both in-studio recording and for outside in the field. Students willing to budget more can greatly gain from their versatility. Bear in mind the prices here may vary according to the country and currency you are using.

At mid-level point, my two recommendations (in the current market) for budget-friendly handheld recorders are as follows:

The Tascam DR-05×2X 2 is typically available for under $120 (See Figure 2.3). Buying used will be far less. With its simple handheld design, as a point-and-record device, it can record over seventeen hours of audio on just two AA batteries, using dual internal condenser microphones. Very useful for recording a single voice, and for interviews. It uses a microSD card.

Very similar to the Tascam recorder is the Zoom H1n, which retails at $120. The H1n offers ten hours of recording time on two AA batteries, recording to a standard SD card. Like the Tascam, it is a simple point-and-record device with built-in microphones and a simple LCD display that shows

FIGURE 2.3 The Tascam DR-05X (Photo: Birgit Reitz-Hofmann/Shutterstock. com).

volume levels in real-time. Both the Tascam DR-05X and the Zoom H1n offer similar functions, and you should check to see details of the latest model when you are ready to buy, as the manufacturers periodically update them.

Of course, you can push beyond these budget recorders to the next mid-range level. Prices will vary worldwide, but it is certainly possible to acquire an excellent equipment package for under $500. For this level, I suggest two more devices.

The Marantz PMD661MKIII 4 is an excellent choice of a handheld device for recording both yourself and another person. You can buy it new for around $350-$400. Older Marantz models can be found in the used market, and if they are fully functional they are solid recommendations. The Marantz is a rugged unit that can handle a few knocks and, with an SD card inside, can record up to six hours of audio in MP3 or WAV format, perhaps even longer depending on the size of your SD card. You will need to have batteries (AA ×4) with you for recording in the field or use a power adapter to plug in at home. Importantly it has two XLR microphone inputs (that's a three-prong input cable connection), so if you are recording an interview or podcast, two dedicated microphones are possible. The VU meter provides quick visibility to see if your volume levels are too low or too high.

Similar in size is the Zoom H6 recorder, which offers more recording inputs than the Marantz PMD661MKIII. You can buy one for around $350. The Zoom H6 offers up to four XLR microphone inputs, each with their own volume control knob. That means you could record up to four people with their own microphone at once and be able to control their volumes fairly easily. A full color LCD display on the front keeps track of the levels. With up to 20 hours of recording time, the Zoom H6 can be used for many recording situations. As with the Marantz, there are older, more affordable Zoom handheld recorders that are for sale in the second-hand market.

Further handheld recorders that students have found useful include:

- Sony ICD-UX570 Digital Voice Recorder, ICDUX570BLK (around $100)
- Zoom H2n (around $200)
- Tascam DR-40X Four-Track Digital Audio Recorder (around $200)

The **microphone** is second on our equipment list. Microphones are like cars. They all get you to where you need to go, but do you really need to get there in a Porsche? A gold-plated microphone is not a necessity to record great audio! However, microphones do vary in their quality of audio recording and need careful evaluation. Remember the second principle that the highest quality audio possible should always be your goal *whatever level* of equipment you use.

At entry level, students are likely to use any built-in microphone that your equipment has. But at mid-level, that is always second best to recording with a dedicated mic. While the Marantz and Zoom models I have described both have in-built microphones, you will greatly improve audio quality when you plug in a microphone. Using a dedicated microphone gives much more control over direction and range of recording.

All microphones are *transducers*, which basically means taking one form of energy and converting it into another. The analog soundwave (your voice) enters the microphone and is converted into an electrical signal that is recognized as audio into a computer or sound board. That electrical signal is then displayed as a soundwave on your screen. Generally, the more you pay for a microphone, the higher the quality of the transducer. By the way, a speaker does the reverse. It takes an electrical signal and converts it into an audio soundwave that you can hear.

Also, beware any microphone under $50 (and many are available), which are cheaply constructed. That can lead to more buzz, hum, hiss, and other unwanted noises, also with less frequency response as well. In my experience, the cheaper the microphone, the less the protection from unwanted sounds. For example, certain sounds make the air move quickly into the microphone, causing a "pop" sound when they are picked up by the microphone's *diaphragm*. This is a disc inside the microphone that vibrates when sound interacts with it and sends that sound to your computer or recording device. These pops are called *plosives* caused by speaking words with the letters *p* and *b* in them. You can feel these plosives by placing a finger an inch from your mouth and then saying "pickled pepper." You'll feel the air hit your finger, and that's what causes it to "pop" into a microphone.

To reduce interference, I recommend using a pop shield or foam windscreen. A pop filter acts as a barrier that stops air from hitting the mic but allows the sound to go through. You can make your own with a pair of tights stretched over a coat hanger! This gets close to recreating what you would find inside a radio studio. Fortunately, pop filters are relatively affordable, about $25 or so. A proven method of reducing or eliminating plosives is to have the microphone at least 6–8 inches away from your mouth when using it and at a slight 20-degree angle to avoid your mouth directly facing it.

When your recording is going to be in the same place every time, recording into a microphone that's plugged into a tethered, or plugged in, computer may well make sense. In this case, you are in essence creating your own basic studio environment (more on that later).

My recommendations below relate to current market costs but should give a good idea of the sort of equipment students will find useful at this mid-level stage.

The Shure SM58 is a rugged vocal microphone with an XLR connection, available for around $100. Used for decades, this mic can take a beating with a deserved reputation for reliability, although it's highly recommended to use a pop shield or foam windscreen when using it, as it comes without protection.

FIGURE 2.4 The Shure SM58 (Photo: dzmat.ph/Shutterstock.com).

Durable and tough, it can also be used as an effective self-defense projectile if needed![1] (See Figure 2.4.)

Some other good microphones that you can use:

- Shure MV7 (around $250)
- Audio-Technica AT2035PK (around $200)
- Sennheiser e945 Supercardioid Dynamic Handheld Mic (around $200)

For a limited budget, a USB microphone such as the Blue Yeti retails for about $130 and is a recommended choice for recording at home with a PC. It records audio at a 16-bit, 48 kHz recording rate, which is considered professional quality audio.

Alternatively, some other USB microphones you could use:

- AKG Pro Audio Ara Professional USB- C Condenser Microphone (around $100)
- HyperX QuadCast USB Microphone (around $140)
- Razer Seiren X USB Streaming Microphone (around $100)

There are many other USB microphones out there, so you have options.

Third, *mic stand* or *mic arm*. Though the coffee mug offers some protection from interference, a proper mic stand really minimizes the problem. A tabletop mic stand works well, is portable for any location, and allows you to find the perfect angle and height for your speaking. But just be careful – surfaces have conductive properties. For example, with a table, accidentally hitting its surface with hands or elbows or even knocking the legs with feet can cause vibrations to travel up the mic stand and into your recording. I once interviewed a local politician who thumped her fist when talking, which rendered the audio unusable in parts. You can reduce vibrations by placing the mic stand on a towel or padding. It may not look great, but it helps.

An alternative to the mic stand that reduces unwanted noise from bumps, knocks, and other problems is a mic *arm* that attaches to your desk, table, or wall. Obviously it is less portable than a mic stand, but it gives options to sit or stand when recording. A floor stand also gives that freedom, though it will pick up even a slight elbow brush.

Four, *headphones*. As we noted at the entry level, headphones make a profound difference to recording. They allow you to monitor, real-time, the recording and recognize any problems as they occur. It is best to record audio with headphones, if at all possible. Volume levels are instantly registered as is environmental interference such as a strong wind.

Like microphones, the cheapest headphones may not provide enough clarity. A general rule of thumb is to look for headphones that cover the frequency range from 20 Hz (Bass) to 20 kHz (Treble). Anything less, and you are not hearing the full range of sound.

Unlike microphones, a decent set of headphones can be purchased for under $50. Don't be fooled into thinking that you need to spend hundreds on cool branded headphones. You're probably paying more for the name than the components inside.

Five, *editing software*. At mid-level, it is easier to edit on a computer than your cell phone. Raw audio needs to be transferred from a recording device, and then *imported* as sound files into the editing program. Those who use computers to record directly clearly have a simpler time importing material.

Chapter 7 will describe the editing process, which is a major part of this book's *developer stage*. In terms of choosing audio editing software, my recommendation is that you use fee-paying *Adobe Audition* (Adobe, 2023). Joining the Adobe Creative Cloud (CC) gives access to this software. Currently, this costs a monthly fee. Some may benefit from discounted or free access through their university or school if they have an arrangement with Adobe. Many in the radio industry prefer using *Adobe Audition* to edit raw audio, and many online training resources assist in your understanding of how to use it.

Advanced level equipment (won the lottery? buy this!)

If you are in the fortunate position that you have the resources to buy whatever equipment you want, then please contact me directly.

Seriously though, more resources obviously enable you to improve quality in your equipment setup at every point. However, you should still be astute in your purchases and avoid ending up with "all the gear and no idea" (Teague, 2020).

First the **recording device**. At this level, remember that the ideal setup involves equipment that can record the highest quality audio and yet still be easily portable. My recommendation is the RODECaster Pro 8, with four microphones, tabletop mic stands, and pop filters for each microphone. This model has become a popular choice with many podcasters, and my students have come to see their RODECaster as a beloved asset (Figure 2.5).

This device enables you to record your voice and the voice of up to three people you're interviewing on separate tracks. Recording independent tracks is important when it comes to editing later because, as you will see, when you have multiple sounds or inputs on one single track, it is difficult to separate them. Recording one track per input facilitates much easier editing. Because the RØDECaster Pro allows you to record multiple, individual tracks on either your computer or to a MicroSD card; it's like having a complete radio studio at your fingertips. You should be able to purchase a RØDECaster Pro for around $600. However, with all the extra

FIGURE 2.5 The RØDECaster Pro. Lots of options (Photo: RØDE).

equipment such as four microphones, cables, stands, and pop filters, you could be looking at a $2,500 + outlay easily.

Another excellent choice would be the Presonus StudioLive AR8c. Costing around $500, the PreSonus StudioLive AR8c Mixer offers options galore. There are four balanced microphone inputs, two instrument/line inputs, and six balanced line level inputs. Connecting via USB, or recording directly to an SD card, this mixer offers plenty of ways to record audio. However, having that many options can seem intimidating. Like dealing with any sophisticated equipment, practical engagement and hands-on learning is the key to growing comfortable with its capabilities.

Other good mixers that can record audio into your computer:

- Yamaha MG10XU (around $230)
- Behringer Xenyx 1204USB Premium 12-Input 2/2-Bus Mixer (around $180)
- Mackie 402VLZ4 4-Channel Ultra-Compact Mixer (around $100)

Second, choosing a more expensive **microphone** opens up wider discussion about ways in which they record. Every microphone has a *polar pattern* that determines how it picks up sound. The more expensive the microphone, the more likely that you can adjust its polar pattern by altering its settings.

Most microphones in this chapter are mono microphones, which typically have *cardioid* and *shotgun* polar patterns (although some give the option to adjust the polar pattern). This means that the sound comes from the center of your speakers or the middle of the sound field. These are fine for recording a single voice, speaking, or singing. For the handheld recorders with built-in microphones, they may well offer the option to record in stereo.

That's a good option if you have it, because for recording interviews, or situations with more people, it's good to record in stereo. A *bi-directional* microphone is ideal for such situations, as the audio is clearly separated into left and right so you can place the interviewer's voice on one side, and on the other, those who are being interviewed. This uses the *stereo field* by placing the recorded voices as separate sounds in a distinct sound space. That's a production technique we will explore later.

Here are the key microphone polar patterns (see Figure 2.6):

So, you can see that *different microphone patterns are good to use in certain situations*. For example, for a microphone to capture the sound of an environment all around you, choosing an *omnidirectional* microphone that captures an environment's ambient sounds with a 360-degree pickup pattern would be a good choice.

As we consider the advanced level of equipment, the Shure SM5B is seen by many to be the best choice for professional recording. It's a hefty

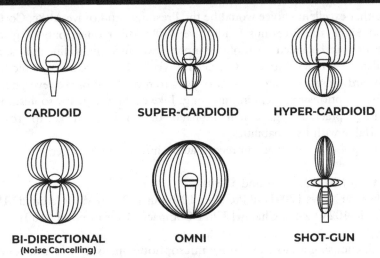

FIGURE 2.6 Microphone Polar Patterns (Image: Mark Williams).

cardioid (unidirectional) microphone that captures the full warmth of human voice and is priced accordingly, around $400 or so. Owning an SM5B makes you feel part of a secret club anytime you spot someone else using one for a podcast, YouTube video, or Twitch stream. Again, using an XLR connection to connect to your mixer or handheld recorder, it's a versatile choice for many audio projects. It is heavy, so you will need a mic stand or mic arm when using it (see Figure 2.7).

For **editing software**, an alternative to *Adobe Audition* would be the more advanced Avid's *Pro Tools* (https://www.avid.com/pro-tools). More often used by music producers and creators, this multi-tracking editing software can be intimidating for those starting out but is an excellent audio editor with many features. It's also typically more expensive at around $400 for the year. Obviously, its many features and capabilities demand a steeper learning curve. Like *Audition, Pro Tools* allows you to export or save your audio in a variety of audio formats, such as WAV and mp3, and has helpful tools to clean up and enhance your audio.

In summary, let's remember that those at the entry level are able to create audio just as adequately as those with more expensive equipment. Yes, with more resources, more complex audio becomes possible. But one quality is essential whatever level you are at. That's the *willingness to develop your skills*. And skills do not depend on equipment; they depend on *you*.

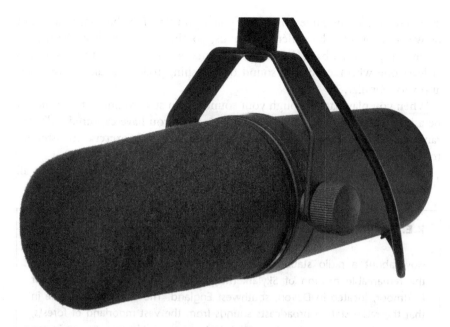

FIGURE 2.7   The Shure SM7B (Photo: Michael V Riggs/Shutterstock.com).

Some of these skills require paying attention to basic elements of recording, like this first exercise, which asks you to notice and appreciate the sounds around you in an entirely new way. Environmental noise is a vital issue.

Chapter 2, R.E.A.L. Exercise #1: The sounds around you

Have you ever considered the sounds of where you live? Your mission for this exercise is to capture the sounds around you, trying to avoid recording any voices, thereby creating a rich montage of your audio environment.

Before you start, walk around and make a plan of what you will record. Consider the following before you hit the record button:

1 **Where is the loudest noise in my environment? Is there a busy road nearby?**

2 **What objects make continuous sounds that I can record?**

3 **What objects make sounds when I interact with them? Think of an old, creaky door or walking on old floor boards.**

4 **What sounds unusual or interesting that will intrigue the listener? Think of different textures and noises to record.**

Try to record about three minutes of sound in total. Hit the pause button in between recording the different sounds, so the sounds play consecutively when you play it all back. When my students do this exercise, there is always at least one who records the sound of a flushing toilet! Creaking doors are also very popular.

When you play back through your sounds from start to finish, there should be a moment when you realize, with pride, that you have captured a diverse range of sounds varying in texture and volume. This exercise in listening to the world around you should open your ears!

As you complete this exercise, remember it's important that you save all the audio files you create in a folder for future playback and review.

R.E.A.L. Moment

How about a radio station that "gives voice to the landscape"? That's the remarkable mission of Skylark (https://skylark.fm), a radio station for Dartmoor, located in Devon, southwest England. The concept is unique in that the radio station broadcasts sounds from the vast moorland of forests, rivers, and wetlands that make up the Dartmoor area. Listeners tuning in can hear sounds of birds singing, bubbling rivers, and wind in the trees. It's a remarkable audio experience, immersing you in the environment, that evokes powerful images in your imagination as you are transported into the heart of nature itself.

Creating the best conditions to record

Critical to the next stage of discovery is making the best acoustic conditions for using your toolkit. Let's explore what that entails.

Soundproofing

Soundproofing is an obvious need. So many factors can sabotage sound quality. Rooms with solid walls and hard surfaces are prime problem-makers, causing serious reverberation. Reverberation is defined as the effect after a sound has been made as audio waves continue to travel through the air, hitting and bouncing off surfaces like walls, ceilings, floors, furniture, or even other people. The greater the reverberation, the longer it takes for sound to die down. In audio-speak, when reverberation occurs it is called "wet" audio. Soundproofing can lead to a pleasant "dry" recording of your voice. As in life, it is much better to stay dry than become wet!

Your experiences in exercise #1 should have alerted you to how many sounds are around you, some of which you may not have been aware of.

The noise of background air conditioning or outside traffic can really interfere, and perhaps you noticed other sounds too.

Soundproofing's goal is to reduce reverberation, either by absorbing the sound or breaking it up with rough or uneven surfaces. Staying "dry." Varying budgets achieve different levels of soundproofing in your home.

Even with little or no budget, you can still create a recording environment that produces clean audio content. It may not look glamorous or professional, but if the result is crisp, dry audio, that's what counts. After all, listeners cannot see the circumstances in which you are recording. At the entry level you need to record in a small space. But avoid bathrooms at all costs! They top the list for reverberation. You can often tell when you are talking to someone on the phone if they are in a bathroom, as shiny, hard surfaces bounce and "boom" their voice.

The simplest solution is to use a closet, especially where you can surround yourself with soft materials to absorb sound. Here crisp, clean, dry vocals can be achieved with a minimum of reverberation. Sticking cardboard egg cartons on a wall may look rather ugly, but they surprisingly help break up reverberation. I have known some students embracing their inner child and constructing a pillow fort, which can also serve well as a sound-absorbing recording space. Another idea is to create a simple vocal booth in a large cardboard box, large enough for you to immerse your head without threat of suffocation. Positioning a microphone within the box, or perhaps through a hole if the box is too small, its soundproofing is greatly enhanced by throwing a blanket over the box as well as your head and shoulders.

You can be more ambitious and create a vocal booth using blankets and PVC pipes for about $200. On a bigger budget still, you can purchase a vocal booth that can be set up at home. But even with just two panels of foam soundproofing you will still be creating a better sound recording environment than recording without it (see Figure 2.8).

Making an effort to cut down reverberation is essential. The assignments in this chapter can all be completed using simple soundproofing methods like these. Soundproofing can make all the difference to the quality of your recordings.

Basic checks for your toolkit

Mistakes happen. When is a great audio piece not a great audio piece? When you forget to press the record button! Particularly at the beginning, when working with new equipment, you need to keep checking the basics to make sure you are on track to achieve quality audio. These checks will soon become second nature, but they always need attention.

FIGURE 2.8 If it's all you have, just two foam panels will work (Photo: Axel Bueckert/Shutterstock.com).

A checklist of some of the easily avoidable mistakes I have witnessed: With your **microphone:**

- Is it too close to the computer, picking up the computer's sound?
- Does any of your equipment cause a buzz or hum that's being picked up by the mic? Sometimes microphones or cables have a buzz or feedback if they are not grounded properly.
- Are your cables plugged in properly?
- Are your recording levels good (not too low, or too loud, about 70% of the maximum volume)? Distortion in a recording that's too high is much more difficult to deal with than if it's recorded too low. Increasing amplification (volume) is always easier. Try to avoid both.
- Are you using a pop shield or microphone guard/filter to reduce "popping"?

With your **headphones:**

- Is your headphone volume too loud? Is audio bleeding through your headphones into your recording?
- Are your headphones set too low? Are you able to hear all the sounds around you that might affect your recording?
- Is your headphone cable a nuisance? Does it obstruct your hands or make a sound rubbing against the table or anything else?

With your **recording device:**

- Are your battery levels okay? Do you have spare batteries just in case?
- Is there enough storage on your recording device or computer to record and save the audio?
- Is the device in a vibration-free place, so it does not pick up unwanted noises?

With your **recording environment** (exercise #1 should have alerted you to these sounds):

- Are there any sounds coming from *within* the space you are in, like air conditioning, heating, electrical hum?
- Is there noise from *outside*, such as traffic and other people?
- Are there sounds coming from other rooms or floors?
- Are there any pets or animals that make a noise? Beware of dogs chewing on your cables!
- Can you mute the house telephone, or cell phone?
- Are you in the best soundproofed location?
- What is the best day/time of the week for you to record?
- If using a phone, consider putting it into airplane mode to ensure you stop notifications while recording.

With your **body:**

- Are you aware of what you are doing with your hands and body when you are recording? (For example, fidgeting or turning pages on a script can often be picked up by a microphone.)
- Is your breathing too loud in the recording?
- Are you coughing or clearing your throat too much?
- When you are recording do you occasionally move away from the micro-phone as you talk, causing the volume to fluctuate?
- Do you often suffer a dry mouth or smack your lips when talking?
- Are you hydrated? Do you have a drink of water on hand to lubricate your throat?

All these common issues can occur, especially when starting to record audio. Only through trial and error can you create circumstances for recording the best quality audio possible at whichever level you are working. Your goal is to produce audio that requires as little fixing as possible in the editing process afterwards. This is where accumulating experience really makes a difference.

Our second exercise seeks to create an audio feature that requires no editing because its sounds are recorded in chronological sequence.

Chapter 2, R.E.A.L. Exercise #2: A day in your life

Building upon your experience of exercise #1, this exercise records the sounds around you as well as your own voice. It will also be a fun exercise to be a storyteller, as you describe a typical day in your life, using sound effects and your voice as a narrator. Before you start, make a plan of what you will record, and even write a short script to narrate the day's sequence of audio material. Consider the following points:

1 **What sounds are easy to record that are part of my daily life? A good start may be recording your alarm clock waking you up.**

2 **Ensure that you alternate your sound effect recordings with narration that explains what is happening. For example, "After I get up, I eat breakfast," could be followed by the sound of milk pouring on cereal, or coffee brewing.**

3 **Try to summarize an entire day, ending with a final sound, like turning off a light switch, or switching off a television.**

Record about two minutes of audio in total, in chronological order according to your script. Again, hit the pause button in between recording, so the sounds play through consecutively on playback. Don't worry about editing the content at this point. Hopefully, your piece will sound satisfying enough as it flows from start to finish.

The little black book (though it does not have to be black and it does not have to be a book)!

You might be surprised that accompanying these sections on toolkit equipment issues, I believe it's not too early to introduce the idea of the little black book. During my first job as a morning show presenter on a commercial radio station in the UK, my mentor suggested that I needed to invest in just such a book. I am so glad I did and now recommend it as good practice for students right from the beginning of their journey.

I used a physical notebook with 250 blank, lined pages. Its hard cover made it durable to survive the rough and tumble of frequent use and eventually travel all over the world. The principle was brilliantly simple: every time I created some audio that *worked*, I noted it down. Similarly, every time I did something that *did not work*, or was a downright mistake, I chronicled that too. Keeping track of the mistakes and triumphs became an incredibly important tool for self-development.

Working with two columns per page, on one side I kept a record of the ideas and strategies that worked, and on the other I jotted down those that failed. In the beginning, I made far more entries in the "mistakes" column than in the positive column. Perhaps that is because it is easier to recognize a mistake – those *oops* moments can sting! Sometimes it is less easy to identify when something has gone well, especially when you are working on your own.

In the early years, I found that I documented mostly technical equipment aspects in my mistakes column. As you develop proficiency in using the equipment and technology, you focus less on simple technical errors and more on content issues. An interesting aspect of this reflection method is that in addition to deepening awareness of your own strengths and weaknesses, it also helps discern skills and mistakes when you work with others.

Personal audio journaling can, of course, also be written in digital form in a Word document or note-taking app of your choice. However you make notes, this journaling process will result, over time, in you chiseling and crafting yourself into a better producer of audio content. Unique lessons learned along the way will improve your confidence. Reflecting on your strengths and weaknesses empowers development like nothing else. Starting with a completely empty notebook, it took me several years to fill it up. After much ink in the early years, the jottings slowed down. And that showed how much *I learned to learn* about myself in crafting audio production. In my journey of self-discovery, the black book had a vital part to play.

Every time you hear some audio or radio that impresses you from someone else, make a note and try to analyze why it worked and what you could learn from other people's production techniques and the way they prepare content. Equally, other's mistakes can serve as cautionary reminders of what you should avoid doing.

This black book concept is an essential personal exercise that you should start today. It requires self-discipline and self-awareness as well as commitment to keep updating it as you learn. **Among your many tasks, please do not ignore this one!** Its importance will become very evident in the *decoder* stage in chapter 10.

This chapter's final exercise asks you to reflect on where you live. When I have used this exercise in class, students have sometimes involved family members and even occasionally have asked "people on the street" for their opinions too! Different approaches to this assignment are possible, so follow your creative instincts. Consider the advice of famous novelist Anthony Burgess (1917–93): "It's always good to remember where you come from and celebrate it. To remember where you come from is part of where you're going" (Friedman & Friedman, 2015, p. 2; Pryor, 2017, p. 111).

Chapter 2, R.E.A.L. Exercise #3: What makes your community unique?
Everybody has to live somewhere. This exercise explores where you live and what makes it a unique place. Describe your community in your own words. You may well love where you live, or feel rather negative about it, and this exercise invites you to record why you feel the way you do:
Consider the following:

1 **How would you describe where you live to a stranger?**

2 **Is there anything exciting or unique about where you live?**

3 **Do you think you will still be living in the same place when you grow older?**

Record for as long as you like for this exercise. Many of us have thought too little about where we live. Taking time may give new perspectives on your home area and where you might like to be in the future.

Play with abandon

In the last chapter I shared my goal that this book will start you on your journey in audio production without worrying about technical issues. I want you to be unleashed and experiment with the new experience of recording sound, entering a safe space to play, fail, and learn. Enthusiasm can evaporate if preparation takes too long. I want to speed up action so that you can hit record and *start communicating.*

As a discoverer beginning to work with your toolbox, you shouldn't worry about mistakes, flaws, distortion, technical pops, and other background noises that will probably appear in your early recordings. Finding your voice and feeling comfortable in front of a microphone comes first. Audio begins with your mouth in front of a microphone! In chapter 1, exercises #2 and #3, you already discovered that within seconds, using the most basic of tools, you can start to record audio. You can experiment without hesitation.

Holly Wagg claims that "regardless of the existence of an audience or the size of the audience, the youth believe that in making a program at a campus-community radio station their voices are legitimated" (Wagg, 2004, p. 275). The simple act of producing audio builds confidence, regardless of whether anyone else hears it. You begin with an audience of one. That is the safest and most creative way. You can certainly play with abandon when no one is listening! We will examine the role of other listeners in chapter 3, but an audience is not needed to realize the importance of the work you can create on your own. Audiences exert pressure that can inhibit self-discovery. You need the safety net of listening to yourself on playback without facing judgment from others. Producing audio for yourself is a catalyst for self-development. Take advantage of the freedom that "for your ears only" provides. Let's leave the whole issue of meeting an audience's expectation until a little later, knowing that your journey should take you to a point where you feel comfortable enough with sharing your work with one.

Final thoughts: *I liked radio so much, I took over the station:* How one student realized his calling and became a mentor to the students who followed him

Picture this: Chicago. A university cafeteria full of busy students eating lunch. In the corner two male students sit at a table. They are freshmen in their very first week of their first year at university. In conversation, one student is about to make a suggestion that will fundamentally change the course of the other student's life.

"It is burned in my memory. That's how important this moment of my life is. It was the second day of school, and I had met a buddy at freshman orientation. His name was Vince. And he was a music fan. I was a music fan, so we were just talking" (P. Kreten, personal communication, August 12, 2021).

Vince asked Peter if he wanted to come with him to check out the radio station he had heard about. "I looked at my watch and said yeah, I got an hour to kill. So we walked to the radio station. And the best way I can describe the first time seeing the studio, it was like seeing in color for the first time. It was like the Wizard of Oz, I was in black and white, and when I walked into the studio ... I was suddenly in the Land of Oz. It was just magical!" Peter walked into that studio carrying the fears and anxieties of an eighteen-year-old at a crossroads in his life, trying to find his place at his new university.

"I was the opposite of what I am today. I was entirely introverted. I had a hard time speaking to strangers. My worst fear in school was the teacher calling me up to say something in front of the class, to give a class presentation. I would get sick to my stomach. I couldn't do it. I was terrified." Very quickly Peter found a warm welcome and a new group of friends. "Joining the radio station was a godsend in so many areas, because it got me a group of friends. For the first time ever in my life, I felt accepted for who I was."

Peter threw himself into learning about radio and creating radio content. "Being in that studio and being on air does something to you. It changes your DNA fundamentally. And it changed my DNA fundamentally. It helped me grow as a person. I'm sure I did terrible radio in the beginning, but it didn't matter because I was learning. And it just allowed me to blossom. I came out of my cocoon because of it. It gave me the confidence to confront other things that terrified me and overcome those challenges," reflects Peter.

Some highlights of that time are cherished by Peter. "My first ever interview was with Ziggy Marley, Bob Marley's son. I also interviewed Yoko Ono and Sean Lennon! John Lennon's my favorite Beatle of all time, and I interviewed his wife and his son! That's college radio right there. I never thought I would have those opportunities."

At this point, I must insert myself into the story. The radio station that Peter was involved with was WXAV 88.3 FM, Chicago, at Saint Xavier University. I was General Manager and witnessed first-hand Peter's transformation as he became more involved with the radio station. He rose to become the Program Director, which was the top student position available. I came to rely upon Peter and view him as a huge success because of all he had learned and done. But all things must pass, and I was to leave the university to take a job in New Jersey on the east coast of America.

Peter recalls the day he found out. "I remember it vividly. It was 2007. You had a messy office at the time. And I walked in, and it was completely clean. And I made a joke. I'm like, 'Oh my God, your office is actually clean! What … are you leaving?' And you looked at me and said, 'Well, actually, I am.' And I was blown away." It was a bittersweet moment though, as Peter recalls: "I was happy for you. But I was devastated at the same time because you and I became good friends. And now my friend is leaving. So, I was really sad."

Not long after, Peter was struck with an idea. "Lightning struck me. I thought, *I have to go for Rob's job.*" A few days later Peter came into my office and said to me that he was going to propose to the university to take over the radio station after I left. Peter remembers my reaction. I was skeptical that they would hire a student who had not yet graduated but nevertheless encouraged him to give it his best shot as he was clearly passionate about the station. Why not?

The next week Peter booked an appointment with the Vice President of the university to discuss the idea. Peter asked him what the plans were for the station after I had left. "To this day, it still blows my mind. He said, 'I have no idea what we're going to do.'" Peter saw an opportunity and seized it. "Give it to me, I know exactly what to do." Utterly convicted that it was his destiny, he presented a vision with confidence and certainty. Peter reflects: "It was really gutsy of me because I was just 23 years old. And I was telling someone that I should become the General Manager of a radio station in the third largest media market in the country. There are people who work their entire lives, entire professional careers, dreaming of getting hired in Chicago, and they never make it. And I was 23, saying not only should I work in the third largest media market in the country, I need to run it."

His argument was persuasive, convinced that after I had left the station, "No one would do as good of a job as I would, because no one cared as much as I cared." He was right. I could not think of anyone else who lived and breathed that radio station more. Says Peter, "I don't necessarily believe in predestination. But there's a part of me that believes I was destined to work in college radio."

So, on a trial basis, the Vice President gave Peter an opportunity to prove himself. Immediately he poured himself into the radio station and mentoring its student staff. Very quickly, recognition came, with *Paste* magazine recognizing WXAV as one of the best college radio stations in the US. Student participation increased, and other broadcasting awards brought further recognition to Peter's leadership. Success has continued to this day. "I take more pride when the students win because we've now won a number of awards from the Illinois Broadcasters Association. I see it as my mission, to give back to the students what you gave me, Rob. I want the student that was just like me, that didn't know that they could have a voice and didn't realize they could do it. And I want them to know that they can do it, and they should do it, and they can be successful doing it," says Peter.

Before long, Peter was appointed full time as a General Manager. He was one of the youngest GMs in the radio industry in the entire country. "It was a vindication, that a 24-year-old kid knew what he was doing," says Peter proudly. Looking back now, Peter marvels at his journey from being a shy, apprehensive student who first entered the radio station with great trepidation and uncertainty and grew into his current role as mentor, manager, and educator at the university. "When we first came to the radio station, we were all outsiders. And it was like, we all finally found each other, and we created our own family. I walked through those doors. And I found my people."

You can imagine how positively I feel about Peter's story. It illustrates what this book is all about. R.E.A.L. qualities marked every step of his journey. He found people who could *relate* to what he had to say, who he could *engage* with, and in an *authentic* and *liberated* way. In short, Peter found a place in which he could comfortably express himself. He found his own voice, and he became more confident. Now he has an opportunity to help others find their voices and create content that is meaningful for them.

As you move beyond day one, you will start to gain self-confidence and realize that there's so much you can record and create; the only limitation will be your imagination (see Figure 2.9).

FIGURE 2.9   Peter Kreten (Photo credit: Alejandra Torres from Epic Lens Photography & Film).

Note

1 Of course, the manufacturer would say this is not a recommended use of its product.

References

Adobe. (2023). *Adobe Audition* (Version 2022.23.5) [Computer software]. https://www.adobe.com/products/audition.html

Friedman, H. H., & Friedman, L. W. (2015). Stranger in a strange land: The importance of remembering and the consequences of forgetting. *SSRN Electronic Journal*. Advance online publication. 10.2139/ssrn.2589389

Larson, D. (2020). *Podcasting made simple: The step by step guide on how to start a successful podcast from the ground up*. AT Publishing.

McKibben, B. (2000). The world streaming in: Free, easy-to-use software turns any PC into the greatest shortwave set there ever was. *The Atlantic, 287*(1), 76–78. https://www.theatlantic.com/magazine/archive/2000/07/the-world-streaming-in/378279/

Pryor, G. (2017). *Origins*. Lulu Press.

Teague, P. (2020). *How to start a podcast: Launch a podcast for free with no previous experience*. Clixeo Publishing.

Wagg, H. (2004). Empowering youth with radio power: "Anything goes" on CKUT campus-community radio. *Journal of Radio Studies, 11*, 268–276. 10.1207/s155 06843jrs1102_11

3

DISCOVERING EFFECTIVE WRITING FOR EARS & AUDIENCES

First thoughts: *Using words as a witness to history:* **How a radio journalist used audio to share important stories from Africa with the world**

Picture this: 1996. Brussels, Belgium. Population: 1.7 million. A student radio station is broadcasting a radio show on Sunday nights that is causing quite a sensation ...

"At 17, I started doing student radio, and I had a show that was an erotic literature radio show," smiles Arnaud Zajtman, who was born and raised in Belgium. It was a weekly show, and Arnaud with the other students creating the show suddenly had a hit on their hands. "We were doing very well among teenagers in Brussels! Talking about and reading erotic literature. Radio was a perfect medium because people could just fantasize and imagine." Radio also offered them legal protection. "Of course, under Belgian law, it's not pornography, because *there's no image*. So, there was no censorship, and anyone could access it. So, we had a lot of 16–17-year-olds in our audience!" says Arnaud. "And that's how I started doing radio, actually" (A. Zajtman, personal communication, July 7, 2022).

From that unusual beginning, Arnaud became quickly involved in serious radio journalism. After gaining an MA in Radio from Goldsmiths College, University of London, he started working at the BBC. "Having French as my first language, I entered through the *French for Africa* language service of the BBC World Service. I was interested in third-world issues, but I didn't know anything about Africa." His knowledge of Africa would quickly deepen. "I joined in June 1998, and in September 1998, I was the freelance correspondent based in Nairobi, Kenya. And I got a more permanent job with them in Congo two years later."

Arnaud found that the medium of radio was massively important in Africa. "It's the main medium for many people. Everybody has a radio. So, I was reporting for the audience that was around me. People would recognize me by my voice. It was

DOI: 10.4324/9781003263739-5

a very big responsibility to report about them, about what they were going through as people living in a war-torn country. In a tremendously rich country in terms of natural resources, but very poor when it came to people's incomes."

Arnaud also found that creating radio was easier than any other medium. "Radio is great, because it's light, you don't need a team, you just go up on your own. It works when it's too dangerous to go and film. It's very quick. You just go to a place, you just describe what you see, often you take notes, you record, and then you do your packages. I've always tried to use sounds, and atmos [atmosphere]. I think you can also do a lot with words just by *describing* where you are. You can do a lot with just writing a good description of where you are, what's around, what the village looks like, what the people look like, how they're dressed."

At this point Arnaud pauses, and then, in a very serious tone, continues. "I think you can do a lot ... even with the *inflection* of a voice ..." As an example, Arnaud shares the story of when he was live on the air for the BBC, in eastern Congo, when he heard something nearby that terrified him. "I was live for the morning program, on this little satellite dish. So, I sounded as if I was in the studio. I remember it being at night and hearing in the background a couple of women shouting and screaming. There had been some shooting during the day ... but it was a very quiet night, and then you had a couple of women screaming briefly. And I was live with this microphone." Arnaud knew he immediately needed to be cautious. "I was whispering because there could be some military, some rebels around, and I don't want to be spotted. And me describing the situation and explaining that I didn't know what happened to these women, but we know that sexual violence is a terrible problem in Congo. So those women were screaming, maybe they've just been raped by soldiers, who knows." Arnaud's live, whispered reporting had an immediate impact. "The producers were like, wow, this was mind blowing, in terms of conveying the atmosphere of the moment."

In that instance Arnaud could only imagine what happened to the women he heard screaming. But in May 2002, in the town of Kisangani, he would be one of the first people to enter the town after a massacre killed 183 people, and he witnessed the devastation. "That was emotionally the most difficult situation." Kisangani was deep in the forest in the middle of the Congo. "It's actually the setting of Joseph Conrad's book *The Heart of Darkness*, from which the film *Apocalypse Now* was adapted." Some soldiers had gone on a shooting spree and killed almost 200 people. Hours after the massacre, Arnaud and a colleague from the BBC were the first to arrive on the scene. "I was kind of leading the investigation. We spoke to the guy from the Red Cross, and to other people and got a clear picture, hour by hour, of what had exactly happened." The story Arnaud uncovered was of indiscriminate killing in the streets all over the town.

You can imagine the sheer impact this had. "I think when you are the only one to report on a story like this, it's very heavy on your shoulders. You feel like you really have the responsibility to tell this story to the outside world." Back in Kinshasa putting together the report, Arnaud was emotionally hit by what he witnessed. "I remember bursting into tears. Sometimes when you report about these terrible things you need to keep a certain distance. It can take a toll on you. I had spent three or four days there, getting all these testimonies because I didn't report until I had the *full story*, then I left because it was too dangerous to be there."

The final story included eyewitnesses interviewed about the massacre, describing in their own words what had happened, as well as Arnaud's storytelling. The world would learn about the massacre because of his work. His investigation into the Kisangani massacre received the prestigious *Prix Bayeux* war correspondent award in 2002. He has since produced work as a documentary filmmaker that has been recognized internationally. In 2019, Arnaud produced a film that won France's prestigious *Prix Albert Londres* award, and also received Al Jazeera's *Human Rights* award.

Today Arnaud reflects on the power of radio. "We tell stories to our children when they go to bed, and for me radio is a bit reminiscent of the stories that you are being told as you go to bed." Radio has an intimacy that makes it a unique medium. "As a reporter, you try to talk to one person at a time. You feel that you are being told the story, just for you. There is that relationship."

Radio can also save lives. "Radio can also inform you on where the nearest health center is, where there's going to be the next food distribution. I think radio gives a sense of community more than other media. It's your radio, you know, you can be a voice, you can have access to it. I think it's important that people have access to their radio, so there is no disconnection. In that sense, I think radio keeps a community together."

"Yes," says Arnaud, grinning, "Radio is a great way of storytelling anything!" (see Figure 3.1)

FIGURE 3.1 Arnaud Zajtman (Photo: Arnaud Zajtman).

In this *discoverer* stage we have already spent considerable time on finding your voice, including giving attention to your two voices (the *outside* voice that people hear and your *inner* voice that only you hear) and the need to learn how to express yourself authentically. Then we explored the necessary equipment needed for your journey, which can be achieved at three different levels according to your budget. That practical chapter also gave details about certain vital requirements for effective recording, like soundproofing. Now, in this chapter we need to learn another skill - discovering the art of *writing for the ear* with natural speech.

Effective writing for the ear

Our emphasis on R.E.A.L. audio stresses how audio *relates* to others as though one-to-one, with *engaging* content while being *authentic* and *liberating*. The exercises so far should have helped you start your journey. But now we must unpack the two sides of creating *engaging* audio. One side involves learning the demanding art of writing words that come across as natural speech, as though you are in a conversation. The other side is understanding who your audience is.

Arnaud's story underlines radio's power to engage with listeners. This often means taking risks to help listeners feel and see things in a different way. Communicating the horror of the Kisangani massacre, weaving together eyewitness accounts with vivid descriptions, required writing a script with the intimacy that gives radio its uniqueness. As he says: "You try to talk to one person at a time. You feel that you are being told the story, just for you. There is that relationship." Central to the power of finding your voice for audio is this ability to see yourself talking with another person sitting on the other side of the microphone with language that comes naturally to you, sounding spontaneous and uncontrived. Actually, the goal is in *sounding* as though you are thinking and choosing the words *as you speak,* even if you are reading from a script.

The heart of this chapter lies in the significant contrast between writing for the eye versus writing for the ear. Most of us first learn to write in school, in college, on paper or laptop, so that you can *see* it. The relationship is *writer to reader.* Only when it is written down can teachers see your first efforts, which need to follow basic rules for writing for the eye. Sentences need to be complete, requiring a subject and a verb phrase. Several clauses may be added so that sentences can grow long. These sentences are then organized into paragraphs that are supposed to contain one main theme each. When writing for the eye these paragraphs can be ordered, providing a sequence of logical ideas like an essay. Often, when read aloud, these essays *sound* like essays, with long, complicated words, and dense, formal paragraphs with a sense of heaviness.

Of course, gifted readers can still energize words written for the eye, but you may have heard audio when speakers sound wooden because they are reading something in this essay style. Its language does not flow naturally with the immediacy of active words delivered by an active voice. It's become dull and flat. Paper has come between speaker and listener. Good audio sounds as though the speaker and listeners are in conversation just sitting across from each other. *Active speech* has different patterns and rhythms aiding that relationship.

In everyday speech, words flow in shorter sentences with informal connections. Contractions of words – *isn't, doesn't, hasn't* – become the norm. Words like *indeed, however, nevertheless*, are likely to be used far less. Writing for the ear breaks some of the literary rules about complete sentences and how they connect in paragraphs. While you should never be ungrammatical, flexing the rules to sound natural becomes an essential skill for audio content.

You may have enjoyed a moment in life when you said something that proved powerful, and made an impact, *almost as if it were scripted like a movie scene*. Such spontaneous events are rare and memorable, but when you write using *your* voice freely and confidently, sounding words out for the ear, you'll have *contrived spontaneity*. You will have *a voice that speaks with passion and without fear –an active voice*.

The secret to writing for the ear is *to test your writing by sounding its words out loud to yourself as you write them*. (We shall consider different kinds of scripts and their demands in Chapter 6). Writing for the ear keeps thinking: "If I was speaking to another person how do I *say* this thought?" Something happens when you read words out loud as though you are going on air. Words change order and emphasis. Key expressions come to you which are colloquial. You discover what words look good on paper but are clumsy off the tongue. You learn to choose and say active words.

Choosing active words

In order to be lively and active, words need to be clear and concise, to help us think concretely and precisely. Concise words avoid cluttering up speech, which easily happens. In many ways we can add unnecessary words. The passive voice can creep in, as when we say "gave encouragement to" instead of "encouraged" or "held a meeting" instead of "met." It is easy to add words like *very* and *really*. Long words which may seem impressive to the eye should be substituted by shorter, familiar words. Rather than using general concepts and vague descriptions that seem abstract, we need to find words that focus on people's actual experiences of life. One of the best ac-companiments to aid precision is the presence of direct stories which provide immediate examples. *Illustrations, descriptions,* and *stories* provide immediate examples of what you mean. Words connect directly to listeners and are not left as some generic comments.

Using words and expressions without obvious meaning can lose an audi-ence. Consider the 2004 *Foot In Mouth Award,* given to former UK Prime Minister Boris Johnson for uttering the baffling phrase, "I could not fail to disagree with you less,"[1] which left the audience completely bewildered. Avoid audience confusion by using plain and direct language as much as possible.

Assume that someone could be listening that you do not know and does not know you. *Radio.co*'s Jamie Ashbrook says that "new listeners have no loyalty. Earn trust by being respectful and creating engaging content" (Ashbrook, 2023, Radio Presenter Fails section). Being too informal and using language that might offend can be risky. You may just lose your audi-ence as a result.

Arnaud's experience also emphasized the ability of words to paint pic-tures. Over 100 years ago, at the very beginning of radio's impact upon society, radio sets were huge pieces of wooden furniture. After they were delivered by truck and hauled into the living room, whole families would gather around these radio sets, mesmerized by stories that would capture their imaginations. Interestingly, when television arrived to provide images along with the audio, some people said they preferred radio because *the pictures were better.* That remains the power of audio. Its words can paint vivid pictures in people's minds. In television and film the director gives you a picture. How many times has an audience been disappointed in a film or television show because the images presented to them did not match the better images in their minds? Audio gives freedom to listeners to create their own pictures.

Active words are like paint colors to awaken the audience. Vivid words impact senses, by giving them a sense of taste, touch, and smell. The moment or situation comes alive in their minds by matching emotions with words. Offer your audience *rich descriptions* that fire the imagination. It's good to use more descriptive and colorful language than when you are talking normally. For example, consider these two opening lines:

- *I'm standing in an old concert hall, with rows of empty wooden seats, and a thick red velvet curtain drawn across the stage. This vast hall is mostly dark, with only the illuminated EXIT signs providing much light in the gloomy darkness. There is a faint smell of dust in the air. There's no one else here but me, standing in silence in a place normally full of people and laughter.*

- *I'm standing at the corner of a busy street. I have to occasionally move as people busily walk past me, some laden with shopping bags, others rushing to get somewhere, others listening to music on earbuds and glued to cell phones. A few feet away, cars, buses, and motorbikes whizz past noisily, leaving strong exhaust fumes behind them. There is a sense of urgency in the air.*

The first example needs maximum description because it is recorded in a quiet space. But with the second you can aid imagination by adding a recording of street sounds. Why not try your hand at the following exercise?

Chapter 3, R.E.A.L. Exercise #1: Hear what I see
Earlier in Chapter 2, exercise 1, you created a short piece using sounds around you. This is a *writing* exercise that requires you to look more closely than ever to describe your environment to the listener.

1 **Choose a location either inside or outside, such as a library, museum, park, or public space.**

2 **Before you write anything down, look around you slowly and fully. Turn around in a complete circle and also look at the ground and what's above you. Take it all in. This should not take more than a minute or so.**

3 **Note down the main features of your location. For an inside location, are there windows, doors, pictures on the walls, or any other items in the location? For outside locations, are there trees, plants, paths, and other features? Wherever you are, is it busy? What does the environment communicate? Is it busy with people or traffic? Is it quiet and isolated, do you feel alone? What does the atmosphere feel like? Write down the main characteristics of the place.**

4 **Now, looking at what you have noted, and writing no more than four or five lines (about 60–100 words) provide a description for someone who can only hear your voice, to summarize your location.**

You may find this difficult at first because it's not easy to prioritize the key features of any location. But as you practice, you will become better at it, and discover that you only need to describe the key aspects of a location for someone to be able to picture it in their mind.

Words that work, and words that do not

Active words express energy and ensure the words we choose keep listeners interested. As author David Lloyd asks, "When you want your listeners to be hungry for what you are about to do, are you using the most appetizing words?". Appetizing words keep people listening.

Avoiding clichés and tired phrases will only improve what your audiences hear. Keep your writing fresh and vibrant, and steer away from phrases and cliches that are repetitive and waste words. Some examples of common phrases that you should avoid:

- *Added bonus* – something that is added is already a bonus
- *Each and every* – saying the same thing, twice
- *Basic fundamentals* – repeating essentially the same thing
- *Free gift* – aren't gifts usually free?
- *End result* – the end usually is the result, same for *final outcome*
- *False pretense* – a pretense is usually false, so why two words?
- *New innovation* – something new is by default an innovation
- *Past history* – the history *is* the past.
- *Null and void* – mean the same thing
- *Advance warning* – all warnings happen in advance of something occurring
- *Major breakthrough* – just say breakthrough, same for *major milestone*
- *Temporarily suspended* – just say suspended
- *First discovered* – just say discovered
- *Unexpected surprise* – just don't

As you create content and start writing, it's good to create and update a list of words and phrases that you should avoid. It can help you stay away from the bad habit of using tired and repetitive language. In conversation, phrases such as these are often said without much thought. Active writing for the ear excises words that waste time and energy. Some words just do not work well, slowing down momentum. Being focused and effective requires you to think about every word that you use, to have maximum effect. Be *intentional*.

Also, be careful about using *jargon* or *slang* words that only a portion of your general audience might understand. Jargon words or expressions that a group or industry may well commonly use may be lost on a wider audience. Similarly, slang that is spoken comfortably in specific groups and regions can confuse others.

It is also important to distinguish between thoughtless repetition and deliberate repetition of *key information*. Since the audience only has one opportunity to understand what's happening, repeating certain key points or moments assists their comprehension. You are simply reminding them of important information.

In conclusion, words that look great on the page should be tested to be great in the ear. Using shorter, easily understood words does not mean that your script has to sound simple or predictable. But when words are fresh and exciting, your audience will want to hear what comes next.

Active words need *your* active voice

We marvel at comedians for being articulate and witty. But, we can easily forget that behind their seemingly easy speech lies many hours of revisions and intensive work to ensure their words are fluent. Earlier I mentioned that the secret to writing for the ear is to *test your writing by sounding its words out loud to yourself.* Using your true voice, your unique style, vocabulary, sentence structure, and manner of delivery adds magic to active words. So, when you write your words down they should be as you talk. At all times you need to make sure that the *process* of writing your script and planning your content does not smother the power of your voice and what it has to say. Audio should come across naturally and authentically.

The more you discover your active voice with your unique characteristics the easier it is to avoid one of the great dangers of imitating someone else. As Oscar Wilde once wrote, "Most people are other people. Their thoughts are someone else's opinions, their lives a mimicry, their passions a quotation" (Wilde, 1905, p. 63). So be yourself, *because everyone else is taken* (O'Toole, 2016).

Jad Abumrad tells a salutary story. Now considered a radio "genius" with a voice well-known to millions of North Americans, Abumrad's work in radio, including the famous *Radiolab* podcast and show for National Public Radio, has received the prestigious Peabody Award and a MacArthur Fellowship. Yet at the beginning he struggled. He did not know what his authentic voice was. In fact, when he started he felt like he had to sound like someone else – in this case, a famous, but dead, news anchor:

> I did the Walter Cronkite thing, so everyone would take me seriously. And then I learned that's just ridiculous. And then I tried to sound like myself, *which took years by the way.* I look back on that period between when I was first getting in, to when someone first recognized me, which was, you know, years went by. And I was largely ignored during that time. I was literally making a show on the AM signal at 8 pm, Sunday nights … No one could hear my show. I was *horribly miserable* about that. But I look back now. And I think, *thank God people were ignoring me.* It gave me a chance to figure out simple things like how do you speak into a microphone and not sound like an ass? What kind of stories are my stories versus the stories other people tell? I got to fumble my way through the dark for a long time finding the answers, and then someone finally paid attention. (Gross, 2021, 26:29)

Fumbling through the dark happens to many of us at the beginning. It is always easier to copy someone else's style than to risk finding our own. But copying is always inauthentic. As Barbara Houseman asserts, "We may try to copy someone else, whom we feel does have a powerful and expressive voice. This never works. Such a voice can never reveal our inner responses. If you wish to find a voice that truly touches an audience, you have to find your *own* voice" (Houseman, 2002).

The exercises in this book are designed to lead you to feel confident with your voice and your sound. Jad Abumrad's success and his work on *Radiolab* was borne out of a period of obscurity in which he learned some important lessons. Give yourself the space and time to be able to experiment and learn about your voice's strengths and weaknesses.

At this point let's have a little fun. Deliberately being someone else is an art that voice over artists and actors have to perfect. They make a living out of performing characters or using their voice for narration, demonstrating great versatility. When you use a voice that is not your normal voice it can be enormously liberating. You are giving yourself permission to have fun and try out styles you would not usually use and possibly discover facets of your voice that you never knew were there.

So, this next exercise is not to be taken too seriously, but it invites you to experiment playfully with your voice. Let's see what your voice can do.

Chapter 3, R.E.A.L. Exercise #2: One script, four interpretations

This exercise helps you to recognize your outside voice and experiment with the pace (the speed), inflection (the way that you modulate your voice up and down), and enunciation (how you say each word). You should record this for personal use!

1 **Look at the three paragraphs from earlier, beginning "The more you discover your ..." and ending "find your *own* voice (Houseman, 2002)."**

2 **First, read *earnestly*, and as close to what you consider to be your normal voice and speed.**

3 **Now read it again, but this time, in as *happy* a tone as possible, and at a faster speed.**

4 **Third, read it as *sadly* as possible at a slower speed.**

5 **Finally, read it as *angrily* as possible at a normal speed.**

You may feel a little ridiculous when trying out these different voices, but that's precisely the point. You are listening, perhaps for the first time, to the range of expressive possibilities for your outside voice. Reading like this provides a good warmup for your vocal cords, before reading any script or recording your voice. It helps to get the mouth physically moving before you speak. It's much like an athlete warming up before they compete!

R.E.A.L. Moment

The Coldest Case In Laramie is a 2023 podcast by Kim Barker, an award-winning *New York Times* journalist. Barker goes back to her childhood home, Laramie, Wyoming, in the northwest of the USA. She paints a bleak picture for the audience to imagine. In a calm, matter-of-fact voice she says, "I've always remembered it as a mean town. Uncommonly mean. A place of jagged edges and cold people. Where the wind blew so hard, it actually whipped pebbles at you, actually pushed trucks off the highway. Laramie stood at an elevation of more than 7,000 feet and got so socked-in by winter storms, it felt like we were trapped. Like there was no way out." It's a painful return as Barker revisits the 1985 murder of Shelli Wiley that has remained unsolved for almost four decades. The way that Barker calmly and clearly explains the story of the grisly murder is a masterclass in storytelling and writing for the ear. She pulls you in, like you are listening to a personal diary, before asking out loud the questions that you may be thinking to yourself. The episodes often end with a twist or cliffhanger, so you want to keep listening to find out what happened next. Good, compelling writing for the ear like this means you can picture in your mind the macabre crime scene and the people she interviews in the town that she herself could not wait to leave when she was younger.

Mind your voice!

Having exercised our voices in exercise #2, we need to add some further advice about our voices. The story goes that John Lennon, then an ex-Beatle, stumbled across a book published in 1970 called *The Primal Scream. Primal Therapy: The Cure for Neurosis* by the psychologist Arthur Janov. This book encouraged readers to purge themselves of repressed childhood trauma and bad memories by using their voices to vent the anger and frustration of those past experiences. To literally cry and scream aloud their anguish, to express and expel the pain from within. Lennon used the technique in some of his music, especially the ending of the song "Mother," released on his 1970 album *John Lennon/Plastic Ono Band*. Listening to that song and hearing Lennon's ragged, screaming voice at the end conveys some understanding of the sad childhood trauma of Lennon losing his mother in a car accident. It's a highly effective use of the voice.

However, screaming like that is not to be recommended if you want to maintain a healthy voice! Indeed, you need to treat your voice as a tool, an instrument, that requires great care. Because their voice is how they make their living, many voiceover artists take extra care to look after their health, and their voice. Being a VO artist means you have to be ready to work at a moment's notice, so being ill and not having their voice at 100% can cost them. Your voice is unique and should be treated with care.

Keeping the voice healthy and ready for action

Like any part of the body, because it is muscle and tissue, it can become strained or worn out. Famous singers such as Adele, Miley Cyrus, and Mariah Carey have all had vocal injuries because they overused their voices. They ended up taking time off to heal and recover. Yet for the average person it's relatively simple to keep your voice healthy and ensure that you are always in a position to deliver something vocally when needed. Some good advice to heed:

- Always drink a lot of water as part of your everyday life, so you are hydrated. Have water available to lubricate your throat when you are speaking for any length of time. In winter or dry climates consider using a humidifier to keep moisture in the air.
- Avoid inhaling smoke, and smoky venues. Smoking and vaping are enemies of healthy voices.
- Try not to overuse your voice. When you know you will be speaking a lot at some point in the day, rest your voice in silence for as long as you can beforehand.
- Avoid screaming or yelling if possible. Don't do a John Lennon scream! At sports games, concerts, or nightclubs it might be tempting, but protect your voice by not pushing it to extremes.
- If it hurts to speak, because of a sore throat or another reason, immediately rest your voice. Never force your voice to speak if you are in pain.
- If you are feeling run down, the voice is often one of the first things to be affected. Always try to get enough sleep and to feel well rested.

Perhaps the most important advice is to pay attention to how your voice sounds and your body feels when you speak. Often we ignore small issues such as a sore throat or minor cough before they get to the point of disrupting our lives. Your voice can sometimes act as a barometer of your overall health, so listen to it.

Managing nerves, the dreaded cottonmouth, and other speech anxieties

When talking with friends we speak freely and without fear. Yet, putting a microphone in front of someone can freeze them. Ironically, the presence of a microphone, the very tool to record sound, can intimidate and silence us. Perhaps it's a feeling that our words will now have more importance or consequence, so we need to take special care in what we say. We worry that we could say the wrong or stupid thing. Being "on the record" is a sobering thought and, as we shall see later, must be taken seriously. What is important in the beginning is that you try acclimatizing yourself to speaking to a microphone. There is no substitute for practicing with an audience of one, so the microphone becomes less intimidating and more of a friend when it's used.

I know firsthand how speaking into a microphone can induce nerves. When I read the news on the radio in the UK for the first time in 1998, I was so nervous, my voice sounded rather like a hyperventilating chipmunk! Adrenaline kicked in, and knowing that many people were listening, I read the script at a ridiculously fast speed. My voice also went up an octave or so. Nervous energy can take the voice higher and higher in pitch. I tore through my script with alarming speed, and sounded like I had just inhaled several balloons of helium.

That voice did not sound like my natural voice at all. After I finished reading, having not paused to breathe properly, my heart was pounding. The experience of being on the air had completely disoriented me. Radio station colleagues looked through the studio window with disbelief and some concern!

Adrenaline can also cause dry mouth, also known as cottonmouth. In stressful situations, salivary glands in the mouth fail to make enough saliva to keep your mouth wet and lubricated. Fear tends to dry you out. When you have a 'sticky' feeling in your mouth and speech becomes awkward, a quick sip of water or any drink remedies that.

Remaining calm and confident is the goal when dealing with nerves. Here are some helpful strategies to reduce speech anxiety:

- Before you start practicing, identify your fears, and write them down. Stating worries often shrinks their importance, for most never happen anyway. Worrying is wasted energy.
- Positively embrace your nerves, and put that energy to good use. Often nerves are an indication that you want to do a good job and will be able to speak with confidence when the time comes.
- Are you able to record or speak in a location which is a familiar, safe place?

- Practice what you have to say, repeating it several times, so there are no surprises that can cause panic when you finally deliver it.
- Ensure the words in your script play to the strengths of your vocabulary and your ability to speak them confidently.
- Focus on what you have to say, rather than how anyone may respond. Don't get ahead of yourself and worry about your audience's reaction.
- Don't expect perfection. Putting pressure on yourself to be perfect adds needless anxiety. Accept who you are.
- Rehearse in front of a family member or friend who is supportive and can offer constructive feedback.
- If it all goes wrong, does it matter anyway? If you are recording something, simply redo the take. Mistakes happen. Don't be hard on yourself.

These strategies should help prevent your body getting into a *fight or flight* state. As you gain more experience, anxiety lessens and you find your best voice more consistently. Practicing speaking as you are gently breathing out so that you can ensure you do not run out of breath. These steps are designed to activate the *parasympathetic nervous system*, as vocal coach Gary Genard further explains, "Our autonomic nervous system is composed of the sympathetic and parasympathetic modes of operating. The sympathetic system is the active version – it's what activates the fight-or-flight response that can induce fear and even a panic attack while speaking. The parasympathetic system is the opposite: it's a calming mode which allows you to rest, rejuvenate, and even reinvigorate yourself" (Genard, 2018, para. 10).

That leads us to our next exercise, which requires you to deliver a news story with authority and gravitas.

Chapter 3, R.E.A.L. Exercise #3: Delivering the news
This exercise asks that you try to deliver a news story as seriously as possible. It involves applying techniques to give your voice authority.

1 Choose a news story currently in the media, most likely from a news website.

2 Copy and paste the words of that story into a blank word document about one page in length. This will be your script. As this is just for practice, and not being broadcast, you do not need to worry about copyright issues.

3 Read the script several times in preparation.

4 Record yourself reading it for the first time. Don't listen back to yourself yet.

5 Now, when you read the story aloud, practice developing a cadence to your speech by varying the inflection of your voice. At the start of a sentence, and at every pause, raise your voice in pitch. When you finish a sentence, your pitch should go down. This emphasizes to the listener that the sentence is finished. It's not a normal way of speaking, but its variations accentuate the script and get the audience's attention.

6 Once you have practiced reading it in this particular vocal style, record yourself again.

7 Now compare both versions. What differences can you identify? How does modulating your voice from high to low affect the way you sound?

Finding appropriate modulation will become second nature as will the whole process of physically making sound as you gain practice. Another good idea to consider is to practice rewriting portions of a script to make it sound more natural as you are reading it. As long as you do not change the meaning, you can always make these kinds of adjustments to make it easier to read and hear.

Who will be your audience?

I've suggested that when you begin the journey of finding your voice you may not require an audience. Play with abandon with the audience of one! Producing audio just for the joy of it is reason enough. Srinivas Rao, author of *An Audience of One: Reclaiming Creativity for Its Own Sake,* puts it succinctly, "When art is not your way of earning a living, you have a sense of freedom to create whatever you're proud to put your signature on, even if it doesn't pay the bills" (Rao, 2018, p. 37). That applies to audio production. Not having to consider what an audience might think about what you have created means the pressure is off and creativity is full-on.

Further, Rao warns, "When we seek approval from others and let them set a standard we feel compelled to meet, we stop listening to ourselves. We understand people have opinions of us, so we dedicate our efforts to making those opinions favorable" (p. 37). Making audio for yourself is all part of giving yourself time with your outside voice. In your own company, you can be as experimental as you like without fear of audience judgment. Keep track of the things that work, as described earlier, in the little black book soyou can include these adventures.

Earlier we considered your voice's *physiology*. Now we consider some *sociological* influences too. Obviously, different social situations affect how we speak. In everyday social interactions with close friends and family, our speech is informal, but a professional work environment likely needs greater formality. Public speaking has its own requirements too, depending on types of audience.

As part of the *discoverer* stage you need to reflect on several issues: a) audio audiences are *different*; b) make a *guesstimate* about your first audience; c) try to *identify their needs* as far as possible; d) gain honest *feedback*.

Audio audiences are different

Producing audio work on air or for the internet contrasts greatly with performing on stage in front of an audience. With one you cannot see your hearers, let alone discern how they are responding. With the other, seeing an audience provides an immediate reading on its key characteristics such as age, gender, and ethnicity. Importantly, you can see how effective your performance is. Yawns, restlessness, and loud sighs with that classic sign of boredom – MEGO *my eyes glaze over* – are utterly demoralizing. Conversely, when a live audience responds positively it gives energy and encourages communication to new heights.

Audio clearly suffers a disadvantage here, though sometimes the type and focus of your audio helps define the listeners. For example, because a college or community radio station may transmit to a community of students or a particular neighborhood, you may have a good idea about age, gender, and ethnicity. Also, we shall see (Chapter 8) that podcasts often focus on specific interest areas that can potentially reach a group of listeners sharing the same interest. That's true whenever a radio show has specific aims, which likely defines its audience.

But, generally, you just *cannot be sure* who will listen. You may well reach people that you had no idea would ever listen to you. One of the joys of audio broadcasting is hearing from someone you do not know tell you how much your audio impacted them. Because there is frequently a gap between times of production and broadcast, this can give a bizarre sense of *deja-vu* as you have long since moved on since you created the audio in question.

Inevitably difficult, trying to define your audience can be very worthwhile, and you should nonetheless try.

Making a guesstimate about your first audience

As you create audio for your first audience, try to guess its main characteristics. How similar are your hearers likely to be to your own age and shared values? Undoubtedly your own interests, values, vocabulary, and lifestyle will connect more easily with some listeners rather than others. Of course, you will never succeed in pleasing everyone.

Each culture has their own systems of communication and ways of expressing meaning. "All these elements together make a composite of their uniqueness. To be successful, it is important to understand what their uniqueness is" (*Public Speaking*, n.d., Values section). Your audience listens and responds to your work through their culture and value system. Obviously, your own cultural experience may differ greatly from theirs. Being sensitive to those differences means taking care about the views and assumptions you present in your work.

Differences in culture and value systems are part of your audience's diversity, which includes race, ethnicity, gender, gender identity, sexual orientation, age, social class, physical ability or attributes, religious or ethical values system, national origin, and political beliefs. In essence, diversity is any aspect that can be used to differentiate a person or group from another.

Creating audio content that celebrates diversity, equity, and inclusion connects content with a wider group who feel they belong in the broadcast. As we learn more about other cultures and communities we learn more about ourselves. Multi-cultural sensitivity is learned through experience.

Your "guesstimate" about your first audience should attempt to ask:

- What is their average age? What demographic are you trying to reach?
- Are they predominantly one gender or an audience balanced in gender?
- Are most of them college undergraduates or graduates?
- Do they share a similar ethnicity?
- How much do you think your own age, gender, education, and ethnicity is similar to theirs?

The more you regularly produce audio content the easier this exercise becomes. Most importantly, its discipline should prevent you from making assumptions and jumping too quickly to create audio in your own image, supposing that what interests you will necessarily connect with your listeners.

So, before you start your project, carefully think about who you are trying to reach, and how best to reach them.

Identify their likely needs

Remember that most people, and therefore most audiences, tend to be self-centered. That's human nature. Think for a moment about the audio you most like to listen to. Why do you make this particular choice? We tend to listen in ways that benefit us and rarely do we give much time to something that fails to interest us. We are not built that way. So, it is imperative to recognize how different they may be from you.

So, you should attempt to ask what does the audience *want* from you? Of course, this moves into the complex territory of assessing a host of psychological factors such as needs, motives, attitudes, and values. Yet, failing to ask these questions can close us off from their needs.

- Is your audience affiliated to a particular group (such as college students, residents of a specific community, a group of similar professionals) where they want to hear their needs addressed?
- What kind of message or content might best meet their needs?
- How might you provide appropriate content to appeal to their attitudes and values?
- Should you beware of particular likes or dislikes, and no-go areas?
- What audio content out there is already popular with your target audience?

Remember, you need to be positive and open to who they are and how they think. When they listen, they should feel as if they are participating in a rewarding experience. You are enriching their lives. Time is the most valuable commodity that an audience has to give you. If they feel intellectually unfulfilled, artistically dissatisfied, or emotionally offended or untouched by your work, they will stop listening. Clearly, you want to come across as someone sensitive to their needs. Audiences quickly ignore speakers who seem to ignore them. Although beyond your control, some audiences will also switch off if they find the topic, your approach, or your voice simply not appealing to them. Don't worry about them, focus on the audience who might want to hear what you have to say.

This next R.E.A.L. moment presents an unusual view. Rather than worry too much about creating audio that engages powerfully with an audience, Rick Rubin urges concentrating on creating audio that pleases the creator first! Audio that is true to our voice! This interesting point of view emphasizes some of the early encouragement in this book about discovering your R.E.A.L. voice and staying true to it. I have included this moment to underline the inevitable tension between assessing your audience and their needs, and your own voice with your convictions.

R.E.A.L. Moment

In January 2023, Rich Roll interviewed the legendary music producer Rick Rubin on his podcast. Rubin founded Def Jam Records and has produced artists such as The Red Hot Chili Peppers, Johnny Cash, LL Cool J, and Adele, among others. Around the 29:00-minute mark, Rubin offers some profoundly powerful advice to those wanting to create powerful content. "Something that cripples artists thinking, 'I have to make the greatest thing ever made to humankind'. And then they basically psych themselves out of being able to make something good. They give into the pressure of thinking it's more than it is," says Rubin. What's his solution to creating without the pressure of an audience? Rubin says it's all about "lowering the stakes, where we're not setting out to make the greatest album of all time, we're not setting out to make the greatest song of all time, we're there to have fun in the studio, we're going to entertain each other, we're going to see if something happens." Whether it's making music, or audio and radio content, if we create for ourselves first, then good things can come from that. Provocatively, Rubin suggests that if we create for ourselves first what is produced will much more likely connect with an audience who appreciates the authenticity, "You have to make it to please yourself ... the audience comes last, and the audience comes last in service to the audience. The audience wants the best thing. They don't get the best thing while you're trying to service them. They get the best thing when you're servicing yourself, when you're true to who you are."

Gain honest feedback

Let me emphasize how learning *to listen to listeners* is immensely helpful on the audio journey. When you are starting out, your first audience may well be friends and family. They are usually willing listeners and will likely affirm us, though you must ask for honest feedback, because it is never too soon to catch problems and mistakes. Guide them by asking some key questions: How interesting was the content? Was it *relatable*, sharing something they did not know? Was it *engaging*, connecting directly with their own experiences? Were some parts unclear? Was I too fast or too slow?

Chapter 10 will consider the responsibility of *decoding* in more detail, but you are in prime position to ask yourself honest questions. Put yourself in the position of your listener. Try to keep open-minded about assessing your own work as you pose those same questions to yourself. You will soon gain a sense of how well you connected with your audience.

In my experience, when friends give you honest feedback, you will almost always find it improves your work.

Final thoughts: *Words can save lives:* How one radio broadcaster used his voice to bring crucial information to his listeners in times of crisis

Picture this: East Asia. Hong Kong. One of the most densely populated countries in the world, with 7.3 million people living on land about 1/4 times the size of New York City. The media culture is vibrant, with television, film, and radio all thriving in the subtropical climate. Born and raised in Hong Kong, Teric Kin-

ho Cheung grew up with a dream of one day working in radio and broadcasting to his fellow Hong Kongers.

"I was born and grew up in Hong Kong and am still living in Hong Kong now!" says Teric. From his early childhood days, the radio was always on and Teric was listening. "I have been a big radio fan since childhood. In the 80s and 90s, DJs and radio personalities were highly popular in Hong Kong. I always dreamed of working in the radio," but he did not know how to make his dream a reality. "At that time, there was no campus radio in my university days" (T. K. Cheung, personal communication, July 21, 2022).

One way to get in the doors of the Hong Kong radio stations was to enter competitions. That strategy paid off. "I did participate in some radio game shows and DJ Contests and thus have chances to visit the radio stations, speak over the mic, meet the DJs, and even join live shows in person!" smiles Teric. Those moments only made him more determined to realize his dream.

In 1988, one year after graduation from university, Teric had his chance. "There was an open position for the full-time post of Assistant Programme Officer in the Radio Division of the prestigious Radio Television Hong Kong (the public broadcaster of the city)." He applied immediately. After grueling testing through written tests, voice tests, and extensive interviews, "I was luckily offered the full-time post and started my 30 year-long career in the radio industry," he smiles.

And what a career it's been. Known for his on-air work as radio presenter and producer, he co-hosted the live Cantonese show *Traveling Round the World,* which was awarded the Top 20 Most-listened Radio Programmes in the city in 2013 and 2014, consecutively.

Many moments in the course of Teric's career demonstrate the power of audio and the uniqueness of the radio medium. When I asked about a specific example he became very serious. In Hong Kong the typhoon season starts in May and goes almost until November. Hurricane-force winds of more than 100 km/hour with gusts more than 220 km/hour can pass directly over Hong Kong, causing flooding and devastating landslides. These are moments of genuine emergency. "When a Tropical Typhoon Signal No.8 or above (highest signal is No. 10, similar to hurricane) is issued, all schools, public transportations, and economic activities are suspended and everybody is supposed to stay safe at home," explains Teric. "In those years before around 2000, all radio stations in the city (including commercial ones) had to joint-broadcast a *Special Typhoon Announcement* every 15 minutes round the clock."

Teric was chosen to deliver these announcements to all of Hong Kong. "That means almost everyone who turned on the radio would hear my voice every quarter of the hour. Also, in those days when being online was not well-developed, I had to stay in a special broadcast room inside the Hong Kong Observatory headquarters. As Hong Kongers were scrambling to get home, Teric would be heading to the observatory. In a state of emergency, Teric knew that his voice had to convey life-saving information. He also knew that he had to write the details as *clearly and concisely as possible*. His very words could make all the difference in a life-or-death situation. It was the perfect example of how radio can be a life-saving tool.

When I asked about his proudest moments in his radio career, Teric does not hesitate, "Together with the tireless efforts of my colleagues, the Community Involvement Broadcasting Service was successfully launched in 2015–16, and it serves to provide a platform for the ethnic minorities, less-privileged, and individuals and groups of special interests to produce proper radio programmes, and broadcast on-air and online." Teric is thrilled that he could play a part getting other people involved in radio, so they could share his life-long passion for creating audio content that impacts lives.

What final advice would Teric give to those wanting to create compelling audio? "You have to be *curious* about your surroundings and the world," he says. "Radio has its own charm and immense power. I like to write my scripts or produce my radio content from the angle of the audience. I use language and terminology they understand. Writing styles or production styles are different for different programme genres, but the content has to have some hooks that keep the audience continuing to listen!" (see Figure 3.2)

FIGURE 3.2 Teric Kin-ho Cheung (Photo credit: Teric CHEUNG).

Note

1 http://www.plainenglish.co.uk/campaigning/awards/2001-2010-awards/2004-awards/806-foot-in-mouth-award-2004.html

References

Ashbrook, J. (2023, April 11). *How to write a radio script that works.* Radio.co. https://radio.co/blog/radio-script

Genard, G. (2018, May 6). *The 5-minute exercise that can make you a fearless speaker.* Genard Method. https://www.genardmethod.com/blog/the-5-minute-exercise-that-can-make-you-a-fearless-speaker

Gross, T. (2021, July 26). *How Jad Abumrad, 'Radiolab' creator and co-host, got hooked on storytelling* [Audio podcast episode]. National Public Radio. Fresh Air. https://www.npr.org/2021/07/26/1020715035/jad-abumrad

Houseman, B. (with Branagh, K.). (2002). *Finding your voice: A step-by-step guide for actors.* Routledge.

O'Toole, G. (2016, April 10). *Be yourself. Everyone else is already taken.* Quote Investigator. https://quoteinvestigator.com/2014/01/20/be-yourself/

Public speaking: Cultural differences and multicultural audiences. (n.d.). Lumen Learning. Retrieved June 27, 2023, from https://courses.lumenlearning.com/wm-publicspeaking/chapter/cultural-difference-and-multicultural-audiences/

Rao, S. (with Dellabough, R.). (2018). *An audience of one: Reclaiming creativity for its own sake.* Portfolio.

Wilde, O. (1905). *De profundis.* G.P. Putnam's Sons.

4

DISCOVERING ADVANTAGES & POSSIBILITIES

First thoughts: *Can you hear us now?* How one student with autism, who found communication difficult, came alive in front of a radio microphone, and then started his own radio station for students with similar challenges

Picture this: 2019. Inside a student radio station, a 19-year-old male student sits in front of a microphone about to go on the air for the first time. This seems unremarkable, until you realize that this person is not used to speaking publicly, let alone on the radio. Something truly exceptional is about to happen ...

"To tell the truth, at the beginning I was nervous and excited, but I told myself not to be afraid," says Giovanni Lenzi (personal communication, January 14, 2022). From Bologna, Italy, and over 4,000 miles from home, he was visiting New Jersey and Brave New Radio on the campus of William Paterson University as part of a summer youth program. "I attended an English course to improve my English." What made the course especially exciting was the possibility of being on the campus radio station. "I couldn't miss this opportunity!" exclaims Giovanni.

Bridget Charlton (personal communication, January 18, 2022), who was the student running the radio workshop, has never forgotten meeting Giovanni. She marveled at his courage, struggling to communicate because of his autism. "When I was told I was going to have an autistic student in my class, I wasn't worried ... as a future speech-language pathologist and also an autistic adult. However, I was also told that if Giovanni couldn't 'handle' the class, or if he was 'distracting' to the other students, they could transfer him to a different course. This was more troubling than anything else. I believe all my

DOI: 10.4324/9781003263739-6

students should have the opportunity to experience radio, so I assured them that I would adjust the class as needed to include and best suit Giovanni. Suffice it to say, he loved the course. He needed to take some breaks during the two days of lectures, and sometimes I needed to rethink how to work on certain skills with him, but overall, the other students were very understanding, and everyone worked together beautifully."

"I am a boy with special needs," says Giovanni. "I found the courage and I put all my heart and soul into it!" He credits those who helped him. "I wasn't alone, because my friends Bridget and Francesco taught me what to do ... to articulate my words and to speak loud and clear. They gave me headphones and they let me talk on the microphone."

As he opened the mic and went live on the air, words began to flow freely from Giovanni in a way that those present had never witnessed before. He spoke so clearly and confidently. Everyone was astonished at the transformation. Bridget was elated. "Giovanni seemed to brighten up on air. It was such a special moment to see Giovanni share his special interest on-air with a live audience," recalls Bridget. Giovanni was elated too. "For the first time, I spoke on radio and my dream came true: I was on-air at a radio station! It was an unforgettable experience!"

Bridget reflects, "I believe Giovanni was able to express himself because he was supported by a strong network of people. From his co-host and fellow student to his other classmates, to his aid, to myself and the other staff at Brave New Radio, Giovanni was outfitted with a battalion of patient, supportive individuals. It was the confidence we had in him and the collective dedication we put forth that helped Giovanni's voice flourish."

How this transformed Giovanni! "The experience at the Brave New Radio changed my life because I understood that I also wanted to broadcast in Italy. For this reason, thanks to the help of my father and some friends, we were able to create our own radio station called Outside Radio." Based in Bologna, Italy, this is not your usual student radio station. It's a place for the *outsiders*, those who might be marginalized, ignored, without an outlet to speak elsewhere. It's a radical experiment in radio. "We are an inclusive radio station, and we talk about diversity as a gift and not as an obstacle to achieve your goals and to realize yourself. We are young, but we have many things to say, and we want to help people to reflect on considerable issues," says Giovanni.

The next year, in February 2020, I witnessed the launch of Outside Radio on World Radio Day, live from the Marconi Museum outside of Bologna. Here wireless radio was invented by Guglielmo Marconi 125 years before. Marconi would likely have approved the occasion.

Reflecting now, Giovanni can speak of the transformative experience of radio. "It is important for young people to find their own voice, to talk about what they think, what they feel, and to transmit relevant messages to other

FIGURE 4.1 Giovanni Lenzi (Photo credit: Greg Mattison).

people. A radio station is the way to do it," he says proudly. Bridget believes she was changed by what happened too. "I'm so glad I was able to give Giovanni an opportunity to express himself on air. This experience has inspired me to continue pursuing speech-language pathology in my career and radio in my free time."

What happened in that student radio station has changed Giovanni's life forever, and all those now impacted by Outside Radio. As Giovanni declares, "I can say that the experience of being on the radio helped me to find my own voice, and I hope that Outside Radio will help other people to do the same" (see Figure 4.1).

This chapter concludes the *discoverer* stage, which is foundational for the rest of the audio journey. I suggested earlier that impatience is understandable because of the urge many have to move quickly to producing creative audio. But omitting this critical process of discovery weakens your personal development.

A key point about the discoverer process: *when you learn more about yourself, you gain insight into who you are, thereby gaining self-confidence.* This is accompanied by another important realization: *as you learn more about yourself, you also learn more about the world around you.* That's because you are *in the world,* and as you discover your place in it, you understand more about how it works. You cannot help but absorb information and knowledge of your circumstances, even as the focus is on self-development. Spending time in the discoverer stage anchors you to knowing *who you are,* and *what you have to say.*

Now, in this last chapter of the discoverer section we need to give some attention to two major aspects of audio production which have been evident in some of the interviews and illustrations: namely, students bring particular strengths to the creative task, and working with a local radio station, when possible, offers immense advantages.

Your advantages and possibilities

I find Giovanni's story quite remarkable. He seemed, as someone with a condition that makes communication difficult, to be the least likely to enjoy the experience of creating audio. To witness and to hear Giovanni's breakthrough with radio was nothing less than inspiring. He's right when he claims, "It is important for young people to find their own voice, to talk about what they think, what they feel, and to transmit relevant messages to other people." I hope this encourages you. You need to know what advantages you have, as a student, approaching audio production.

What students bring to the microphone

I am convinced that students bring many distinctive assets to creating audio content. The students I teach are often teenagers and young adults. Sometimes it is assumed that because of limited life experience, they are idealistic and naïve in their worldview. Certainly, I have witnessed both overconfidence and self-doubt in the classroom, which testifies to a sense of an identity that is not fully developed. Students can question the value of their own voice, and that can lead to self-doubt and a spiral of silence. It is true of all of us that we can think too highly or too little of ourselves, and that can be demonstrated with agonizing candor in the classroom.

However, we should never disqualify or invalidate what students have to say because they do not have extensive personal histories or experience. Their gift is in seeing things *afresh*, finding ideas and suggestions that are "outside the box" of older people's worldviews and paradigms. Here is no jaded or institutionalized thinking. It is a mistake to dismiss their views.

It's also a mistake to underestimate the difficulties they may be facing. Many students exist in a continual state of economic anxiety and instability. A student recently confided that, in addition to being in school full time, he needed three part-time jobs to make ends meet. Students are acutely aware of the thin margins of life resulting in bare survival for some of them. They can therefore be on the cutting edge, engaging with many issues and topics, especially those relating to fairness, equality, and justice.

So, responsibility to shine a spotlight on these sometimes ignored areas of culture and society can fall upon young students and their generation. Their work uncovers stories and issues that no one else is aware of, or particularly concerned about, and exposes them to a larger audience. By doing so, the students experience "feelings of social relevance" because they create "publicly available cultural products" (Jacquay, 2019, p. 175) such as podcasts and radio programs that other people listen to. They lend their voices to important causes and issues.

What students can learn together

I find that students are incredibly encouraging and supportive of one another and want to hear what each has to say. I remember one student struggling at the microphone with nerves and the group rallying around to give support. Working in teams can provide students with a support structure that encourages everyone to succeed in their efforts to reach a common goal (Wood, 2017). When students work together, they overcome obstacles.

At this point I want you to take advantage and get involved if there is a college radio station near you. Throughout the world, college radio, as it's popularly known in the United States, takes many different forms. In the UK it's known as *student radio*, in Latin America it's known as *university radio*, and in India, it can also be known as *community radio*. Despite the difference in names, all these stations have one thing in common – they provide access for many people to have their first experience of radio broadcasting and producing. If not for college radio, many people simply would not have access to a radio station environment, which is typically the domain of professional broadcasting companies and off-limits to most people.

From my involvement with college radio, I have witnessed firsthand how students can be transformed by their experience with creating radio. College radio truly is "an alternative medium of learning and engagement" outside of the classroom (Ibrahim & Mishra, 2017). Laor's (2020) study of how students are positively affected by college radio supports this idea. He found students arrived with "very little faith in themselves. However, after some time broadcasting and working at the radio station, they developed higher self-esteem" (p. 349). He concludes that "college radio represents a precious platform and opportunity for self-expression and fulfillment through original content, creativity and unique production opportunities" (p. 350). Lives are changed and career trajectories altered when students get involved with radio.

Community radio gives another opportunity, sharing many similarities with college radio; it likely has more resources and represents community interests with a range of presenters. Community radio stations are typically run by and for a community, and many small towns across the world have thriving stations that are the heart of their neighborhood. Volunteer vacancies or even applying for jobs at such stations can provide serious hands-on opportunities as well as demanding high levels of commitment.

Working in college and community radio provides the first opportunity for many people to work in teams and focus on creating different content such as news, music, or sports broadcasting. Working in a team is an important learning opportunity, because collaboration helps develop skills, not least of which is the art of listening and finding consensus with others. Such empathy with each other drives effective *teamwork*.

This is fertile ground for students to forge relationships and friendships (Jacquay, 2019). As much as any team sport, there can be a powerful bonding experience in the camaraderie of broadcasting. That's why I am a strong advocate for getting involved with a student or community radio station as a catalyst for developing you as a person. They are places where the key questions in chapter 1 can incubate and grow. In finding your voice you should be trying things for the first time. You will identify interests and dislikes. You will experience success, and failure too. Failing together with other people can be enormously valuable. "It is not when things come easily that we appreciate them, but when we have to work hard for them or when they are hard to get," asserts author Simon Sinek (2017). He argues that failure or tough moments "are the experiences we remember as some of our best days at work. It was not because of the hardship, per se, but because the hardship was shared ... the camaraderie, how the group came together to get things done" (p. 279).

So the wonder of student and community radio is that you are trying new things *with other people*. Even if you fail together you are still learning. You are on the same *discoverer* journey as them, learning about who you are, and what you have to say.

A word to those without access to student radio

I realize that some of you will not have a college/student or community radio station anywhere nearby. I applaud those who are on their own, working with the basic entry-level toolbox with a desire to create audio. My aim in writing this book, and devising the four stages, is to provide the basis for *everyone* to develop the same skills and outcomes, to find their voice even if they are on a solo journey. Admittedly, the process is easier with the help of accessing a radio station, but you can achieve so much working through the exercises in this book and applying them carefully. You may not have a formal framework for trying out new things with other people, but you can benefit from informal relationships with family and friends who can provide similar help, especially when it comes to assisting you with content. Ultimately, a journey of self-discovery is necessarily an individual quest, even with the assistance of others.

Podcasts are one of the most significant areas for the soloist to create audio. You will see later in this book (Chapter 8) how this popular audio format has developed dramatically, and it encourages those without access to a radio station to pursue their audio journey. The point is, there is so much that you can do on your own, and not having access to a radio station should not prevent you from finding your voice and making content that expresses it.

At this point I should mention an adventurous option for those unable to find an opportunity in a college or community radio station. We are living in a time of such technological advancement that you can take matters into your own hands. Apps like *Clubhouse* and *Beem*, available on Android and iOS, let you livestream your voice as if you were presenting a radio show. This allows anyone with a smartphone to start creating content and distributing it to an audience. I am sure the range of apps like these will only change and increase in the years ahead.

I like the story of how in 2000, the early years of the internet, Bill and Rebecca Goldsmith decided to create one of the first web-only radio stations in the world, calling it *Radio Paradise*. Prior to its launching, "Bill had spent much of his life involved in the broadcast industry. But Rebecca, who was new to that industry, taught Bill that a lot of what he learned in the competitive, ad-saturated world of commercial radio needed to be *un-learned*" (https://radioparadise.com/info/who-we-are). The result was a radio station created by them, playing music that no other radio station would, a station "that breaks more rules than it follows." It was a massive success. Radio Paradise is listener supported and has been going for over 22 years. It's a model for those who decided to do live radio their own way and to connect with an audience that appreciates their uniqueness.

Many have followed their example with a range of websites that allow you to create your own station or channel:

- Airtime.pro
- Broadcastradio.com
- Live365.com
- Radio.co
- Radiojar.com
- Radioking.com
- Shoutcast.com

Bear in mind that these internet radio providers will likely charge you a monthly fee to use their platform, and there may also be issues to consider such as paying music royalties.

Creating your own radio station or streaming channel has the tremendous advantage that you can choose exactly how you want it to sound. That freedom is exhilarating! But the downside to running a channel successfully is its hugely time-consuming nature. Developing your own station or channel is perhaps best left until you have built up radio experience, but it's worth keeping the possibility on the back burner.

As we come to our first exercise of this chapter, think about how you can use your voice to convey excitement, tension, and energy. Of course, you are still recording this exercise for your ears only.

Chapter 4, R.E.A.L. Exercise #1: In that moment ...
For this exercise, you are to bring alive an important moment in your life, and tell it as a story with a clear beginning, middle, and end.

1 **Think of an interesting true story of a moment of your life. Perhaps a time of great triumph, or victory against all odds.**

2 **Write down the key points of your story, remembering any important details.**

3 **Practice telling the story using brief notes as talking points to guide you.**

4 **Record yourself telling the story, from start to finish.**

5 **Listen back when you have finished recording and give honest feedback on how you used your voice to convey the story's dramatic moments.**

This exercise should move you closer to understanding how your voice *is a tool that you can use to connect emotionally with others*. It also may reveal how much of a storyteller you are! Of course, it might seem odd that you are telling a story for no audience to hear, but the purpose is in understanding what decisions you made in how to tell it and speak the memory into life.

Valuing college/student/community radio (where possible)

Learn by doing

For those who can take advantage of a radio studio, this is a big plus. It's a great place to discover who you are in the process of learning about audio production. Much like a laboratory, college radio is a place where students can experiment and tinker with ideas and equipment to produce content. You learn by doing, using equipment that has been provided for you, which otherwise you probably do not have access to. Mistakes unfortunately occur throughout any professional career, but I say to the students, this is a place to make those mistakes for the first – and hopefully last – time. Often, it is as important to learn *what not to do* as it is how to do something correctly.

Typically, studios comprise two rooms. The first will be the control room, where most technical equipment is located. The second room is the vocal room or booth, which is an empty space just for recording voices with microphones. Both rooms will be soundproofed, especially the vocal studio. The first equipment you'll likely encounter in the control room will be a mixer, or some version of a mixing board (essentially larger versions of the RØDECaster Pro and PreSonus StudioLive AR8c Mixer). Typically, there is also a computer or digital audio workstation (DAW) that is connected to the mixer. This computer will have audio editing software installed.

The mixer controls the inputs such as microphones, CD players, vinyl turntables, and other equipment. A whole variety of inputs go into the mixer before entering the computer. The mixer will have an output for speakers that can be quite impressive in size, so the producer in the control room can listen to the live recording and its playback and editing. All this equipment can make a radio studio quite intimidating at first, but as you learn how to use it, it becomes a vital tool in skilled hands. Sometimes, with a one-studio situation, especially true for small radio stations, the equipment and the microphones might all be in one room.

The contrast is night and day between a professional studio and a home-made recording space like a closet, cardboard box, or even improvised soundproofing that we saw in the last chapter. Having access to a working environment with soundproofing and equipment readily at hand gives license for imaginations to roam.

This next assignment could run long because it invites you to explore your family history. Much depends on the kind of responses you get from your questions, and whether family members are enthusiastic participants. Take heed of the words of Henry Wadsworth Longfellow (1807–82), the famous American poet: "A single conversation across the table with a wise man is better than ten years mere study of books" (*12 Best Henry Wadsworth Longfellow Quotes*, n.d.). You may uncover stories and information that you never knew, material that you will want to keep.

Chapter 4, R.E.A.L. Exercise #2: From my grandfather to my father, this has come to me
Our experiences of family history vary dramatically. Some may have personal family circumstances that are painful to recall. This exercise invites you to tell the story of your family in your own words, seeking to focus on the positive aspects of your upbringing. If you feel comfortable doing so, ask family members what they remember about their family growing up and record them sharing their memories. Consider the following:

1 How has your family changed since you were born?

2 What memories do your parents or relatives have of family life when they were younger? What was life like back then, before you were born?

3 Are there interesting stories, or pivotal moments in your family history?

Keep recording interviews as long as you are hearing good material, for often this exercise can open people up to share at greater length. That's when you may find yourself learning about events and people in your story that surprise you. Again, save all the audio content, as you may return to it in the future.

College radio's important mission

College radio's mission is to *educate, empower, and serve those marginalized in our local communities, on and off campus* (Hilliard & Keith, 2005). I love stories that prove just how much college radio has provided an outlet to rally ignored or marginalized communities on college campuses. For example, Harrison (2016) found that "at a time when institutions were slow to adjust their organizational structures and curriculum requirements, when university administrators, by and large, lacked the conviction and insight to institute effective inclusivity measures, Black college radio represented a central node in a Black student support network" (p. 143). It was in college radio in the 1980s and 1990s that Black students "through their involvement in and around college radio programming, authored their own means of supporting one another and alleviating feelings of isolation." College radio is more than just having fun; it's a place that gives a voice to the community.

Ellen Waterman (2006) provided another example, when she explored how even though women were under-represented at Canadian campus and community radio stations, those few women who were involved established an important community for themselves. They found and created a space in which they encouraged each other to find their voices on the air. That is how college radio has the power to serve those marginalized in our communities.

Unlike commercial radio, which has become a place for highly polished, homogenized programming that seeks the largest possible audience and is perhaps risk-averse to experimentation (Hilliard & Keith, 2005), college radio is mostly noncommercial and is not pressured to be commercially viable in its programming. It is liberated from having to play the same small number of songs on a heavy rotation because it needs to keep their audience. College radio can afford to include voices and programming that would not be heard anywhere else. It empowers those marginalized in our communities and gives a voice to people who would never be heard on commercial radio or other forms of media. In many ways, this is college radio's superpower.

This role that college radio has cements its place on the spectrum as an important form of alternative media. If it were to disappear, there would be significant consequences for the rest of the media landscape, especially because college radio is still considered a stepping-stone for those wanting to work in the radio industry or media generally. But it is also a place where countless generations of students have gone to discover themselves, learn about radio, discover new music, and find a community that accepts them. This is a place that will accept you too.

R.E.A.L. Moment

I asked my friend Carlos Araya-Rivera from Costa Rica whether he could share a story about how one of his students at RADIO-E was impacted by his radio station. Carlos is a professor and academic advisor at the Universidad de Costa Rica. He was delighted to tell me about a student named Geovanni Castillo, who certainly found that radio helped him discover himself.

"I have to accept that at first I had no idea of the great contribution that radio would generate in my personal and academic life," says Geovanni, who collaborated for three years as promotion director and announcer in RADIO-E at Universidad de Costa Rica. Geovanni studied Library and Information Science and got his degree in 2023. The last three years coincided with the global crisis of COVID-19, and he highlights that during these difficult moments, "radio became the space that allowed me to put aside many of my worries, a marked place of learning and constant motivation to investigate." His experience at RADIO-E was fully demonstrated in his research work for his Licenciatura's degree, in which he proposed a digital marketing plan for public libraries in Costa Rica, in which he used the case of the management of social networks in the student station. In this way, he recognizes that the extracurricular activity at the station opened up new opportunities for him. "Radio was an ideal space that allowed me to develop soft skills that I now apply in my personal and professional life," remarks Geovanni. "Without fear of being wrong, I have to say that radio was the best complement in my academic courses."

I like how Geovanni mentioned that without "the fear of being wrong" he was able to learn and grow in new and unexpected ways. The radio station was a place for him to "put aside" his worries. It's in circumstances like that, we feel more able to communicate authentically and with liberation.

Student radio also serves communities ignored by big media

Big media is not naturally suited to covering small-town issues that affect relatively small communities because they seek the largest possible audience. Localism in radio has diminished somewhat because of the deregulation and ownership changes in the radio industry in recent decades (Hilliard & Keith, 2005). Often this has left college (and community) radio stations to serve as a stronghold of localism, serving communities ignored by big media. College radio can therefore focus on local news, events, and sports that form the social fabric of any community. Often students are the only ones who can cover certain local stories in depth, even though only a small audience ultimately hears that content.

Working in partnership with the local community, college radio offers a showcase of a community's diversity and uniqueness. Because some college radio stations also have community volunteers alongside the students, these volunteers reflect the community's unique identity in their programming content.

A proud history of producing alternative radio content: Opportunities and dangers

College radio has earned a reputation for discovering music and being a great influencer of taste. It continues to play music that no one else does and champions local and unsigned artists. Lull (1985) contends that the playing of rock music on college radio "is an extension of the emotional state" of many students, and "an effective agent of resistance" (p. 365). Students view their choice of music as an important act of expression. They also know that commercial radio is offering something very different, and *inferior*, in their opinion. Wall (2007) writes that "although the dominant form of music radio relies upon centralized, computerized programming based upon highly developed market information, [college] stations felt that there was something important in the handcraft of choosing music" (p. 51). Being musically independent is a badge of honor for college radio.

College radio is also known for taking risks and may experiment even at the risk of alienating its audience. However, there are opportunities and *dangers* here. It's possible for a student to discover a story which has serious repercussions. Encountering real life situations that are weighty, students may not be aware of all the potential dangers they face, legal or otherwise. My advice is obvious: safety first is always a priority. Never work alone if you have assignments that could take you to places where you could feel unsafe. Later I shall describe the critical role of mentors such as advisors and professors who can help guide and shepherd students through some potentially difficult situations.

In summary, today college radio has the potential to be the last bastion of uniqueness on the radio dial (Sauls, 2000). It is bursting with ideas and music that are defiantly out of the mainstream. It is also on the internet, as many do not possess FM or AM licenses. Even with these limitations, Callahan (2005) suggests that college radio offers fresh opportunities. Such "limitations enhanced the credibility of these stations because they were run by young people with a love for radio and music, particularly music that was fresh, innovative, and free of the taint of mainstream formula" (pp. 99–100). Being an outsider can have its advantages too.

For all these reasons and more, getting involved with a local college or community radio station can be a very valuable experience.

Chapter 4, R.E.A.L. Exercise #3: *Unheard among us*

This exercise asks you to think hard about where you live, and picture unique story possibilities that can emerge from your surrounding community. It is a vital *preliminary* stage about writing down ideas and sources to create good audio. This exercise is a springboard to some major work later. Please give it your best attention.

1 **Think of an issue or topic that is <u>unique</u> to where you live. It could be about a new construction project, a local business, or a community initiative. What stories are not being told in the media?**

2 **Make a shortlist of up to three issues or concerns about this topic/ issue that would merit creating a story.**

3 **For each story idea, identify the reasons why it deserves attention. Why should people be interested to hear about it? What details might be new to many people? Are there local secrets that should be shared?**

Hopefully, you may be surprised at how easily you can generate story ideas that no one else has thought of. Always keep your notes, you will definitely need them later.

This exercise is the starting point for a larger project that we will also call *Unheard Among Us.* The idea is that we highlight the important voices that often go unheard in our communities. This project will grow ever more important as you move through the *developer* stage. We will be returning to this exercise and developing it further, in exciting ways.

So, poke life

Steve Jobs once shared this vision for young people:

When you grow up you tend to get told the world is the way it is, and your life is just to live your life inside the world. Try not to bash into the walls too much. Try to have a nice family life, have fun, save a little money. ... The minute that you understand that you can poke life and actually something will, you know if you push in, something will pop out the other side, that you can change it, you can mold it. That's maybe the most important thing ... once you learn it, you'll want to change life and make it better, cause it's kind of messed up, in a lot of ways. Once you learn that, you'll never be the same again. (Silicon Valley Historical Association, 2011)

Poking life can lead to surprises and a desire to bring change. When students ask in class: *Why do things have to be this way?* they are on the way to poking life, perhaps questioning what seems unfair, discriminatory, or bafflingly, needlessly complex. Because of their constant exposure to social-media-fueled celebrity, many students perceive the world as hyper-competitive, and that money and fame are prerequisites for success and happiness. Some may even feel this pressure so acutely that they already sense they are a failure, because meeting these expectations seems an impossibility. Pushing back against these frameworks can be empowering.

It is vital to remember that *a good idea is a good idea regardless of where it comes from.* Just because a good idea comes from a student, that should never mean automatic dismissal. In the process of developing self-identity and poking life, students often surprise themselves with their insights and boldness. They are going to be the ones who will inherit the world in the future. They should be listened to. The world is a better place by having their voices in it.

Creating audio content can play a significant role in the developmental process. *Anyone* willing to learn – even if they are on their own, even with limited audio equipment, even if they are older – can experience this process.

R.E.A.L. Moment

In southern Bangladesh, a community radio station called Lokobetar FM 99.2 was established in 2011 in the town of Barguna (Lokobetar 99.2 FM, n.d.). The name Lokobetar means "People's Radio," and the station is exactly that: a passionate bastion of community programming and a place where people from all parts of the community can create radio content that reflects their culture. Mohammad Shazzad Hossain (Genilo et al., 2016) described it as having the most basic of facilities. Just three rooms – an office, a training room, and a studio. They do not even own the building but rent it from the Mass-line Media Centre, a non-governmental organization where the "overall objective is to remain an advocate for freedom of opinion, expression and free flow of information in the media" (p. 152). Despite the lack of resources, they are making a huge impact. My favorite story is about a child living near the station who "is good in poetry and has written a book on poetry." The station asked the child to produce his own poetry show, and so "the child mainly recites the poems from his book" on the air. I picture that child in front of a microphone reading from his poetry book. That's R.E.A.L. right there – a child experiencing the liberating thrill of sharing his soul to the world.

As we come to the end of this chapter, and the end of the *discoverer* stage of the journey, reflect on what you have discovered so far. Your voice, your identity, your story are all unique, and *you have what it takes* to find your voice, develop it, and share it with others. The author Susan Orlean asserts that "self-analysis is crucial to developing a strong voice ... You can't invent a voice. And you can't imitate someone else's" (Orlean, 2007, p. 158). Indeed, you must be yourself. As someone once said, "Be who you are and say what you feel, because those who mind don't matter and those who matter don't mind" (O'Toole, 2018, para. 1).

Final thoughts: *We will not be silent:* How one student courageously told the truth for herself and other victims of domestic violence and won national recognition for her radio story

Picture this: It's 2015. A classroom with 15 students. A professor stands by the whiteboard. There is complete silence. The class has just heard some audio played to them by a fellow student, Meg Cassarino. Most people are in a state of shock.

"I was always a very outgoing person. ... if somebody needed a friend, I was going to be that friend," says Meg Cassarino (personal communication, January 28, 2022). It was in that media production class that Meg played her final media project. I was the professor teaching the class. Meg was well liked by her classmates, and no one was expecting to hear what she had just played to them.

"I thought of myself as a confident, strong person, and I ended up in this relationship that ... ended up being emotionally abusive. And then it went on into being physically abusive, and then sexually abusive. And I remember thinking to myself, *how did this happen?* I never thought I'd be the type of person that this happened to." So, in this final class project, she had an idea to shine a spotlight on these issues that are often hidden from public view.

Meg knew that some women strongly believed that being in such an abusive, toxic relationship would never happen to them. "I started thinking about how that's a stereotype. *Oh, I've never been in a relationship like that*, or, *once they hit me, I'd be out in a second!* And my thought process was to show people that it doesn't just start out with physical abuse, it normally starts out as emotional abuse." Meg knew she wanted to show that it's not a simple situation for a woman to be in. "By the time you're at that point, you're in over your head and don't know what to do. And there's so much more to it than what most people think is black and white. And it's not. And I wanted to use this opportunity to show people it's a much deeper issue, and it happens to a lot of people, and people that you wouldn't typically think that it would happen to."

Meg could have chosen to do this as a video project but decided against it. "I chose audio as the form because I knew that if I tried to do anything else, getting participants would be hard. And I also think that sometimes audio is better, because you really have to listen to what the person is saying." She called the piece *Survivor*, and it was a radio documentary, running about ten minutes in length.

Meg put the word out to friends and a local group on social media for survivors of domestic abuse, looking for stories to include in her project. Including others' stories would show that she was standing in solidarity with the other women. "I put out my own story and was like, 'Hey, this is something that I went through, and this is something that I want to kind of shed light on. So, I'm going to *handle it with care*, because I've been through this before. So, I know that you're worried about safety for yourself, you're worried about safety for your family, and I know that there's a lot of emotional issues with it. So, I promise that I will put your story out there with care, but I'll also protect you.'"

Naturally, there were many fears. Yet many women did come forward, despite these real concerns. Why did they take that risk? "They just wanted to help people in any way that they could," says Meg. She was right about doing an audio-only project. "That definitely got more people to volunteer for it. There's one person that I did change the pitch of their voice a little bit to help protect them. But if it had been a visual project, I would not have had as many people speak about it, definitely not."

None of the class were expecting to hear this. After it had finished playing, I remember the shocked silence of the classroom. The horror of what these women had endured, sharing stories of violence and rape, and the fact that one of the voices *now sat among us*, made such emotional impact. Meg remembers how unprepared she was for the moment as well. "I just remember being like, *I didn't think about the fact that I was going to play my own story for a bunch of people right now* ... . *Oh, my God, I wish somebody would just say something.*"

Soon the silence was broken by an outpouring of praise by her classmates, who were moved by Meg's courage. "It did give me a confidence boost because I was able to talk about it. And I was okay, I didn't crumble, I didn't cry, the room didn't explode!" remembers Meg. But it also struck her that in that classroom, "people sitting right next to me could be stuck in something like this and not know how to get out and help. I wanted to help people understand it better, so that it didn't happen to them. Or if they knew somebody that it was happening to, they could better help them. Domestic abuse and sexual assault happen so frequently that I bet you there's somebody else in this room that has experienced that, and I hoped I just gave them some sort of strength," says Meg proudly. She also wanted to make a vital point: "I called it *Survivor*. Because a lot of people get in that mindset of, *you're a victim*. And my whole point was *you're not a victim, you're a survivor*, this happened to you, but you are not defined by that, *you survived!*".

That year, I never heard another radio piece like it in any of my classes. When it came to submitting entries for the *Intercollegiate Broadcasting System* national student media awards, I asked Meg about submitting it in the category of *Best Radio Documentary*. She agreed but told me that she felt it would not achieve anything. A few months later she was announced as a top five national finalist for the award. Then, at the awards ceremony in New York City, Meg won first place in the entire country. She had produced the *Best Radio Documentary* of 2015. She was not even present. As a graduate she was already busy in her new life. So, I sent an email to let her know she had won, and *by the way, when are you going to come by and pick up this huge trophy?*

Meg recalls the moment she got my email. "I remember reading that email, and I started to cry, because I was like, this story *actually made a difference to other people*. And I reached out to the people in my project that had talked with me. And they were just so amazed, that … what happened to them could make a difference in some way, shape, or form. And to get recognized for that, it was pretty cool … I was overwhelmed!"

This award made a huge impact on Meg. Creating the *Survivor* documentary was so important for her. "It was therapeutic," she says. "It gave me strength, and I took back control that was missing for so long. Using my own voice helped me take my power back." So, after earning an MBA, she spent time traveling the world, visiting Cuba, Peru, and other countries in Europe, Africa, and South America. "I started doing these trips, and I was able to talk about my story and help women that were experiencing the same, and in cultures where they don't really have a voice at all. I've been able to really help a lot of people and get them out of situations … We're taking our lives back. Okay, this is what happened to all of us, but you're not alone!"

Looking back now to that class project in 2015, Meg reflects, "For me, it was more than just a class project, I wanted it to change somebody's life. In radio, you can focus on the important aspects, on telling the powerful story and not worrying about what people are gonna think, because people can't see you. So, you can be authentic, and you can be real, and you can get as honest as possible. So, radio is a beautiful avenue where you just be as authentic as you possibly can!"

And what message does she have for anyone who might think about using audio to tell their story? "Everybody's voice matters. And it doesn't matter if you went through something as traumatic as I did, *everybody has a voice that matters.*"

References

12 best Henry Wadsworth Longfellow quotes. (n.d.). The Cite Site. Retrieved June 27, 2023, from https://thecitesite.com/authors/henry-wadsworth-longfellow/

Callahan, M. (2005). *The trouble with music.* AK Press.

Genilo, J. W., Bhowmick, B., & Hossain, M. (2016). Giving voice to the voiceless: Community radio of Bangladesh. In V. Kumar & J. Svensson (Eds.), *Media & communication in sustainable development* (pp. 142–163). Society for Education & Research Development. https://www.researchgate.net/publication/338175483_Giving_Voice_to_the_Voiceless_Community_Radio_of_Bangladesh

Goldsmith, B. & R. (2023). *Who we are.* RadioParadise. https://radioparadise.com/info/who-we-are

Harrison, A. K. (2016). Black college-radio on predominantly white campuses: A 'hip-hop era' student-authored inclusion initiative. *Africology: The Journal of Pan African Studies, 9*(8), 135–154. http://jpanafrican.org/docs/vol9no8/9.8-X-9-Harrison.pdf

Hilliard, R. L., & Keith, M. C. (2005). *The quieted voice: The rise and demise of localism in American radio.* Southern Illinois University Press.

Ibrahim, B., & Mishra, N. (2017). College radio as a mechanism for participatory learning: Exploring scope for radio based learning among undergraduates. *Online Journal of Communication and Media Technologies, 7*(1), 51–70. 10.29333/ojcmt/2579

Jacquay, G. (2019). *Is this thing on? The learning possibilities for participants at a college radio station* [Doctoral dissertation, California State University, Stanislaus]. http://hdl.handle.net/10211.3/214425

Laor, T. (2020). The added value of college radio: student self development, fulfillment, and confidence. *Higher Education, Skills and Work-Based Learning, 10*(2), 339–354. 10.1108/HESWBL-07-2019-0089

Lokobetar 99.2 FM. (n.d.). *Home* [Facebook page], Facebook. Retrieved June 27, 2023, from https://www.facebook.com/Lokobetar

Lull, J. (1985). On the communicative properties of music. *Communication Research, 12*(3), 363–372. 10.1177/009365085012003008

O'Toole, G. (2018, August 30). *Those who mind don't matter, and those who matter don't mind.* Quote Investigator. https://quoteinvestigator.com/2012/12/04/those-who-mind/

Sauls, S. J. (2000). *The culture of American college radio.* Iowa State University Press.

Silicon Valley Historical Association. (2011, October 6). *Steve Jobs secrets of life* [Video]. YouTube. https://youtu.be/kYfNvmF0Bqw

Sinek, S. (2017). *Leaders eat last: Why some teams pull together and others don't* (Rev. ed.). Portfolio/Penguin.

Wall, T. (2007). Finding an alternative: Music programming in US college radio. *Radio Journal: International Studies in Broadcast & Audio Media, 5*(1), 35–54. 10.1386/rajo.5.1.35_1

Waterman, E. (2006). Purposeful play: Women radio artists in Canadian campus and community radio. *Atlantis: Critical Studies in Gender, Culture & Social Justice, 30*(2), 76–87. https://journals.msvu.ca/index.php/atlantis/article/view/781

Wood, J. T. (2017). *Communication mosaics: An introduction to the field of communication* (8th ed.). Cengage Learning.

PART II

Developer

As we move from *discoverer* to *developer*, you are transitioning from the private, reflective work of looking within, to considering an outside audience for your work. You have a better sense of who you are and what you have to say. You will now consider the role of an audience, and how to create content for them. You will learn about the processes of developing a variety of content, including how to conduct interviews, and planning, recording, and editing your content.

DOI: 10.4324/9781003263739-7

5

WELCOME DEVELOPER

Interviews – The key ingredient for making the meal

First thoughts: *Is this World War Three?!* **How one radio journalist experienced a life-changing event**

Picture this: The morning of September 11, 2001. Edgewater, New Jersey. A busy city by the Hudson River, right across from New York City. It begins like any other day …

"That particular day was primary day, so I was going in late," remembers Glenn Schuck (personal communication, January 28, 2023), reporter and anchor for 1010 WINS, the all-news radio station for New York City. "So, I had to be woken up to the news. I looked out of my window to see what had happened to the World Trade Center, that it was on fire, and I could see it across the river." Schuck could not quite believe what he was seeing. "It was almost like you thought it was surreal. *It couldn't have been real.*" But then his professional training as a journalist kicked in. "You looked at it as a news person, and you're like, 'Okay, we have a tragedy unfolding here. But I need *to get there* and worry about the consequences later.'"

Getting into Manhattan was going to be almost impossible. Roads and bridges were closed. Mobile phones were not working, and the last thing most people would do is move into a disaster zone. "It was frightening because you start seeing *fighter jets* coming overhead on the Hudson River and everything else like, *was this World War Three happening?!!*"

Luckily Schuck and some other reporters found a man with a boat who was willing to take them across the river into Manhattan. "He wouldn't take us for free. He took any money we had in our pockets, about $1,000. He took us over to the Chelsea Piers area. We run down towards the World Trade Center as thousands of people run past us." Schuck remembers the smell of the air,

DOI: 10.4324/9781003263739-8

"You could smell gas. I don't know if it was gasoline or natural gas, but the whole city smells." Eventually he encounters Mayor Rudy Giuliani, who was already on the scene.

Soon after, Schuck managed to make a phone call to his radio station. "They said, if Giuliani is there, stay with him and don't leave his side. As this is happening the one building collapses, and then the other, but I stay by him." In the heart of tragedy and destruction, hours seemed like minutes. "I never left his side, wherever he was, from that Tuesday morning until Thursday night. So, I guess it was about 70 hours straight." Without sleep Schuck did not even manage to call his parents. "I panicked ... I hadn't even spoken to my parents, they might think I'm dead! I never connected with them *for days*. I didn't have a cell phone that was really operating. I only finally connected with them, I think, on that Thursday, and then when I called my mother she wasn't panicked, because she said, *Hey, we knew you were OK, we heard you on the radio!*"

Schuck had an important job to do. Interviewing Mayor Giuliani and other public officials about the disaster, he was able to share important information with the listening audience. At a time of confusion and terror, his reporting was providing vital information.

He remembers a pivotal moment. "The thing that I'll never forget was the morning of September 12. They organized what's called a press pool with one radio person, one TV person, one print journalist. They couldn't have every reporter down at ground zero, there's no way. So, they selected me as the radio person. We were the first reporters to go to ground zero with the mayor." What he experienced will stay in his memory forever. "They took us to the middle of the West Side Highway, which looked like hell on earth. I mean, the sky was red. The smell was terrible. It was just complete devastation. Like a nuclear bomb had gone off. And there was nothing left. I mean, there's nobody talking. No sign of life. That's the first time I think I was really afraid. When I looked at that I said, *there's nobody alive here.* These memories are seared in my head, like I will never forget, almost every detail of what I saw."

Schuck viewed his role as a radio journalist as having two purposes. First was describing what he saw. "This was well before social media, so I had to paint the picture of what I saw. And that was hard to do." The second job was to interview key officials to gain information about listeners' loved ones. "The first couple of days, people had no idea if their loved ones were alive or dead. Our job really was to inform people." Schuck's interviews provided vital personal information.

So, what advice would Schuck give to someone learning about interviewing for audio and radio projects? "Get experience. I always take students out and say, just go up to a fellow student and ask them about the subject of the day, or how hot do you like your coffee? Or, you know, what do you think of those gas prices, or whatever else and *just have a conversation.* Because a lot of people don't like approaching strangers, right? When

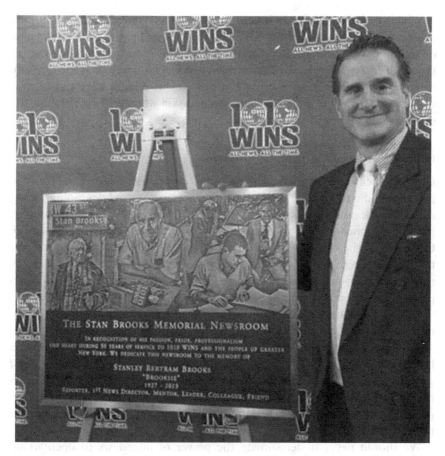

FIGURE 5.1 Glenn Schuck of 1010 WINS in New York City.

you do interviews, 99% of the time, you've never met them before. I always tell young people that you can't take it personally if you go up to someone and they tell you to get lost or whatever." Going through the experience of being rejected helps you grow as an interviewer. "Once you know you can have that banter and meet a stranger and talk, then that's half the battle!" Before our interview is over, Schuck shares one last piece of advice, "Stan Brooks, who was the first news director at 1010 WINS, was my mentor, and he would always tell me to persevere with people. *Don't get discouraged!*" (See Figure 5.1).

Moving from *discoverer* to *developer* now enters the practical stage of creating audio, which will be the focus of the next three chapters. The aim has been to encourage you to experiment freely as you progress through this journey, keeping note of successes and failures in your little black book.

While you have engaged in hands-on recording, we now move to the much more complex tasks of applying what you have learned to the specific demands of creating your own audio project. First among these tasks is focusing on the art of *interviewing*, one of the building blocks for developing the majority of audio projects. It is so important it deserves its own chapter and, as you will see in chapters 6 and 7, it is an assumed skill when moving through the eight-stage audio production process.

Interviews matter – The key ingredient

Glenn Schuck's story at the beginning of this chapter is a stellar example of the power of audio to make an impact through interviewing and describing. Being chosen as the sole radio journalist on 9/11, in the epicenter of the disaster, gave him a once-in-a-lifetime opportunity for creating extraordinary audio. Operating at the highest – most dramatic – level, his story is unique. We are unlikely to ever face a situation like his, but I highlight his experience to inspire us to take these next three chapters about the process of audio production seriously.

Earlier we considered how listening to radio or any audio allows the imagination to roam freely, stimulating mental images of situations, places, and people. Audio has an ability to take you to deep places of intimacy. When listening to an audio conversation you can often feel as though you are *right there* as people talk. So, in audio production, it is no surprise how significant a role interviews play. After all, they are the easiest way to generate interesting material. Solo talk into a microphone is hard work, but a riveting conversation makes the minutes fly.

We should never underestimate the power of interviews to open us up to learn about other people's experiences, insights, and stories, sometimes in extraordinary, unexpected places. Interviews are the perfect form of *infotainment,* simultaneously entertaining while giving information. Listeners can learn without realizing they are learning. In an age of social media apps that can share viral content with lightning speed, public figures know that just one interview or moment can be seen worldwide within minutes. The downside is that many public figures are now more guarded because they know any unwise words will also be widely heard!

We have already noted that there are two general types of audio. When it comes to interviews, there is a world of difference between **live** interviews occurring on air, with no second chances, and **pre-recorded** interviews! With the first, when it's done, *it's done*. With the second, if mistakes happen, you have a chance to pause the interview and make changes or even restart a question. And, of course, as we shall see in the production process, you can always edit until you are satisfied.

Occasionally there is a third, rare type of interview which is a **pre-recorded interview conducted as a live one**. Although you are pre-recording the interview, you must prepare and conduct it as if it were live, without the safety net of being able to stop and recalibrate if necessary. An interview like this might occur if you have very limited time with someone and essentially have one shot to do the interview.

All types of interviews require *diligent preparation*. Obviously, live interviews increase pressure on the interviewer's quality of preparation. It hardly needs to be said, but live interviews are best left until more experience is gained. Rather, we'll begin by considering pre-recorded interviews, and later (in chapter 9) we shall explore the live radio environment.

Also to consider is how you will conduct your interview. With the pandemic lockdown in 2020, many journalists shifted to online interviewing rather than the traditional in-person environment. For many, that change is now permanent. So let's consider *how* you will perform the interview:

- **In-person:** The traditional method of getting an interview is in-person, with the person in front of you. That makes for the best quality audio but can require a lot of time and effort to make happen. For big-name interviews, that can easily be a whole day spent on just a few minutes of audio!
- **Live on the air/streaming:** For a radio show or podcast, you may well have an interview on the air as you are performing your show. A guest may connect or 'call in' with you via online video or some other way.
- **Telephone:** Probably the easiest way to get an interview, but the worst audio quality, especially if it's a regular phone call. Many audio professionals avoid telephone interviews, and they are considered as a last resort. Plus, you cannot control much about the caller's possibly noisy environment, and you will not get any non-verbal cues about how the interview is going.
- **Online (Zoom, Skype, or video app):** Now preferred by many audio creators, at least you can see the person you are interviewing, and the audio quality has improved significantly in the last five years, but you are still at the mercy of the quality of the interviewee's webcam microphone. This is the best compromise between being in-person and a telephone interview. *Note:* good eye contact is still essential for video interviews, even though you might just be using the audio only. Many of the courtesies of in-person interviewing are still required.
- **Phone app:** I recently did an interview for NPR station WBUR, and they sent me download instructions for their special audio app. I followed their detailed instructions carefully and the resulting audio was almost as good as if I was in the studio with them! There are many phone apps now available that you can explore.

- **Sent audio:** There are times when you need some audio from an interviewee, but they are either too busy or they prefer to record their answers
to your questions and then send them to you as an audio file. This is not
technically an interview, as you will have no real time influence on what
they say. But if it's someone you know and trust, and the audio you are
seeking from them is not the key focus of your piece, this is still better than
having no audio at all.

Whatever way you are conducting your interview, your objective will always
be the same: *you need to finish that interview with the content you need.* How
you get the content you need depends on how well you perform as an
interviewer, as we shall explore next.

The dance: The accepted conventions of interviewing

I need to introduce a metaphor to describe the relationship involved in interviewing: It's like a *dance* between two people. That provides an instant
picture in your mind! Like dancing with a partner, interviews only work well
when both parties *want them to work.* You cannot force someone to dance
with you. It takes two to tango. Both sides should be invested in a happy
outcome. Interviewers want to create interesting audio, while interviewees
want their messages and stories to be heard.

Often interviewees have a particular angle they want to stress which,
hopefully, makes for wider interest. With celebrities it is likely to be promoting
their latest project. Those representing organizations will be keen to present
their official version of events. Anybody who has a story to tell wants to come
across well. But these angles can also raise red flags. That's why, like a dance,
interviews need rules and conventions, with moves understood by both parties. Two dance conventions apply to interviewing.

First, *one leads and the other follows.* Without this order, a dance can end in
disaster. Poor moves, stumbles, sometimes even falls, can end up with
ungainly heaps on the floor. Lead-and-response is the basic rule for dance and
for interviewing. The interviewer's stance is: *I get to ask you questions, and you
get to answer those questions.*

This can be delicate, because there are probably questions to which listeners
would like clear answers. Obviously, interviewees want to avoid areas where
they will feel uncomfortable. But, these may be precisely the topics where
listeners want some probing! Depending on the person being interviewed,
and the interview's purpose, it might be important before you start an
interview to ask if there are any issues off the table for discussion. You may be
instructed not to talk about certain things beforehand, or told to specifically
stick to certain topics only.

Sometimes an interviewer may cross into a forbidden area unintentionally with no ill intent. However, when interviewers enter a field of questioning that they feel is perfectly relevant to the interview, but the interviewee disagrees, then conflict is inevitable. This is the stuff of dramatic high-profile interviewing which can capture headlines. Interviewer and interviewee in battle! As new developers of the art of interviewing, we need to avoid such conflict and ensure our dance steps complement each other.

Second, like dancing, *interviews have a performative aspect.* People can play roles. Whether that's being a celebrity, official spokesperson, or corporate representative, when interviewed, people may seem to be *very different* from how they first present themselves. Why? Because *this is for an audience.* This may well prompt you to question what is real and what is fake. That's why interviews are like a dance, because people mostly know their clearly defined roles and what responses are needed to the interviewer's questions. At best, such interaction results in a tidy, pleasant interview that leaves everyone happy that the dance has gone according to plan.

With growing experience, you will want to push with more incisive questions – to create interviews that talk deeply and persuasively about things of real substance because that's what the audience wants to hear. You'll want to reach a point where floodgates open as someone really opens up with authenticity. Listeners are able to quickly tell if an interview is worth listening to - when it strikes them as fascinating, intriguing, funny, or even horrifying. That is the ultimate goal of R.E.A.L. audio.

Some necessary realism

Let's keep our feet on the ground and admit that getting a really powerful, floodgate-opening interview is rare. Yet, I need to add that in my experience, the magic of impactful interviews often comes as a surprise, and cannot be planned for. When the moment does hit you, you can recognize, in real time, that something remarkable is happening right in front of your ears. But expecting that something remarkable *needs to happen* in an interview will likely increase the probability that it will not happen. Remarkable moments are organic, and their authenticity rings true because they are unexpected. You must not measure your ability as an interviewer by the number of times your interviewee has become emotional or shared something extraordinary. Only someone like Oprah Winfrey could reasonably be expected to deliver content like that!

Each interview you conduct is unique, and depending on the topic of your interview, the outcome could vary considerably. For example, consider the difficulty of interviewing someone who has been through a tough experience, or even mourning the loss of a family member, compared to interviewing someone about winning an award or receiving recognition. Delicate, serious topics will need to be handled with great care, and as you gain experience as an interviewer, you will become more capable in adapting to the emotional intricacies of each interview situation. Let's be real, and recognize that a good interview is one where you have asked your questions and received answers. Anything more is a bonus.

Most of us will never get the chance to personally meet celebrities or important public figures that we follow and admire. The closest we get to know them is when they are interviewed by others. This is why many of us enjoy watching interviews of other people. But, be encouraged that you have many interview opportunities out there. Hundreds of stories surround us, stories from people who live in your community, or share your workspace. More stories than we could ever imagine. The challenge is getting those people to talk or be interviewed by you, encouraging them to share in an interview dance.

We should begin by interviewing 'ordinary' people around you, who are not considered famous and will likely speak more openly. In my experience, the best and most enjoyable interviews are sometimes with people who are not famous, and are not media trained to the point of being overly guarded. Yet, remember, *extraordinary things do happen to ordinary people*. All the time. A listening audience may even find such stories far more relatable than listening to an unreachable celebrity, because they could imagine it happening to them. As empathetic beings, we always think about what we would do if we were in the same situation as the person in the story. Would we have made the same decisions? We become emotionally drawn in as we listen to someone telling their story.

I generally teach students to *get out of the way* when someone is telling their story. It's your role to ask the questions that the audience would want to ask, to go places that the interviewee might have forgotten to mention or never considered before. So you *facilitate* the best possible storytelling. One way of getting out of the way is to remove your voice in the final version or edit of your audio piece, leaving only the person or people you have recorded telling their story without your narration or explanation. That can be very effective to bring an audience closer to the people and their stories in your piece. However, that can be hard work to pull off in practice, as it's often necessary for your own narration to help frame and provide context to what your interviewees are saying and to assist an audience's understanding.

Preparing for interviews: Essential do's and don'ts

Interviewing needs your best conversational ability. Remember Glenn Schuck's advice, to get out there and interview as many people as possible, to become more comfortable with talking with strangers and other people.

Develop curiosity in other people. What makes them tick? What do they think about a certain issue? The greater your skills as a *listener*, the greater the quality of conversation.

Since all human beings are different, you will need to adapt and adjust your interviewing approach for every person you interview. As you see later, Marissa's story at the end of this chapter tells us that as you do more interviews and gain experience, you will develop your own list of do's and don'ts. You'll also develop more confidence! R.E.A.L. audio is all about discovering more of who you are, and the interview dance mightily sharpens up skills as you engage in the lead-and-response with an interviewee. But, to ensure the interview dance leads to good and lively conversation, diligent preparation is needed to shape the questions. Interviews can fail for many reasons, but careful research always repays the effort.

Let's go through some important steps in preparing for an interview.

Keep your goals clear

You must have a main purpose in mind for the whole project, and your interviews must fit that purpose. Your goal decides the kind of content you need, which drives the selection and content of particular interviews. The overall goal explains *why* you are doing these specific interviews. Why are you talking with these people and not others?

It could be a simple goal like, for example, telling a person's story. Here the goal aims to achieve an account full of color and personal detail which is accompanied, probably, by observations from others along the way. Or, it could be a more complex goal, following a story in your community or connected with some changes in your neighborhood. This will likely involve more explanation, with several interviews, perhaps presenting different points of view.

Selecting any interviewee is open to risk. Of course, you choose them because they appear to suit the goal of your audio project. But will they share in the task and contribute to this overall goal? Will they be interesting and natural? Who might provide the basic facts? Who will provide a balance between different points of view if necessary? Will the tone be formal and serious or fun and conversational? Hard-hitting or entertaining? Always the interviews should fit into *an audio piece of interest that will hold listeners' attention throughout*. Choose carefully to keep attention levels high.

Fortunately, audio interviewing has two advantages. First, it encourages interviewees to share in conversation for longer blocks of time, allowing for greater intimacy and the likelihood of increasing relaxed sharing. Many interviewees feel more comfortable when they know they will not be seen. Second, as we shall see, you can always edit out interviews and content that do not meet your goals.

The importance of doing prior accurate background research

Interviewing people about *themselves* and interviewing people about *factual situations* are both areas requiring careful prior research.

First, when you start interviewing people you are likely to know something about them and perhaps their story. Your starting point probably emerges from their personal life, the company they work for, the town or city in which they live, or their hobbies and interests. It could involve almost anything. Interviewing people like this still requires careful preparation, but it is often less onerous.

When you know little about them, accurate background research is critical. Social media provides some helpful biographical information. What's their job and how long have they been in it? What are their family circumstances? Do they have specific interests? Questions like these help you see the world *from their perspective* and develop an *empathetic approach*. Some research is obvious. For example, ensure that you know the correct pronunciation of their name – mispronouncing the interviewee's name gives the worst start! Make sure you know the correct pronunciation for all names, places, and businesses/organizations if you are going to bring them up.

When a person is well known, conducting background research becomes much easier. Often a quick search online will instantly yield thousands of results, and then your biggest problem may be choosing what to read and focus on. It's easy to be overwhelmed with information on someone famous. To prevent information overload, focus on reading or listening/seeing no more than three or four of their most recent interviews. You can quickly see a pattern or selection of frequent topics. Admittedly, looking at previous interviews can make you feel inadequate and ask yourself, *how will my interview add anything that isn't already known about this person?* That's only normal. Try to push past those concerns and continue planning your questions as you normally would with any person you interview. This is where the time spent preparing for an interview really makes a difference. The more time you spend on research, the more confident you will feel about what's going on in their lives *at the moment of your interview*. That can provide vital context for your questions.

Getting the context wrong can be disastrous. For example, in 2014, the famous actor Samuel L. Jackson appeared on a Los Angeles morning television show (KTLA) to talk about his new film *Robocop*. The interviewer, Sam Rubin, made an embarrassing and insulting error. "Did you get a lot of reaction to that SuperBowl commercial?" Rubin asked Jackson, referring to a car commercial that starred the Black actor Laurence Fishburne. He had clearly mistaken the two. Jackson immediately picked up on the mistake (Tha Artist Network, 2014). "I'm not Laurence Fishburne," said Jackson after an awkward silence. "We don't all look alike! We may be black and famous, but we don't all look alike!" Rubin, realizing his mistake, apologized and tried to move on, but Jackson was having none of it. "There's more than one black guy doing commercials. I'm the 'What's in your wallet?' black guy," Jackson said, referring to his Capital One commercials. "He's the car black guy. Morgan Freeman is the other credit card black guy. You only hear his voice though, so you probably won't confuse him with Laurence Fishburne." The moment went viral around the world because of the interviewer's error and how the interview fell apart as a result. Proper background research would have avoided this embarrassing moment.

Second, when you are interviewing people about *factual situations*, the advent of *fake news* makes careful fact-checking essential. Knowing with some degree of confidence that the information you are relying upon is fact-checked provides the best, ethical approach and is considered due diligence. This way you avoid the dreaded "fake news" stories that are readily available online.

As Deepak Adhikari (2021), editor of *South Asia Check* asserts:

> Almost everyone knows that you can't trust everything you read, see, or hear. False information in the media or online can be small and insignificant, even a simple or honest mistake. But the spread of misinformation and disinformation can erode democratic institutions, promote authoritarian regimes, and undermine people's ability to make informed decisions (para. 2).

> Fortunately, with fact-checking, there are easy-to-learn methods, processes, and tools to expose and push back against false information in all its forms (para. 3).

Joe Rogan, a famous podcaster and media personality, once made the claim that some Australians were considering a new law banning its citizens from growing their own food. This story was circulating online and got Rogan's attention. After expressing shock and horror about the proposed idea to his millions of listeners, his producer tried immediately to fact-check the story. After coming up with nothing to contradict it, Rogan, *live on his show*, said, "It's got to be a real thing ... it seems too good to not be ... damn it, it better not be fake ... it might be fake" (Cassidy, 2022, para. 11). Rogan had been tempted to take, at first glance, a story that seemed too outrageous to ignore, and a story that supported his worldview. All while broadcasting to an audience of millions.

Many fact-checking resources are out there to help avoid such moments. The Craig Newmark Graduate School of Journalism at the City University of New York suggests starting with these four questions when evaluating a story's accuracy:

- Who says?
- How do they know?
- Are they biased?
- What do I not know?

(Craig Newmark Graduate School of Journalism, 2023)

Fact-checking also involves examining the story's date of publication, the URL to see if it's been altered or changed from what you would reasonably expect, and whether the details of organizations or people being quoted are accurate.

Inevitably, one further complication to the interviewing task arises from the interviewer's own perceptions and beliefs, which unwittingly bring bias. For an effective interview dance there should be trust both ways. In early days, you lack the experience needed to confront, *in real time*, false or misleading information. Growing experience not only alerts you to your own bias but also gives you the confidence to recognize it in others.

Finally, remember we live in a world where opinion and information freely mix. The term *fake news* is used for almost anything that people personally disagree with, and so there is distrust everywhere. It's important to distinguish between a fact, which is a proven truth, and an opinion, which can represent the views of an individual or organization. Opinions are not necessarily grounded in facts. While you may not be producing work that can be considered journalism, and do not have to abide by accepted journalism standards, you should still be aware of using any information that is not fact-checked, sourced, and authenticated, and it contains obvious bias. This is not just an issue of presenting truth, but if you are seeking to build an audience, you should make the extra effort to ensure that the information you are using is as factual and truthful as possible. Your audience will appreciate that due diligence, and your attention to matters such as these only helps build your credibility and reputation.

Over time you will develop your own interview style and, if you are careful about issues of truth and factual information, you will build a reputation. Do your best to make sure it's a good one!

Chapter 5, R.E.A.L. Exercise #1: Family first
This first exercise seeks to gain interview experience, which will help prepare you for the rest of this chapter.

1 **Get permission from a family member to interview them about their childhood.**

2 Think of at least ten questions that you want to ask them, such as *Where were you born? What was your first childhood memory?*

3 Having prepared, then record the interview as professionally as possible.

4 Include an introduction and an ending.

As you will experience, this exercise gives you good practice for what's to come. You can listen to your interview after this chapter to see how you might have improved it.

It's all about the questions: Crafting questions for maximum effectiveness

Another vital part of preparation involves crafting your questions. Questions are the tools needed to access the content that will be natural and interesting. A well-crafted question starts the dance sequence. Suddenly the interview is flowing beautifully. Questions are like dance cues. Just what will you ask? Giving serious thought to your questions makes all the difference.

Engaging in a recorded conversation has a peculiar dynamic. You always need half your brain to listen to what they are saying, while the other part of your brain is thinking, *What am I asking next*? When you first start doing interviews, you are so preoccupied with concerns such as, *Is my recorder running? Is my microphone working? Is everything going well? How is my battery? Am I getting good sound levels?* It's easy for these concerns to take over your whole brain, to the detriment of your interview. You'll need to train yourself to keep listening, even while you are juggling all these thoughts. Actively listening is an art that good interviewers develop to be flexible with the next question.

To begin, make a list of all the possible questions you would like to include and then question your questions! Try and avoid questions that can be answered with a simple yes or no, or one-word answer. Questions that invite explanation are better, such as starting with *how, why, where, who, when.*

There are three kinds of questions: *Soft questions* need to be scheduled for the beginning of the interview. They ease the first dance steps together. No one expects a difficult question to begin with, unless you only have one shot at asking a single question when you have to take it.

Key questions lie at the heart of why you are doing this interview. Be careful if you are thinking, *I need this person to say this.* Do not try to predetermine the outcome of the answer. This can limit the possibilities of other content that might be more important.

The third kind of question is the *unexpected one*. Perhaps one of your key questions leads to the interviewee making an admission, or revealing something that is game changing. This needs a follow-up question. When you read Marissa's story at the end of this chapter you will see this was a lesson she had to learn. Sometimes you can miss stunning pieces of information because you are focused on the next question on your list. Failing to pick up on it because you are distracted loses a huge opportunity. Never switch off your active listening! That's a lot to take in, but it is part of the interviewing role. The unexpected question can make the interview stand out.

Dynamic interviewing needs you to stay open to changing the story or the narrative. Don't be rigid, and be alert to unexpected openings. An apparently difficult interview could perhaps end up being an astonishingly positive one, and a seemingly great interview can sometimes fizzle out as mediocre.

Make sure your questions are written down. It may seem impressive if you are able to commit your questions to memory, but having them in front of you is a safety net. Perhaps you want to confidently ask the first question without looking at your notes, fine. But there's no shame in tracking your written questions throughout the interview. In fact, having notes written down gives you a reference point and reduces moments of tension, should they arise.

I also recommend writing down *twice* as many questions as you think you will need, just in case. Those extra questions can be a lifesaver if you burn through your other questions quickly. It's always better to be over-prepared than under-prepared. Remember, everyone you interview will likely be a human being (although a feature on animals could be great audio)! To remind yourself that they are just as human as you are is a great leveler. With a famous interviewee, being a fan as interviewer will certainly aid the feel-good factor, but it might inhibit any difficult, critical questions that should be asked. In some circumstances, the celebrity might respect you more if you ask the tough question, you never know.

As you write your list, consider these questions about questions::

1 Is this question easy or complicated to answer?
2 Will this question be expected by the interviewee? If not, could it be a problem?
3 In terms of importance, on a scale of 1 (least) to 10 (most), how vital is it that you include this question?
4 Where in the interview should this question be asked (start, middle, near the end)?
5 What will your softball questions be at the beginning, to help the interview start well?

This process will allow you to sort and order your questions. You'll now have an idea of how you would like to structure the different parts of your interview. Let's next understand the different stages of an interview.

The five stages of an interview

Typically, you will be interviewing one person, which is considerably easier than when you are faced with two or more people. When interviewing multiple people there are not just technical issues to consider. You will need to *try to be fair* and offer everyone an opportunity to speak, though in practice, some people are more willing to speak than others. Always seek to be sensitive to anyone who perhaps needs encouragement to speak.

After you have set up recording equipment and taken sound levels with your microphone, you are ready to begin. The interview might be a stand-alone interview that forms the whole audio piece. Or it may form part of a wider project involving other interviews. Whatever its role, interviews follow a set of stages and questions. Some are obvious – a start, middle, and end – but two more stages are also necessary.

Before you get to the interview, you may also engage in **pre-interview** communication. Your interviewee might ask about how you envisage your interview might progress with a number of suggested topics. Be careful, as you need to weigh such requests that can help build relationships and clarify how the interview might proceed, with providing too much information, such as telling them your questions before you start. You will have to judge how much to share, but a pre-interview engagement can help everyone feel more comfortable and establish expectations.

The **start** of your interview involves an *introduction* and *first questions*. The introduction is always necessary, to ensure listeners know who is going to be interviewed and to set the scene. Who are they? What is their role or capacity? You have two options here. You can describe who they are in front of them, which can sometimes be nerve-wracking. Or you can decide to record that later for the final edit, and go straight into the conversation. Of course, a live interview always requires the first option. Consider yourself lucky if you ever interview someone so famous that you get to say, "This person needs no introduction!"

These first questions should be relatively easy, or softball questions. Only when you begin carefully to establish a good rapport can you seek to attain something that will come across as R.E.A.L. audio. Perhaps you are entering their world and seeking to *relate* it to your audience, or the interviewee's experience is one with which the listeners can readily *engage*.

The **middle** stage is the heart of the interview, where you have placed the key questions. Having developed a relationship of trust, you aim to secure interesting content in line with your big goal for the audio project. When the goal is relatively simple, like telling a person's story, the questions need to probe the interviewee's key personal details to establish why it's worth listening to. Gaining interest and color from their answers needs interesting and colorful questions. More complex goals like telling a story in your community, which will be the focus of your audio project, requires much more explanation with several interviews, some of which will offer differing views.

The **end** stage wraps content up. Sometimes it's obvious that you have both exhausted the conversation as it draws to a natural close. At other times, the ending can be quite abrupt, especially if the interviewee has insisted on hard time limits. Then the ending *might be out of your control.* A golden rule is to make sure you do not leave any key questions to this final stage, when time runs out.

The final, fifth stage is **staying aware** after the interview of two issues: of the interviewees themselves, and essential technical matters. In all your communications with those that you interview, your conduct before and after the interview is important. Remember to thank people for their time, and to provide them with a copy of the interview if requested. Transparency in your communication and purpose will always be appreciated! Further, keep in touch with significant interviewees' progress and story, because you never know when your relationship with them could lead to further interview possibilities. That could simply mean staying alert to any story with their name in the news, and keeping a record of their phone number and email address.

Technically, always remember, an interview *is not done until it's done.* You need to be engaged from the first spoken word to the last. That means confirming it's been recorded, that you have checked the file to see it's recorded properly. Up until that point, it's not 'in the can'. With live interviews there is at least the relief that once it's done, it's done. It's wasted energy worrying about it. This is raw audio that becomes an essential component in the production process ahead. You should always save the interview as a full, unedited audio file, and make a copy as a backup, just in case.

Chapter 5, R.E.A.L. Exercise #2: Planning questions for an interview
For this second exercise, your goal is to interview someone about an upcoming event happening in your community. That could be an event organizer or public official. You are to get as much relevant information as possible about the event.

1 Identify the key information and questions: *What time is it? Where is it? Who is organizing it? Is there a story behind the event and the interviewee's involvement?*

2 Identify some good softball questions to start the interview.

3 What key questions will help you achieve your goals?

4 *Where can your audience go to find out more information about the event?* This is a positive question to end the interview.

Helping the dance to be a success

To complete the interview dance without any missteps, several aspects need attention. Some are more obvious than others. In this section we will cover the importance of getting *permission*; choosing an appropriate *location*; considering *time limits*; understanding *body language* and knowing when to *stay silent*; what to do when things *go wrong*; and how you know you have *done a good interview*.

Permission

It's vital that you establish the professional nature of the interview from the beginning, when you get their consent to be recorded before you record anything (Dennis, 2023). Verbal permission is okay , but signed, written consent is better. You should always be up front with the interviewee about the intended use of the interview content. There are many examples of release forms online, and you should choose one that best fits your purposes. An example is included as an appendix in this book.

Remember, a consent form protects you from any future allegations that the interviewee did not give permission to be interviewed or recorded. So, it's important that you take a few seconds to get it signed before you hit record.

Location

Finding a good location for your interview is essential. Often you are given little choice because you need to meet on the interviewee's turf. When you are invited to another location, remember the advice in chapter 2 about avoiding acoustical problems. Try to ensure that you use the best area that is less noisy and more private, enabling both cleaner audio and also a conducive space for sharing conversation.

Sometimes an acoustic space is less suitable. A busy high street or train station may convey the interviewee's context, and add ambient flavor to the audio. But remember, microphones attract interest and if it's a public place, a small crowd may gather. For a straightforward interview, it's fine to do that openly. However, if you want more thoughtful responses, interviewing at a Starbucks or somewhere else like that is far less appropriate. So, think carefully about where you will conduct your interview, as it affects emotional openness. Nothing inhibits personal sharing like a crowd.

Time limits

Typically the more important the person you are interviewing, the less time you will be allowed, and it will be strictly enforced. There are rare exceptions to this, but do not expect to be given more time than was offered to you. If anything, expect less.

The last section about going onto someone else's turf gives me the opportunity to name drop! In 2013, President Joe Biden was then Vice President. The White House press office told me in advance that I would get absolutely no more than ten minutes with him for my interview on student radio and student issues. Imagine my horror when most of that time was spent on introductory pleasantries and just the first question! Luckily, and surprisingly for me, Biden liked to talk, and I ended up with more than thirty minutes with him. He was passionate about the subject – yes, student radio! – and gave me so much more content than I expected. However, that is unusual with most VIPs and celebrities. Commonly, you will wish you had more time for more questions.

So, it's always best to expect that you could have less time for an interview and need to prioritize your questions accordingly. Hopefully, you will have one key question that is extremely important and probably one or two others also of high significance. These must be asked. They are the reason for the interview! Bear in mind that the interviewee may disagree. They might consider your important questions to be less important or irrelevant! Even though you need an opening soft question, when time is short the unmissable key questions must not be missed out on.

Of course, at the other extreme, time limits prevent an interview going *too long*. Sometimes the floodgates open because your questions trigger something, and the interviewee says, *I need to talk about this*. This could signal a long interview! If something resonates with them, it could provide interesting material, but you *have to get the content you came for*. Beware letting them go off track unless you have what you need for your project.

Experienced interviewees may try to use techniques to control the interview. They could go on too long and answer questions you did not ask. Or, they could give one-word or one-sentence answers. Allow a few beats or seconds between questions, to allow the interviewee to finish what they are saying before you speak. Voices that overlap or talk over each other make editing the interview later a difficult process, as you cannot separate recorded voices when they are speaking at the same time on a single audio track.

Understandably at the beginning there is some degree of anxiety about working with time restraints. Using a stopwatch, and remembering to start it at the beginning of the interview, helpfully keeps track of time. Otherwise it can become a blur. But, with practice, you will develop a sense of timing and know roughly how much time you have left. It's so satisfying when you know you have asked the key questions, so you can relax and enjoy the rest of the interview.

Chapter 5, R.E.A.L. Exercise #3: Identifying the highlights

For this third exercise, there is no need to record something new. Instead, we are going to use some previously recorded audio. This exercise will demonstrate your ability to identify the most important moments in your interview.

1 Go back to your first interview in this chapter (exercise #1). It is likely that the interview is several minutes long.

2 Listen again to your interview carefully. Your task is to identify the top three moments in the interview. Were there certain answers to your questions that were noteworthy? Was there a moment where you reacted to something that was said that you are proud of? Was there a question that you delivered perfectly?

3 Try to then order the three moments in terms of what you consider most important.

4 Reflect on these three highlights. What does that say about how well your interview went? What larger lessons can you take away from these moments?

This exercise can be challenging, as it can be difficult to identify what went well, but if you follow your gut, you will know which moments went so well that you can say *I nailed it*, and with increasing practice it becomes easier to recognize your triumphs.

Body language

Our body language communicates far more powerfully than our words. We pick up on other people's body language the second we meet them. We can sense anger, frustration, nervousness, and apathy from their movements and gestures. We can also sense happiness, excitement, and enthusiasm from their smiles, wide-eyes, and vigorous handshake.

In the interview dance, remember there is mutual reading of each other's body language! When you have prepared diligently, you should arrive at an interview feeling confident and positive, and that will show in your smile and body posture. Similarly you will readily read how pleased and ready they are for the interview.

When you start asking questions, body language gives real time feedback. You can see how they are responding to your questions and to the direction of the conversation. Body language reveals how well we are listening. One classic way of describing listening identifies five different levels:

- *Ignoring listening* – the most basic level, spending zero effort
- *Pretending* – at least giving the appearance of listening
- *Selective* – listening to parts only
- *Attentive* – actively listening, truly engaged
- *Empathetic* – the highest level, requiring the most mental and emotional energy

Most of us are, at best, selective listeners. But when you are interviewing, attentive listening is requisite and achieved by eye contact and body language signals, such as nodding in affirmation.

Interviewing famous people complicates reading body language. You may well see an immediate change in personality the second you start interviewing them. They are then on guard, on their best behavior, knowing they are going on the record. Don't take that personally, especially if they are aggressive or unfriendly toward you, compared to their demeanor before you started the interview. In my early radio career, I occasionally hoped that famous interviewees would be so impressed with my interviewing skills that we would become friends. Sadly, this is fantasy. Especially if you consider how many interviews these people do everyday. What may be an important moment for you, is immediately forgettable for them. You need to stay as confident and positive as possible.

Knowing when to stay silent

Generally, interviewers on audio need to be silent once they ask their questions. Of course, something may naturally prompt laughter, for example. But the natural tendency to validate what they have said, by saying *sure, right, thanks* is forbidden. Instead, keeping eye contact, just nod to indicate that you have received and understood their answer. This will convey to your interviewee a level of professionalism and save time later editing out your valueless contributions. As stated previously, when voices overlap, that's hard to edit out later.

Sometimes silence itself can be a powerful tool. When, for example, you are dealing with noncooperative subjects, you need to be quiet and wait. Ask your question. Let them give you the rehearsed answer, but then sit there quietly and see what comes next. Some people feel compelled to fill silences and continue talking. Occasionally when something emotionally powerful has been said, a moment of silence seems only appropriate before you respond. Silence is not to be feared, unless you are doing a live radio interview and after a few seconds a dead-air alert is triggered at the station! But, we will address that situation in chapter 9.

When things go wrong: strategies for saving the situation

Despite your best efforts, occasionally interviews do not go according to plan. Bluntly, sometimes the interviewee does not want to dance with you. At least not in the way you started the first steps. Yet, because the interviewer leads the dance, you can hopefully guide the conversation back into safe territory.

Sometimes a major disconnect occurs because the interviewee is unsure about your aims. So, be explicit. For example, say, "What I really need is a quote from you encapsulating your feelings on the issue," or, "I really need you to walk me through the chronology of this." By giving the interviewee guidance, it reminds them of their obligation to the interview process. After all, if they have agreed to give you the interview in the first place, there should be some willingness to talk with you.

Very occasionally in a tense situation you may even temporarily cede control. Let them lead the dance. Invite them to take the mic, to speak freely, stating their opinion and perspective. By offering them this opportunity, you will demonstrate your good faith and desire to salvage the interview. After listening to them, a fresh opportunity may open up to ask your questions.

Unfortunately, and more rarely, you may discover early on that the person really does not want to talk. If that's the case, there's little you can do to persuade them otherwise. Similarly, if a person gets angry or insulted at a question you ask and starts to walk, you have a window of just a few seconds to try and deescalate the situation. But when voices are angrily raised and there is even the hint of possible violence, stop the interview and leave immediately. It's not worth risking your safety for the purpose of an interview.

Dealing with contentious territory is difficult. No one, especially a public figure, wants to talk about stuff that's controversial or embarrassing for them, but sometimes you need to ask the obvious direct question. That's your job. Before it gets to that point though, you can ask them, "Is this something you are comfortable talking about? Should we move on?" This also demonstrates sensitivity on your part, that you recognize the interview is in a difficult moment.

If conflict does occur, you may end up with an interview that becomes infamous. That may be good for viral hits on social media, but future interviewees may well see that and decline to be interviewed by you.

How you know you have done a great interview

By the end, you want the interviewee to feel that they came across well in a good dance. You do not want them to feel misunderstood or exhausted by the experience.

As you gain experience, you will realize in real time the gems in your interview. Those moments when something is said that's so relevant that it practically jumps out and appears as a printed quote in front of you. When that happens you will know they made the lights light up. You've got what you wanted.

However, in my experience, nine times out of ten, if you finish the interview and feel unsure in your gut, *did I get what I needed?* it means you probably did not! It might be possible to save the content by some creative editing later on that may then lift it to above average listening.

R.E.A.L. Moment

In 2017, British interviewer Alison Hammond interviewed Ryan Gosling and Harrison Ford about their upcoming film *Blade Runner 2049* for ITV television (This Morning, 2017). In the interview, Hammond is so laid back and funny that soon all three are laughing raucously. She starts the interview by saying, "Bleak, dystopian, an absolute nightmare to be honest with you ... that's just my interviewing techniques!" Soon the notoriously serious Harrison Ford is smiling and laughing uncontrollably, and Ryan Gosling cannot control his mirth either. "This is not the introduction we were promised!" smiles Ford, as Gosling can barely contain himself. It's an interview of such fun and joy that many consider it to be one of the funniest and most entertaining interviews Ford and Gosling have ever done. That's because of the sheer enthusiasm the interviewer brought to the interview, and the interviewees connected with that infectious authenticity to create a remarkable moment.

As we come to the end of this chapter, know that you are capable of getting interviews that have great content. As you gain more experience, you will also develop your own unique interviewing style, as you keep track of what works and what does not in your black book!

This chapter has introduced you to one of the vital components for creating your audio project: conducting an interview. The next two chapters journey through eight stages in the production process during which the skills of planning, collecting audio including interviews, editing, and preparing material for a script are all dependent on the kind of thinking and questioning that we have just focused on. I shall be using another metaphor, that of creating a meal, and just as the main ingredient of a meal has its own nutrients and taste – whether it's salmon, steak, chicken, or stir fry – each interview you do has its own character and will constitute a key ingredient of the meal.

Final thoughts: *The courage to speak:* **How one student came out of isolation to find her voice to then tell other people's stories**

Picture this: March 2020, Passaic, New Jersey, USA. A single woman, aged 20, sits alone in her apartment. Marissa Banks is a student who, like many other people, is under the COVID-19 lockdown. The world is shutting down, she's locked down at home, and there is a sense of fear everywhere.

"It was pretty miserable," says Marissa. "I was super sad. Honestly, I used to just sit in silence and darkness, praying that COVID would end like literally any day. And it was not looking like it. Living by myself, I wasn't really speaking to many people. My parents occasionally, but they were maybe an hour and 45 minutes away from me. So, I was just by myself, during all of COVID" (M. Banks, personal communication, May 15, 2022).

Only the week before the COVID lockdown started, Marissa had started training at her university radio station, WPSC Brave New Radio, at William Paterson University. A professor, Dr. Diana Peck, felt that Marissa could offer a lot to the radio station, especially with her interest in current events and news. "I remember the first time I was at the radio station. There were a bunch of people sitting at the tables. It was a very happening place. I walked in feeling uncomfortable only because I've never seen people so happy. So, I was like, *oh, these people were really happy to be here. This was cool!*"

Marissa became immediately involved. But then COVID hit. "I had just started my first week, we got sent home, and then we couldn't train." The university shut down all in-person classes and activities, and everything became virtual, lasting days to weeks and then months on end.

Eventually, by the summer of 2020, the radio station had figured out how to bring people back with safety protocols to broadcast safely on air once again from the main campus studio. "When I got the message that we could come back, I was still anti-social, because I had spent so much time not talking to people and being sad. I didn't want to answer the message. And then ironically, I *accidentally* started typing. My subconscious probably saw me typing out the response, 'Okay, yeah, sure.' And I came back."

Being back made so much difference. "Coming on air was refreshing because I felt I was talking to somebody. I could be like, 'We're all going through this.'" The ability to use the radio to communicate her loneliness and share her experiences was deeply healing for Marissa. "I think honestly, everyone who was here needed that, but I definitely felt like I needed it more than I think I can even put in words. It was pivotal during COVID." Her radio experience helped her face loneliness in her own apartment. She describes her weekly approach: *I can keep doing this a little bit longer because I have this outlet to go to at least once a week. All right, I've now just got to make it back to Tuesday.*

As Marissa became more involved with the radio station, opportunities opened up. "Coming back, we were doing a complete revamp. There were a lot of positions open. And I'm like, *all right, I love it here, so I have to figure out how I want to help in some way.* I really loved the news because during COVID were the Black Lives Matter protests, and a lot of different news stories were breaking. I always liked writing and knowing what's going on. When I saw the news director position, I was scared at first because I was like, *what does this entail?*" Learning that this position would mean interviewing people to get stories and information, Marissa saw she faced a huge obstacle. "I had done *zero* interviews. And even though I'm an extrovert, I'm an introverted extrovert. So I get anxiety sometimes when talking to people. I was so nervous!"

Marissa tried to work through her fears. "What if I go to interview them, and they don't like me? But I think getting the role made me feel like it's for the team. It's bigger than just my anxiety. I need to do this because this interview is important. And we need this story. I'm going to have to just work it out, internally."

At that time Marissa found a potentially huge news story on her doorstep. News emerged that the university would be making layoffs. Marissa was decisive. "People need to know about this. What's going on? Who's doing it? How do people feel about it? We need a voice from everyone involved, because it's not just the professors - the students are losing their professors. The administration claims there is a huge budget deficit. Okay, well, how big is it that you have to lay off these people?"

Gaining answers meant that Marissa would have to conduct some potentially difficult interviews. "I was like, this is uncomfortable, this is a touchy topic. I don't want to get Brave New Radio shut down, because we might be teetering into uncomfortable zones."

She plunged into the story, giving everything she had. "I had to learn on the spot. The one thing I think I forgot is that when you ask someone a question, follow it up." Marissa discovered how interviews can go into unexpected directions. "I'm like, okay, these are my questions, but if you're giving me something good, if you have some details that I wasn't aware of, I need to get some more information about that."

Marissa admits that when they first aired the finished story, "I was shaking in my boots!" The resulting story examined the issue from all sides and was a piece of radio journalism that Marissa could be proud of. It deserved to be heard by a larger audience. In fact, the radio station submitted it for *Best News Feature Story* for the national 2021 Intercollegiate Broadcasting System Awards. Marissa had low expectations but she admitted, "Even if we don't win, it was a winner to me, because it was our first huge story."

Exceeding her expectations, Marissa and Brave New Radio did win first place for her story "William Paterson Layoffs." It was a moment she'll never

FIGURE 5.2 Marissa Banks.

forget. "I was screaming in my car, because I was streaming it on my way to the award ceremony and I was running late. I was like, *we did it!*"

Since then, Marissa has grown more into her role as news director, and especially in her ability to conduct interviews. "You know when you've done a good interview, or when you've been a good interviewer, when you leave with more than what you expected," she says. "I think, as a professional, I had to learn really quickly," she says. "I found my voice in general doing radio, but I kind of got to learn who Marissa was and how I wanted to be perceived and how I wanted to say things. I think my confidence in who I am as a news director, and just a member of the station, is completely different from when I first walked in."

What a story of transformation! Truly finding her voice. Today she says, "I'm used to talking! I'm used to getting up and being, *this is who I am, period!*" (See Figure 5.2).

References

Adhikari, D. (2021, June 10). *Get your facts straight: The basics of fact-checking.* The Kit: Exposing The Invisible. https://kit.exposingtheinvisible.org/en/fact-checking.html

Cassidy, C. (2022, May 18). Joe Rogan's rant about growing food in Australia: What did he say and is any of it true? *The Guardian.* https://www.theguardian.com/australia-news/2022/may/18/joe-rogans-rant-about-growing-food-in-australia-what-did-he-say-and-is-any-of-it-true

Craig Newmark Graduate School of Journalism. (2023, April 25). *Fact checking & verification for reporting.* City University of New York. https://researchguides.journalism.cuny.edu/factchecking-verification/fact-check-your-work

Dennis. (2023, May 23). *Why and when to use a podcast release form for your guests (with template).* Castos. https://castos.com/podcast-release-form-guest/

Tha Artist Network. (2014, February 12). *Samuel L Jackson Blast news anchor for confuseing him with Laurence Fishburne full interview* [Video]. YouTube. https://youtu.be/OdxMkQhq58g

This Morning. (2017, October 4). *Ryan Gosling and Harrison Ford lose it at hilarious interview* [Video]. YouTube. https://youtu.be/bAb8KIhgVAI

6

PREPARING THE MEAL IN THE KITCHEN

Developing tasty programs

First thoughts: *Go Easy on Yourself:* **How one radio station manager coaches her students to produce their best attempts at audio content and avoid the pitfalls of program preparation**

Picture this: Eva Gustavfsson is sitting in her radio station, K103 in Gothenburg, Sweden, while I sit in New York State, USA.

Eva Gustavfsson (personal communication, February 6, 2023) describes her city: "Gothenburg is on Sweden's west coast. It's a harbor city. You can probably compare it to places like Liverpool or Seattle with its working class, rain, but also a very vivid music scene that we've had over the years. It's a university city as well. It has two universities, Gothenburg University and Chalmers University, and we're operating together with both of them. We have about 750,000 inhabitants."

Eva has been station manager of K103 since 2007, and I ask her what the radio station's primary mission is. She pauses before speaking precisely, "Our focus is to make any person who wants to tell a story, *ready for that*." I ask her to explain what she means about telling a story. "*Story* is making a DJ music show, creating news, interviewing interesting people, or having discussions with your friends about topics that you feel are relevant for our listeners. You should be able to make it happen so that you can get *your* voice and *your* opinion out to the world. Because youth is often overlooked but has a lot of things to say!"

It's obvious that Eva's passion is not only to create content herself, but also enable others to discover their potential to make content too. "We try to give people tools and encouragement and the support. So that you can do the best

DOI: 10.4324/9781003263739-9

you can with the knowledge that you have, and learn from the older ones … who've been here before."

So, what does Eva teach the new recruits about storytelling? "On the personal level, you know, you're talking about something that you've been thinking about, or you've been worrying about, that is helping to tell your story to a bigger audience, and maybe also knowing that there will be people out there who will be benefiting from hearing this story." But does that also help the person telling the story as well? Eva strongly agrees. "When you feel lonely and it's like, *this is only happening to me*, if you tell your story to people, you also feel less alone." That's the power of relatable audio.

Eva sees the transformation with those who first walk into her radio station. "Sometimes it's remarkable about the people who come to us. Because they're intrigued by something, they're curious about radio as a medium. But when you meet them, you kind of think, *you're not really cut out for radio, because you're super shy*. It's a struggle to get them to speak into a microphone. And it's like, *why do you want to be in front of a microphone? Because it feels like you don't want to be in front of people at all*."

Eva pauses, and then smiles. "But then *they try it out!* And they learn and they get better and better. And you can feel that they gain confidence, *in life in general*. You can see that these people *bloom* in a way. And when they've left the station, they're leaving with more confidence and more tools to face people. And especially the person that I'm thinking of today is a teacher who every day stands in front of an audience in school. And I could not see that happening when I met him the first time. So, I think that is super!"

I also share with Eva the eight-step production process detailed in this chapter and ask her which is the most important stage. I receive a simple answer: "*1. Plan.* Failure to plan can result in failure just as much as doing too much planning. Some people overplan, you know, have a *plan and plan and plan* and then you know, *there's never a show*." Can she give me an example? "Yeah. Last semester, for example, I had one team. They did so much prep, they were here for four days and prepped, and they went out and did three interviews. And then everything just imploded because energy ran out. And that never saw daylight. Or like the team who recorded too much material and then spent three weeks editing that, and in the end, they only did *one show* last semester. So, I mean, you can also do too much!"

What final piece of advice would she give to those starting out in audio production, to find the right balance and approach? "*Don't be too harsh on yourself in the beginning*. Because if the first thing you do is the best thing you do, then everything else you do in the future won't be as good. And you're *supposed* to improve. So just continue doing it, and you will get better over time" (see Figure 6.1).

FIGURE 6.1   Eva Gustavfsson (Photo credit: Eva Gustavfsson).

How might you begin?

Whenever I interview enthusiasts like Eva, who have experienced the wonder of encouraging others along the audio journey, it reinforces my desire to encourage you. Especially in these next two chapters as we move into the heart of audio production. This chapter's title of preparing a meal can be a helpful metaphor for creating audio. Hopefully, it stirs imagination as well as activating taste buds. It invites you to see a range of options, and also stresses the need for careful preparation with a planned sequence of actions. Above all it is practical; its process ends up with something for others to taste and see. Or in our case, hear!

But it is less helpful if it only conjures up visions of chefs in white, barking instructions to assistants in gleaming kitchens and five-star restaurants. As I described in Chapter 2, I want no one to be excluded. Those three levels of equipment began with basic equipment: a smartphone using free apps for editing. Only the most expensive level was able to spend large amounts of money on the checklist, with multitrack recording devices and high-end microphones. Some readers will also have access to a college or community radio station which will enable them to experience working with more expensive equipment. We noted the many advantages that students have when they are given access to a radio station in Chapter 3.

Other readers do not have that advantage. As we follow through the planned sequence of actions it is important to realize that *everyone* should be able to follow them, whatever their level of equipment. Even with basic equipment the idea of creating a meal for others follows certain stages. Essential principles and strategies apply for all levels of entry. Never forget who you are as you find your voice (Chapter 1). This is the essential tool that makes the rest possible. Sophisticated equipment is secondary to your uniqueness! It is up to you what recipes or content you will create for the delight of others and yourself. Like a chef, if you are producing something to be shared with other people, you will be hoping they enjoy or resonate with what you have created for them.

Chapter 2 also emphasized the two key principles. First, *the type of content always determines the tools needed for its creation.* At the *discoverer* stage, we focused on creating basic audio content that is relatively simple to produce without the need for editing. Now that we move to the *developer* stage we shall need to edit material. The process becomes more complex, yet you can still accomplish much with basic equipment.

The second key principle is: *recording the highest quality audio possible should always be your goal whatever level of equipment you use.* Let's remember that poor audio quality wastes time and energy as we create an audio project for others.

When you prepare a meal two big questions must be asked: 1) What will guests expect on the menu? 2) How will you create the different courses?

Renowned *Iron Chef* Esther Choi once said, "When I create any dish, literally the first thing I think of is, what is the purpose behind this dish? Why am I putting this ingredient in it?" (Beltis, n.d., para. 23). Famous chefs successfully bring to their cooking their unique culture and worldview. They have made their own journey of discovery, learning who they are, and what particular qualities they bring. Rather like a chef, you will have favorite ingredients that will distinguish you from everyone else. Your ingredients are discovered and developed as a result of *finding your voice*. From the exercises so far in this book, you are beginning to get a sense of *who you are*, and *what you want to say* with your voice. Your identity, unique from anyone else, is the key bedrock ingredient to anything you create, its own distinctive flavor!

As you listen to the audio and radio work of others, you can learn from their distinctive audio ingredients. You will realize how they have developed their voice and how they decided to use it. You may consider their choices different from what you would make, but that's the point. *They are not you.* When you start, there are advantages to following the "recipes" of more experienced chefs. As you become more comfortable using different ingredients you will be able to take more creative control of your audio dishes. You will learn different audio production techniques and you will apply them when it comes to creating audio content.

As any chef knows, preparing a meal requires a sequence of planning and activity. Creating audio similarly has a production process that has an *eight-stage sequence*. The diagram that follows (Figure. 6.2) is an essential framework for much that will follow in this book. In my classes at university, I teach this process as being fundamental to audio production, and several students who've gone into the audio industry have contacted me to let me know that they still use it everyday.

THE PRODUCTION PROCESS

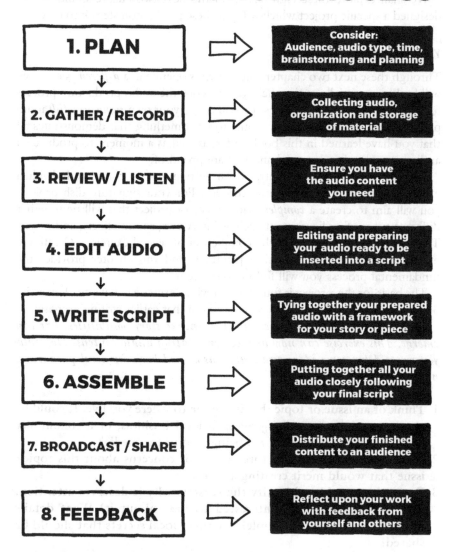

FIGURE 6.2   The eight-stage production process.

First, its sequence applies to whatever levels of equipment are available. Second, it applies to whatever type of audio production you are involved with. Whether it's pre-recorded content such as a podcast, or a live radio show or streaming broadcast, the eight steps assist you in your preparation. The fundamental difference applying the process to live broadcasts versus a pre-recorded project is that you will likely be playing in *real time* your edited audio content to the audience. So it's essential, like pre-recorded content, that all your audio is fully edited and ready to go.

We shall explore these eight stages in the next two chapters, and I have designed a specific project which will put these production steps into practice.

Your signature dish

Through these next two chapters the exercises operate in a *different way*. They will build sequentially as they help you practice the audio production process for real. Through these exercises you will create your own *signature dish* audio project. This project has the potential to be something that demonstrates all that you have learned in this book so far, as well as a moment to produce an audio piece that is substantial and you are proud of.

So far this book has concentrated on getting you to complete individual exercises that produce standalone content. For your signature dish project, you will aim to create a *complete* audio piece or project that will tie together different types of audio content such as interviews, sound effects, and music. That content will come from the completion of several exercises. Creating a more complicated piece will take planning, and this chapter provides the fundamental process you will follow to create it.

The basis for this project is found in a previous exercise in Chapter 4, exercise 3: *Unheard Among Us*. Let me remind you of that earlier writing exercise:

Reflect about where you live, and the unique story possibilities that can emerge. This exercise can now be used for creating audio content. Hopefully you wrote down some ideas and sources as a good basis for developing a signature project.

1 Think of an issue or topic that is unique to where you live. It could be about a new construction project, a local business, or a community initiative. What stories are *not* being told in the media?
2 Make a shortlist of up to three issues or concerns about this topic/issue that would merit creating a story.
3 For each story idea, identify the reasons why it deserves attention. Why should people be interested to hear about it? What details might be new to many people? Are there local secrets that should be shared?

You may be surprised at how easily you can generate story ideas that no one else has thought of. Always keep your notes; you will need them later.

This exercise was designed to provoke you to think of possible stories which could be the basis for an audio project. You may well be the only person who is producing content on the topic or issue you have selected. You are giving an opportunity for the unheard among us to be recognized.

To inspire you for ideas, consider the following topics:

- **A new or proposed building or construction project in your community**
- **A local news issue such as a recurring or ongoing problem**
- **A special upcoming event like a concert or exhibition**
- **A story about a local organization, such as a community group or sports team**
- **A profile about a resident who has an interesting story**
- **A history of where you live and imagining its future in changing times**
- **An exploration of the mysterious, ghostly, and urban myths about where you live!**

As you can see, the possibilities are many, and these are just a few suggestions. Some of my students are especially excited about the last suggestion, and dive into exploring spooky ghost stories and local myths and folklore! Having taught in New Jersey for many years, I now know more about the "Jersey Devil" than I ever wanted to know! (Jersey Devil, 2023) Whatever topic you choose, it needs to be something that *excites you*.

Now let's tackle this chapter's first exercise about interviewees, and the first step in creating content for your signature dish.

Chapter 6: R.E.A.L. Exercise #1. Choosing an interviewee for *Unheard Among Us*

Now that you have completed the chapter on interviewing, let's put that to immediate use. I will assume that you have decided the focus of your *Unheard Among Us* piece. Your goal in this exercise is to secure an interview that fits in with the goal of your project. It's up to you whether that interview is conducted in-person or via telephone or internet (such as Zoom or Skype):

1 Identify someone locally that you need to interview about the topic or issue that you have selected for your *Unheard Among Us* project. Will you be interviewing them as an individual, or will they be representing an organization or group?

2 Find out how best to approach them. Do they have a website? Is there an email or telephone contact? Can you see them in person?

3 Explain your purpose as a trainee interviewer seeking to conduct a substantive interview for your project about the particular issue.

4 Seek to be as professional as possible, from the moment of first contact to the final "thanks" email after the interview.

You may find someone who never does interviews, and you will need to provide as much information and guidance as possible for them before you interview them. Or you may find that the person you interview has extensive experience of being interviewed and will provide a solid dance partner, as long as you have done the necessary preparation! The only concern is that they might decline to be interviewed if you are not representing an official organization or outlet. But go for it! Typically, if you interview people who live in the same place as you, they can be enthusiastic and willing to talk about your proposed topic. You will be a local as they are, and that can build trust between interviewer and interviewee.

After you have conducted this interview, you now have *one key ingredient* for your signature dish project. That's a great starting point, and we will continue the project shortly. Now let's look at the whole production process, to learn how audio projects are made (see Figure 6.2).

With your first interview for *Unheard Among Us* now recorded, you have already begun the first two stages. You will follow the steps in the production process to complete your project. Typically you will conduct an interview once you have gone through these early production stages, but you now have a head start.

This production process sequence will structure the rest of this book and hopefully your work beyond it. This chapter will describe and explore the first three stages:

Stage 1. *Plan for what you will need to record*
Involves answering a series of questions about audience, audio type, program types, use of time, scope of brainstorming, and mapping out an outline.

Stage 2. *Gather/record your content*
This requires collecting key types of audio and developing habits of effective organization and storage of material.

Stage 3. *Review/listen to your content*
Ensure you have what you need.

Let's explore these stages further.

Stage 1. Plan for what you will need to record

Eva Gustavffson declared this to be the most important stage: "Failure to plan can result in failure just as much as doing too much planning."

For chefs in the kitchen, planning their meals depends greatly not only on their skill level and reputation but also on who the guests are and their expectations. Beginners start with simpler menus so that skills and reputation may grow with practice. For your *Unheard Among Us* project, your plan will have to consider: *what* topic or issue am I focusing on, *who* will I interview about it, and *how* will I put it all together, including my own contribution? A plan is therefore essential before you do any recording.

You need to face several questions as you plan each audio project:

Who is likely to be your audience?

Just as chefs need to think carefully about who is coming to the table, creating an audio project requires giving attention to those who will hear it. Unless you are creating audio content just for yourself and friends, any larger, outside audience will have *expectations that need to be met*. Lessons learned in Chapter 3 about visualizing listeners are bedrock disciplines for deciding the kind of content needed and how to best present it.

At all stages of planning, you need to keep asking whether each part or chapter of your project is strong in its *interest* and *relevance* for your audience. Boring bits should be rooted out. The following questions help to keep the audience constantly in mind:

- What do I want my audience to *understand* at any given point of my project?
- How do I think my audience will *react* at any given moment?
- What will my audience be *expecting* to come next?
- What does the audience need to *feel* at the end?

That last question is crucial. An audience left hanging without answers or a satisfying closure will be frustrated, although that might be your goal! For example, if you are producing a series of episodes or broadcasts, you may intend to keep them listening because you finish each episode with an intriguing cliffhanger or raise new, unanswered questions, which keeps them hooked to hear more.

Will you use pre-recorded or live audio?

The contrasting types of audio we have already met require different planning skills. "**Pre-recorded**" audio content is recorded material edited into a final piece for later broadcast or distribution. A podcast or radio documentary, for example, would therefore require a *pre-rec* script. Such a script might contain phrases such as, *"This week on the podcast we explore the history of ...,"*

"The information, opinions, and recommendations presented in this podcast are for general information only ...," "The opinions in this piece are my own and do not reflect my employer's ... ." The script is written in a way that indicates it's a pre-recorded piece, not a live broadcast. Such a script usually is meant to be read word-for-word, without the improvisation that is sometimes required by live broadcasting.

"**Live**" audio is an event or broadcast happening live, in real time. A live radio show, or a live webstream (such as announcing a sports game) would require an as-live script. It might contain phrases such as, *"Hello and welcome to another live episode of ...," "Right now we are standing outside the ....," "Joining us is our special guest ... ."* The script needs to be written in a way for it to be used for either live radio, or to sound like it was live when you recorded it. A *live read* is designed to be read straight on the air. Some experienced live radio presenters may prefer to have just bullet points or key words and phrases written down rather than a whole script, word-for-word. It depends on the situation. A live script has a degree of flexibility necessary for any happening during a live broadcast. Hosts will likely prepare a safety net of backup content in case of unforeseen circumstances. As we shall see in Chapter 9, dead-air scenarios kill presentation. It's like presenting a main course with obvious spaces on a plate where food should be!

Preparing pre-recorded content can be far more time consuming to produce, but there is an assurance that when it's shared with an audience, every second is taken care of. It is highly likely that you will choose pre-recorded audio for your project.

R.E.A.L. Moment

Back in my radio days as morning show presenter on Connect FM in Northamptonshire, England, it was the early days for using computers to broadcast live and automated radio content. One morning, I noticed that a strange "clicking" sound was happening every few seconds for EVERY song! It was so obvious. Music was about 60% of my show! Listeners started calling in, "Is there something wrong with my radio or with you?!" they asked. Not knowing what to do, I rebooted the computer and went to my backup plan of having listeners call in to discuss a local news topic for about ten minutes. That bought me enough time for the computer to reboot and reload, and to my immense relief the problem was solved! Sometimes you just need to restart something, and even computers need a break sometimes! Having a backup plan saved my show that day.

Which kind of audio content form best suits your project?

As suggested it is likely you are choosing to create pre-recorded audio to begin your journey. For example, you may decide that for your *Unheard Among Us* project you will ultimately interview five people alongside your own narration and present the finished piece as a pre-recorded documentary feature. But that's just one option.

You should be aware of the great range of possibilities that are open for pre-recorded pieces. What follows is like the wide range of options that a skilled chef can offer. Just as different forms of cuisine call for very different ingredients and styles of cooking, this list includes a vast variety of audio options. Just think of some of the content you can create, from very simple production pieces to those that are elaborate and complex. Contrast pizzas and hamburgers with haute cuisine! But as you look at this range of options and see the potential for what you can create, keep in mind that, at first, we need to take easy steps. Remember the key principle that *the type of audio content you create significantly impacts the required structure and design you will need.*

Different categories of audio content include:

- **Interviews.** Typically an interview requires two people (interviewer and interviewee) but can also involve several people at once. It typically has a scripted introduction and ending, and your as-live interview in between. Chapter 5 is devoted to interviewing.
- **Livestreaming**. This is effectively broadcasting live to an audience. In Chapter 9 we will explore the role of radio broadcasting, but with the emergence of so many streaming platforms, you can now stream live audio content around the world. For example, consider the following platforms/websites: *Clubhouse, Facebook Live, Instagram Live, LinkedIn Live, TikTok Live, Twitch, Twitter Spaces, Vimeo, YouTube Live.* The preparation for livestreaming is similar to broadcasting on a traditional media outlet, and just as demanding in ensuring you have enough material to fill your time whilst also being interesting and engaging for the audience.
- **News stories**. News stories bring together the audio clips you will have from various interviewees or sound recordings (these are also called *packages* by radio stations) and tie them together with your voice as an anchor or reporter. Your job is to present stories to the audience in ways that are easily understood. Needless to say, your stories should also be bias-free and accurate with a formality that fits news telling, which covers a variety of often serious subjects. Though writing for the ear often encourages informality, news stories require great care. Uncluttered words and communicating seriously should match the gravity of your content.

When reporting, journalists typically consider the Five W's: *who, what, when, where,* and *why.* None of these questions should be omitted in your content, so that audiences are given essential information and context.

Different kinds of news stories include:

News bulletin/newscast – presenting a selection of news stories within a specific time.

Hard news stories are about contemporary events. Very time-sensitive and pertinent.

Soft news is about an issue that's topical, and less time-sensitive than hard news.

Editorials present opinions and points of view about an issue in the news.

Features and documentaries – much longer pieces, see the next point.

- **Personal pieces.** This is material of personal concern and creation. The majority of the exercises in this book, so far, have been this type of content. For many students, this will be a good place to start, and I shall assume this type of audio in the exercises I have designed in what follows.
- **Podcast.** This format will be covered in extensive detail in Chapter 8, but a podcast can also include many of the various types of audio content in this list, from an interview to documentaries and features, for example.
- **Radio program.** This format will be covered in extensive detail in Chapter 9, but a radio program can also include many of the various types of audio content in this list.
- **Social media audio.** These days it's possible to create and easily share your audio online in spaces like Soundcloud, Mixcloud, YouTube, and other online entities. The key to ensuring the largest audience possible hearing your audio *is making sure they can see it.* That's why having a video component to your audio is essential if you plan on sharing it via social media on places such as Facebook, Twitter, TikTok, SnapChat, and Instagram. Visually appealing content, even if it's primarily audio, is still important when it comes to sharing on social media. Such content attracts followers to repost and share your material, so that it may go viral and reach a large number of people. There are always new apps emerging that will enable you to take your audio content (usually a short excerpt) and convert it into a video clip that can be shared. For example, check out services such as Audiogram, Descript, Headliner, and Wavve. Search for the one that's best for you.
- **Sound art and design.** This type of content is artistic, creative, experimental, and unconventional. Sound artists create experiences and work using interesting sounds, music, and words. From thought-poems, soundscapes, and aural atmospheres, this type of content utilizes the full sound spectrum and spatial audio to immerse the listener inside an

experience that can move and enlighten. Some of these pieces can be elaborate, and therefore best attempted once you have acquired competency in several areas of audio production.

- **Spots: commercials/public service announcements (PSAs)/promotional.** Typically, any of these last a minute or less. Radio broadcasts and podcasts have commercial spots as well as PSAs in their programming. Don't be fooled into thinking that it's easy to create such content because it's short in duration. Often you will find it challenging to fit in all the information within the given time. For a commercial spot, typically found on the radio, you will have to meet the requirements of the client. A PSA should communicate key information in a way that grabs the attention of listeners. PSAs focus on important public issues such as public safety, health issues, and environmental concerns and are produced by non-profit organizations. This contrasts with commercial radio spots that are designed to sell products. But both will likely entail many drafts before a final script is written.
- **Documentaries/features.** Resembling news stories, their content is usually much longer and deeper in scope. It's also probably the toughest type of content to create, as you will create a script that must bring together all your audio clips, while providing context and understanding for the audience in the process. An hour-long documentary might have over a hundred audio clips to arrange! Inevitably it's an audio format that requires intense concentration and work. Also, like the news stories earlier, you will probably be using language that's more formal. Arnaud Zajtman's radio work in Africa (Chapter 3) is in this category.
- **Drama and comedy.** This is the most demanding kind of audio content, for unlike other formats which often piece together audio clips or other content, drama and comedy require focused writing and planning, rather like a playwright at work. The script is everything. It requires creative writing in which each sentence plays its part and high-level skill is required. If you are attempting this, involving others can help.

As you review all these different types of audio content, you will realize that the contrast between recording a personal diary entry versus producing serious journalism, for example, will be massive. The amount of time needed to complete such a personal piece would be considerably shorter than a longer, more structured production. That's why it's advisable to start with a project that has clearly defined goals, and nothing too complicated at first. The importance of time is therefore crucial. This cannot be overstated. I think the hardest thing for students to understand is the importance of focused time on a project.

However, don't get too bogged down with planning that you never actually produce any content. *Project paralysis* is real. Remember how Eva warned about two problems: "Some people overplan, you know, have a *plan and plan and plan* and then you know, *there's never a show* … . Or like the team who recorded too much material and then spent three weeks editing that, and in the end, they only did *one show.*" As you become more experienced with producing audio content, you will get better at estimating the time you will need, and quicker in creating content as well. At the back of your mind you should always be prepared to ask the perhaps feared question: *what do I need to change if this plan is not working?* Changing your plan is not an admission of defeat or failure, it's a realization that you need to make adjustments to ensure your project's success. Don't fall for the *sunk cost fallacy* (The Decision Lab, n.d.), when you are deterred from making a fundamental change because you've already done so much work and spent so much time. If you know in your gut that something *isn't working*, you are always better off in following the right path, even if that means starting over.

Crucially important is always considering your audience in your planning, by asking yourself what *you* would want to know if you were listening to it. Ensure that you plan to take the time to explain or unpack your content, so it's fully understood by an audience.

The key to selecting which *type* of project you will undertake requires thinking about your purpose – why are you creating it in the first place? It is best to begin with one-off projects like *Unheard Among Us* rather than anything bigger in scope. That way, you can more easily complete a project, experience the resulting sense of achievement, and keep your enthusiasm intact! It is likely when you start that you will be working entirely alone – presenter, producer, and editor all in one. So, it's even more important that you create a project that you can complete successfully. Be careful of biting off more than you can chew!

How much time will you have?

This important question has two parts. First, *how long will your audio piece last?* Second, *how much time can you give to the project?*

For beginning discoverers there is often no time limit. The content takes as long as it needs to seem complete. Working without a time constraint is a necessary freedom when you are learning and makes the process more enjoyable. However, producing audio becomes a far more difficult task once you start to create content to a specific time requirement, which becomes the norm when you prepare program material. Working in audio professionally means getting used to meeting deadlines, and that requires practice. Deadlines introduce a degree of pressure. Sometimes, if too much material has been produced, cutting out content can lose important information. But, at the other extreme, sometimes too little material means stretching content to fill the time. Audiences can generally detect "filler" content, just as they can deduce that something has been cut down and stuffed into a smaller timeframe than it deserves. They can tell if an idea is rushed or overdone, just as someone can taste if a meal is undercooked or burnt.

Producing consistent content that is as strong at the end as it is at the beginning, including the middle, comes down to effective planning and structuring your material. Experience plays a part here too, and getting used to completing projects informs your ongoing craft. Always keeping the time limit in mind sharpens skill in planning.

The second question of *how much time can you give to the project?* is critically important too. In the early days of creating audio, it's easy to grossly underestimate how much time you will need to complete an audio project. Any project that is pre-recorded will take much longer to complete than something that's live and instant. One of my audio professors once gave me a rough estimate that *for every 15 minutes of pre-recorded audio material produced, you need at least one hour of production time*. Of course, it all depends on the level of your production skills. Gaining more experience, especially in editing, can shorten the equation. What is certain is that the longer and more complex the project, the more time you need to give for its production. Nearly every student arrives at the realization that it took longer than they ever imagined to complete their audio project.

In my early experience of audio production, I also struggled with the importance of keeping track of time. It's only natural when you are starting out that you spend more time than necessary on simple tasks. Gaining competence with the process and equipment takes time and practice. Don't lose patience. Be assured, as you become more experienced with the procedures and methods of creating audio, you will become more efficient and quicker in your abilities. Take some heart that creating audio content is considerably easier and less time consuming than creating video or film content!

In addition to growing familiar with the production process, you need to build in time to be creative; to be "in the zone" as we say. Being in the zone eats up time like nothing else. When you are totally absorbed in a project the clock races and time evaporates. Adrenaline kicks in and our creative juices fuel concentration and purpose. This experience has so many bonuses because when you are in the zone, creativity is exciting and fulfilling. It may not happen too often, but when it does you can lose all track of time. It's incredibly easy to become detached from the reality of the ticking clock.

From *day one* it is helpful to keep an eye on the ticking clock, to keep checking for improvements you are making in the amount of time taken. One brilliant technique to help ensure you meet any deadline is to create an additional personal deadline two days or so before the actual one and work to meet that instead. That way, if needed, you have an extra buffer of time to add polish and corrections to your final piece. Developing personal discipline with time reaps big rewards in the future. Never procrastinate!

For those thinking of a future in a professional broadcast environment such as a radio station or podcasting studio or similar, you can imagine how failing to keep track of time can be fatal to your career. Failing to produce content to a deadline, or not delivering content to the specified length required, are scenarios that can have serious repercussions. It is never too early to learn that predetermined lengths matter. Basic time limits determine structure. Students sometimes produce content without considering the time limit. As we move to producing a specific piece of audio, time limit matters. For your *Unheard Among Us* project, you need to determine how long you will give yourself to complete it. Two weeks, one month? Once you have decided, stick to that decision.

Have you brainstormed an outline?

When chefs plan a meal they have guests in mind and ideas about what courses they should prepare. As we have progressed through these early stages, it is vital to settle on an outline for your project. The word *settle* can disguise a busy and confusing time, where you think through various possibilities.

Brainstorming is a good way to describe this settling process. Most of us find it easier to brainstorm using a blank page and throwing down on it all kinds of possibilities. It can be scary to start with an empty page. Jotting down different ideas, stories, pictures, and words that might relate to your topic quickly fills up that page. Let the imagination fly. Genuine, free-wheeling brainstorming releases blue-sky thinking. It can begin small, like writing down words and phrases that immediately come to mind as you think of your subject. Give yourself time to write down an increasing range of possibilities, the wilder the better. Even just writing down emotions and feelings can be as helpful as writing down specific places, names, and objects. At this stage, if you can think of it, write it down!

The different ways in which a person's creative juices flow is highly personal. Some people need quiet and paper; others need noise and action. Often taking a break and coming back to a project refreshes the gray cells and prompts renewed creativity. Sometimes revisiting unused brainstorming ideas can trigger fresh inspiration. You can also collaborate. Some students find "thinking out loud" with others can be immensely stimulating. Others prefer to work alone. Either way, always keep track of any brainstorming notes.

You should feel *liberated* to include as many ideas or approaches as possible, without any thought as to how to realize them. Indeed, if you limit your ideas because of their perceived impracticality, you may inhibit the flow of ideas that could lead to the answer you seek. My initial belief in 2013 that President Obama really should be supporting World College Radio Day led to him writing three letters of support and the White House inviting us to visit twice during his time in office! Dream big! Sometimes you may come up with an idea that ultimately will not work, but leads you to an idea that will.

Hopefully, you will end up with far more ideas than you can use. This generative process enables your own voice and experience to make an impact. If you have completed the self-discovery exercises in this book, no one else will fill that blank page like you! It's R.E.A.L. in action. No one else has to see what you have come up with either. It's brainstorming with *your* audience in mind. After a brainstorming session, you can then sift through all your ideas and start to *identify* what's possible. This is when you next envision an initial **outline** for your project, incorporating one or more of your generated ideas from your brainstorming.

At this stage, you need to make some decisions. Sifting through the results of your brainstorming effort tends to sort ideas roughly into two categories: ideas that are **achievable** in your present situation and ideas that are **future goals** to work toward. By focusing on what you can do right now, you will not be paralyzed by the prospects of putting together a project that is too complicated and ambitious. At this stage in your journey, you need to focus on the first category, achievable possibilities. Overreaching with ideas that are likely to be complicated can knock your confidence. Keep focus on ideas that your skills can bring to life *now*.

The outcome of your brainstorming should be an overall achievable **goal** or **focus** which requires an **outline** to get there. That goal is an issue or topic which will be the primary focus of your project. An outline is a rough, broadstroke overview of the sequence of points/events that will likely be in your audio piece – what you have essentially decided to include and exclude. For example, for your *Unheard Among Us* audio, you may decide to put together a story about a new business in town, and you know that it will feature several interviews, but nothing more specific than that at this point. So, at this stage an outline is necessarily vague, and you will still have to nail down exact details. Once you have identified the topic and what you would like to achieve in broad principle, it's time to get more detailed.

Your outline now becomes a step-by-step **plan** for how you will structure your audio piece. This is no longer an outline; it has become a **content plan**. You are getting more specific in your thinking now, carefully considering what specific content you will need. For example, you might decide you will begin with an introduction followed by an interview with someone who presents their position on the topic. You could then decide to follow that with an interview with someone who presents an opposite point of view. That adds interest and balance for your piece and demonstrates that you are thinking about how you are exploring and presenting the issue or topic.

For example, here's an example of a basic outline for your piece:

Intro to discuss the issue → Interview #1 → Interview #2 → My own take → Interview #3 → Interview #4 → Outro with my conclusion

Of course, every project you create will be different and unique from anyone else's. Your individuality and voice come through in what you plan and produce.

See Figure 6.3 for an overview of the brainstorming process.

From initial **brainstorming** (what will my chosen topic be?) to **outline** (what needs to be in it?) to a **content plan** (how do I structure/arrange my material?), decisions will be made to more clearly define and focus on what you will need to do. As you develop your project, you are adding further details at each stage for what you want to include in your content, and you are building a structure and sequence for your piece.

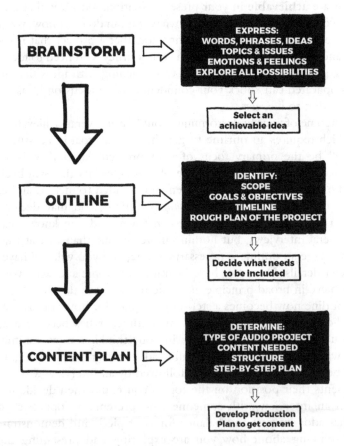

FIGURE 6.3 The brainstorming process.

Note, a content plan for how to *structure your audio piece* is different from your **production plan** on *how to get and produce the content for it*. Your content plan is your audio wishlist and structure, your production plan is all about *where* you need to go, and *who* and *what* you need to get and do in order to make your content plan a reality. The production plan emerges after you have done the work of finishing your content plan.

Putting this newfound knowledge to work, we'll now continue the next *Unheard Among Us* exercise, which will follow through the eight stages of audio production. This is the heart of this book's practical work. I want you to learn by doing. The *Unheard Among Us* project will likely fall in the audio category of *personal pieces*. To benefit from this process you need to set aside some time to do this next exercise.

Chapter 6, R.E.A.L. Exercise #2: Planning your *Unheard Among Us* signature dish
After completing exercise #1 in this chapter, you already have one recorded interview. Let's build on that. Continuing the same *Unheard Among Us* assignment, let's now create a more substantial piece that builds on your ideas and further develops your content. You are looking to develop a piece that more fully explores the local issue or topic that you have selected.
To develop your plan, you now need to answer the following questions about what you imagine your project could be:

1 **Is your audience for this piece an obvious one?**

2 **Will you use pre-recorded material? Will this be a live broadcast instead? (For this *Unheard Among Us* exercise it's assumed it will be pre-recorded.)**

3 **How long will you aim for your piece? Fifteen minutes is a good target to aim for.**

4 **How much time will you have to create it?**

5 **Have you brainstormed an outline? Be as creative as you like. Think carefully about what elements you need to make it a complete production. Are multiple people required to be guests or interviewees? Make a list of those you would need to participate.**

This exercise will probably require a few pages, but it's important at this stage to understand that even a simple audio project needs a plan. That's why having a structure for your piece is rather like a chef preparing a meal, having a strong foundation for you to build upon.

If you are aiming for a final, edited 15-minute piece (for example), think about what you will need. Also, consider how your voice as host or narrator will tie all your audio content together. At the end of this exercise, you should be able to imagine what your completed *Unheard Among Us* project will be!

Stage 2. Gather/Record your content

At the end of stage 1, your brainstorming of various possibilities should result in an outline of your audio project. Next your outline needs more details, and so you will develop a content plan of the sequence of main points and audio that will structure your audio piece. This is still likely to be a wishlist because so much depends on this next stage of gathering and recording content. These two aspects, gathering and recording, obviously belong together.

Gathering enough good material is the minimum goal. You need to ask key questions:

- **How much of my voice will also be included?**
- **How many people do I need to interview, if at all?**
- **Apart from interviews, what other types of audio will I need? (see list that follows)**

After you have made a list of what you'd like, reality kicks in. You may find something you planned to gather is not feasible, or if it is feasible, recording it might not be possible. Think, for example, of an interview with someone that you would like to include. They may not cooperate, or if they see you, may refuse to be recorded. Inevitably, changes will be made to your plans through no fault of your own. My students quickly learn that adapting to unforeseen events is a normal occurrence!

The question about how much of your own voice will be included is pivotal. What other audio elements to include should be easier to consider. Sound elements such as music and location ambience add interest and excitement to your piece. Think of sound elements as ingredients to spice up your audio recipe! And, as with most recipes, choosing a blend of ingredients gives more subtlety and flavor to your audio.

Your voice

When you first develop your content plan, a key decision concerns how much your own voice is going to be involved. As you thread together the different parts of your audio piece will *you* be the narrator? Depending on your content, you will need to make decisions on how you will approach the recording of other people's voices and stories.

Those who work in audio and radio production know that there seem to be two common models of narration when it comes to presenting a story. The first, which seems to be predominant in the USA and the UK, is having a host or narrator that ties together the content, offering explanation and agency to the piece. The second approach, which seems to originate from Europe, lets the interviewee voices speak for themselves, and there is no host or narrator, such as yourself, to shape or interpret what they have to say. Essentially, the narrator gets out of the way and lets the interviewees speak for themselves.

From experience, producing such European-style material is difficult, because you are entirely dependent on the interviewee's effectiveness as storytellers, and there is an enormous temptation to insert your own voice to clarify, add context, or accentuate what they are saying. Either way, the way you edit someone else can, to a certain extent, also assist in an audience understanding more clearly what's going on (that will be explored in the next chapter). But when it's not your story, but someone else's, you will need to make decisions on how you will approach the recording and presentation of other people's voices and stories, and whether you need to get out of the way to do so. These are the tricky questions that the *developer* must consider:

- **Your voice:** How much of your voice will be in it? Will you be the primary narrator, or will you let the audio speak for itself, or have someone else narrate? Will you remove yourself from the piece, or be integral to it?
- **Your intentions:** Are you ultimately seeking to emotionally move (creating *relatable* content) your audience or persuade them to a point of view or understanding (*engaging* your audience)? How does your story convey emotion to support your intentions? What is your overall goal?
- **Key moments:** Considering your intentions, what important moments can you identify as being pivotal in your piece? What essential information needs to be understood?
- **Your style:** Will your piece be conversational in style, or more formal? How does your approach affect its accessibility for an audience? Will your style be more traditional or experimental?
- **Your structure:** Will you structure your piece as a singular standalone piece or have episodic chapters, each with their own opening and conclusion?

Before this point, so much of the *discoverer* journey was about finding *your* distinctive voice, and it may be that you will now have an opportunity to employ an active voice. How much do you see your project as telling a story? Gathering content involves you thinking about your own role *and the role of others* that will be included in your content. You will need to ensure that you are fair and honest about how you use their voices and handle their contributions.

Before you consider sound effects, music, and the use of other audio material, work out how much of the gathered content you will need to provide yourself. Once you have assessed that, you can now determine if you will need to sprinkle in other ingredients such as sound effects, music, and archival recordings. From experience, I know that beginners to audio production may try to use too many things when they first start. That's a simple case of too many ingredients spoiling the dish. A *less is more* approach is best to begin with and will not overwhelm you or over complicate your first projects.

Sound effects

Ultimately, the power of audio lies in its intimacy with the listeners and their ability to connect with the creator's work, through words and sounds, the silences between the words, the emotions expressed, and the stories they hear. Sometimes communication is not through words at all. The sobbing of a mother who has lost her son to a drive-by shooting does not need words to convey the searing grief that she is experiencing. Communication sometimes does not need understandable language to be effective and affecting, for sound is a language all in itself.

Once a student played the sounds of their back garden at night, with no human voices but the sound of loud crickets, light winds rustling leaves in the nearby trees, and ominous hooting owls. It was an evocative soundscape that immediately transported the listener to the darkness of nighttime. Sound effects can transport the listener to a place in their imagination.

Whether we realize it or not, we all have our preferences for aural input. The sounds of nails on a chalkboard or screeching brakes on a car are instinctively unpleasant to hear. A police or ambulance siren provokes concern. Sound is rarely heard with neutrality because we automatically attach value and meaning to it – whether we like it or loathe it, whether it triggers memories or specific thoughts. Sounds have power to stimulate reactions in the brain, and we must be careful about the choices we make. Do not assume that your audience will feel the same way that you do. You should never underestimate the impact that your content can have.

Some sounds are easily available, such as footsteps walking down a corridor; a closing creaky door; the sound of busy traffic outside; the sound of rain and the outside environment during a big thunderstorm. Though professionally recorded sound effects are available, these will be for a cost. Certainly, at the beginning, it is far more fun to create your own sound effects.

For example, to create the sound of footsteps you can record yourself walking inside or outside with your recording equipment. If you want to create the sound of a key turning in a lock, that's also easy to do. Many sounds like these are not only enjoyable to create but will have the advantage of consistency in your audio recording. Purchased professional sound effects have likely been created on different audio equipment than yours that may give too much contrast with your own production.

While the moviemaking business spends millions of dollars on building elaborate sets and locations to convince the viewer that they are watching something genuine, audio does the job affordably with sounds helping to provide a rich picture. Remember that painting words in someone's imagination *gives better pictures*, and sounds greatly help add color.

R.E.A.L. Moment

Audio's ability to evoke feelings of terror – to make your heart beat faster – is the reason the podcast *Scary Horror Stories by Dr. NoSleep* (Cummings, 2011–Present) has built a dedicated audience. Describing itself as "the most terrifying horror stories on the internet," this US-produced podcast uses audio to maximum effect. Narrated by the mysterious Dr. NoSleep, each episode is full of ominous and dramatic music, and spine-tingling sound effects such as screams and knife slashes. Definitely not recommended for children or listening to late at night!

Music

Music holds a prime place in the claim that sound is a language all unto itself. Certain sounds appeal to us based on our prior encounters with them. Sounds, and especially music, can function like emotional bookmarks that remind us of specific times and places when we heard them. Listeners' ears perk up because music dynamically accentuates emotional impact. Movie makers rely on its power.

An enormously wide range of music is available online. However, most of it is copyrighted to generate royalties for its creators. To use such music requires all kinds of legal permission. We shall cover the issue of gaining legal permission later in this book. At this stage, we shall wish to include music affordably. Happily, many royalty-free music websites do offer music that you can use in your piece at minimal cost, though always double-check that you have all the permissions and have paid the license fee. Again, as with sound effects, if you have the option to record your own music, it's more satisfying and more fun than just downloading a music track. But, admittedly, it is so much easier just to click a button and download some ready-made music.

Because music has such emotional power, you should heed a few warnings. Conjuring up emotions of happiness, joy, sadness, and even fear should be used judiciously. Too much music can drown out your voice and dominate your project. Also, I often see students using music in their projects at a volume that is far too loud, which drowns out the audio and diminishes the quality and impact. Music is a very effective emotional trigger, but you need to think carefully when using it.

Archival recordings/file management

Archival recordings are previous audio recordings from other sources, such as soundbites of another person speaking. Again, such sources can add interest, excitement, and energy to your audio. However, bear in mind that just as with using music, you will need to obtain legal permission because of copyright issues. Using anything created by someone else is likely to need permission. There is such a thing as a *fair use policy*, where you are allowed to use archived recordings in a certain, limited way, and we shall return to that later on.

Over time, you will be creating your own archives. Even during this first sequence of exercises, you may record audio, or even edit audio, you will not use on that occasion. At the start of this book, I recommended keeping all of your digital audio files in a folder on your computer for safekeeping. This should be true for any new audio project that you are creating. Create a new folder for that project, but you should also be developing additional folders within it. When you organize your audio content like this, it's called **file management.** When you start a new project create a new folder for that project, which should also contain the following subfolders:

- **RAW Audio** – for all the unedited recordings you have. All the recordings should be stored here to begin with, making sure that they are labeled as being unedited (RAW) for example: *interviewRAW, soundeffectsRAW, NarrationRAW.*

  - As you listen/review your RAW audio, you should create two additional folders *within* the **RAW Audio** folder for you to sort them: **Good Audio** and **Unused Audio** (for any audio that you have decided you definitely *will not* be using in the final piece, but you might find it useful or important later on). Although these raw audio files are not yet edited, you will be able to sort them into these two folders as you listen to them. It will save you a lot of time later if you know what files you will definitely need.

- **Edited Audio** – for any audio that you have edited from the RAW Audio folder. It's important not to overwrite the original RAW file, but save a copy in this separate folder with the suffix EDIT as part of the filename. For example, *interviewEDIT, narrationEDIT, IntroEDIT.* It is not a bad idea to get into the habit of appending _v1 or _v2 to files as soon as you start to edit them. That makes it easier to go back quickly to find an earlier version if needed.

- **Other Audio** – for any sound effects, music, and audio from elsewhere/ not directly recorded by you.

- **Documents and Scripts** – for any text-based documents that contain scripts, ideas, or notes. Note, there are now many free web-based utilities and software editors that will automatically transcribe audio for you, and you should keep your transcripts in this folder.

These folders also constitute a content checklist for your project. Organizing your work with a regular backup routine is also a vital habit to develop. Saving a copy of your work on an external hard drive or online in the cloud protects you if your computer fails. Such backups can save the day, if your work gets lost, corrupted, or accidentally deleted. You may consider these to be rare events, but they do happen!

Sticking to this organizational method for all your audio will also help you save time and be more productive when it comes to creating your project. As you shall see, time quickly becomes of paramount importance for most audio projects, and being able to quickly find the audio you need is crucial. Good file management habits can make all the difference!

This stage of the production process also includes **recording your content**. That means organizing and conducting your interviews, going into the *field* (outside) to record sound effects and environments, and searching and locating music and other audio that you want to use. If you use just a smartphone to record your material, you will likely have to keep track of the recorded files on your phone, and ensure that you keep track of what specific recorded audio tracks contain. This can be easily done with a notebook, or by creating a note on your smartphone. However you do it is up to you, but it is important to do because you can quickly lose track of what you have recorded. Otherwise, transfer your content to a computer as soon as you can, making sure you place the audio in the folders described earlier.

Gathering enough good material is essential to producing a finished audio piece. This requires careful preparation. Nothing disappoints quite as much as recording some beautifully crisp and clear audio that proves to be irrelevant. Also ensure that nothing spoils the recording process such as an unplugged cable or dead batteries. Keep on top of the technical aspects of recording. Failure to gather content thoughtfully and record effectively results in wasted time and can lead to the failure of what you imagined for your audio project.

Chapter 6, R.E.A.L. Exercise #3: Gathering additional content for *Unheard Among Us*

Following on from exercise #2, apply this next stage in the production of your signature dish project to help develop your content plan:

1 **Are you able to gather the necessary interviews for your *Unheard Among Us* project? The more people involved as guests or interviewees, the more effort will be needed to record your material, as you contact them and make arrangements to interview them.**

2 **What different types of sounds will you need? In addition to the interviews you will be conducting, make a list of all the other different types of audio you need. For example, do you need to record ambient**

sound from the location that your project is about? What sounds can help bring your project alive to a listener?

3 Recognizing the power of music, will you be using any in your piece?

4 Will you need to use any archived material? Start researching what you may need, and what conditions there are in you using it (consider any required copyright and royalty permissions).

This stage can be time consuming, and that's because you are now collecting the main ingredients of your project. Remember the mission of your piece – to explore a local issue or topic – and consider the different types of audio required for the finished piece. By the end of this exercise, you are ready to go to the next stage in the production process.

Stage 3. Review/Listen to your content to ensure you have what you need

Once you are sure you have recorded and gathered the content you need, go to the next step of **reviewing it**. That means listening to what you have recorded, making notes, or *logging* your recorded interviews by providing brief notes about important moments in an interview. For example, revisiting your interview with a family member from Chapter 5's exercise "Family first" would be perfect for this. Your interview might be logged like this:

00:35 – *Interviewee describes their job*
02:37 – *Description given of first major problem at work*
06:36 – *Story about solution to work problem*
10:39 – *Important realization about how the business world works*

The same can apply for all your recordings, especially those recorded for the *Unheard Among Us* piece. Logging your content saves time overall and is enormously helpful in allowing you to quickly find the audio moment you need. For example, with the recording of an outside environment, note the specific times that certain sounds like traffic, animals, or windy trees can be heard. This doesn't take much time to do and saves enormous time later on when you are trying to locate a particular moment that you want to use. Do not forget to then save this file in your *Documents & Scripts* folder inside your project folder.

Another benefit of listening back to your audio is picking up on things you might have missed the first time. Often you will discover problems that you did not notice (a siren or airplane sound in the background or a noisy environment, for example). Or, you may find that you forgot to ask an important question, or cover some important area of content. In either case, that might mean you go back to step one and begin again.

Also, remember the general rule that *if you feel unsure after an interview whether you got the content you need, you probably did not!* When your review of material gives you a gut feeling that you have what you need, you can enjoy a sense of satisfaction.

So, after you have recorded and gathered all the audio material you need – which is raw unedited audio at this stage – now listen to everything you have. It's like a chef reviewing the ingredients they have laid out on the kitchen table to ensure they have enough for what they want to cook. At this stage, you may well find that you are missing key ingredients, and that will require you to go back to the previous stage to get the audio material needed. Let's apply that step to your *Unheard Among Us* project.

Chapter 6 R.E.A.L. Exercise #4: Let's hear what you have
Following on from exercise #3, apply this next stage in the production of your signature dish project. Let's assume you have now spent some time and gathered all your audio content, including interviews, sound effects, ambient recordings, and even music. Make sure you have all the ingredients you need to start creating your dish.

1 Listen back to all your collected audio for your *Unheard Among Us* project.

2 As you listen to what you have collected, sort the material into *two* folders that are in your *RAW Audio* folder: *Good Audio* (audio that will be used) and *Unused Audio* (audio that will not be used). In this process, you should also consider moments or parts of your audio recordings that you will want to use, and make a note of the time code for those moments (for example *"12:07–13:45 can be used"*). For any audio files that contain at least one moment that you will use, make sure that's in the *Good Audio* folder.

3 As you decide what audio you will use, create a document that lists all the audio files in your *Good Audio* folder, and the specific times in those audio files that you will use. Save that document in the *Documents & Scripts* folder.

4 After you have completed reviewing all of your collected audio, are you missing anything? Do you need to go back to stage 2 to collect more audio?

Remember, at this stage you are probably missing your voice in these audio files (not including your voice in any interviews you are using). That's because your narration will be recorded later once you have a script you can read.

If you are satisfied with what you have, it's time to move on to the next chapter, and the next stages in the production process. You can feel assured that you have the necessary ingredients to put together your *Unheard Among Us* signature dish.

Final thoughts: *We Have Two Senses*: How one professor created an educational podcast during the pandemic lockdown that has grown into an award-winning production and training ground for his students

Picture this: I am watching a podcast called From Suarez's Basement *on YouTube. A man sits in front of a basement brick wall with some bookshelves in the background. He's talking into the camera with infectious energy.*

Francisco Suarez (personal communication, March 24, 2023) is an associate professor at the Communication Department at the State University of New York at Oswego. He is an enthusiast! As a child growing up in Venezuela, he tells stories of how he used to make films with a VHS video camera, posing his *Star Wars* figures to tell stories. As a fan of *E.T.* and other films of that era, Suarez was intrigued by the idea of how people work with each other to tell stories. "Whatever we are watching on those screens ... it's all produced by a group of people that come together to tell a story. So, for me, it was the idea of telling the story, but more than that, just creating the fantasy world. When I was a kid, I used to spend more time *creating* the universe of the game than I did *playing* the actual game!" A strongly visual person, he had a major adjustment to face.

Later Francisco got the opportunity to work in radio, and he hosted a weekly syndicated Spanish radio show called *Voces de Nuestro Mundo*, broadcast on 62 radio stations nationwide. He discovered the major difference: "We have two senses that are the most important systems in our body – the capacity to *see* but also the capacity to *hear*." For his Hispanic audience, "I needed to *describe* to people in the audience what I was seeing. And it took a little bit of time to understand that." But what an important discovery he made. "The Hispanic population is the number one consumer of radio in the United States. I realized that because I'm Latino, I'm very much involved with the difficulties that immigrant people have in this country. I saw in this radio show a platform, where I said *wow, this is actually quite powerful*. I have the chance to communicate with an audience that is out there seeking advice for immigration, health of the family, and economics. And so, the radio became something that I really fell in love with."

This experience helped Francisco set up his own podcast show in 2021. "With the podcast, I follow the same principles that I learned through my experience with the radio show." Starting during the pandemic, he interviewed guests over the Internet from his basement. At that time, everybody was at home under lockdown, and Francisco wanted to create cheerful and interesting content with a focus on discussing the visual image, both on television and the big screen.

His first guest was a Pulitzer Prize-winning reporter, and he continued to attract big names, though he also gave his students the opportunity to both appear and create content. His passion for helping students partly drives the podcast's focus. "Yes, it's great to have a conversation with the editor of *Star Wars* who's won an Oscar, and it's great to have these experts, but can we establish a good educational, informative conversation?" He's even created learning resources and a mentor program for his students. "I don't let people feel like they will be wasting half an hour of time if you listen to the podcast, or if you want to be one of our guests. I want you to be sure that your conversation with me has a very important value and that value is to *educate*, to *inform*, to *entertain*. So, I need the listener to understand that what I'm doing is for my students and the value of education. I don't need 500,000 followers or whatever, I need quality more than quantity."

It's been a strategy that has paid off big time. In 2022, the podcast won a Silver Signal Award in the category of Educational Podcast. The International Academy of Digital Arts and Sciences selected *From Suarez's Basement* as the Best Educational Podcast at the 2023 Anthem Awards. Clearly the podcast is effective and successful. When I speak with Francisco, I get the feeling of a person completely at ease with himself. "I think I have reached a point in my life where I am so secure of who I am and what I want to accomplish, understanding the power of words and the power of communication."

What advice does Francisco give his students? "I say to them, your optimal responsibility with yourself as a human is to get to a point in your life that you really are *true to who you are*. That's when you know you have found your voice" (see Figure 6.4).

FIGURE 6.4   Francisco Suarez (Photo credit: Francisco Suarez).

References

Beltis, A. J. (n.d.). *28 chef quotes to fuel your culinary fire*. Toast POS. Retrieved July 2, 2023, from https://pos.toasttab.com/blog/on-the-line/best-chef-quotes

Cummings, D. (Host). (2011-Present). *Dr. NoSleep* [Video podcast]. Patreon. https://www.patreon.com/drnosleep/posts

The Decision Lab. (n.d.). *The sunk cost fallacy explained*. Retrieved July 2, 2023, from https://thedecisionlab.com/biases/the-sunk-cost-fallacy

Jersey Devil. (2023, May 15). In Wikipedia. https://en.wikipedia.org/w/index.php?title=Jersey_Devil&oldid=1154918721

7

IN THE OVEN

Developing audio cooked to perfection

First thoughts: *200 Euros will do:* How one person helped create the first radio station of its kind, armed only with sheer determination

Picture this: Lahti, Finland, lies 100 kilometers to the north of the capital city, Helsinki. Here Ari Hautaniemi lives and works. He's the co-founder of LiMu Radio, a radio station that only exists because of his and friends' efforts.

Ari Hautaniemi (personal communication, July 31, 2022) works at Lab University of Applied Sciences in Lahti. I first met him when he visited my radio station in New Jersey to see how it all works. He smiles as he describes Lahti: "It's a small town of 120,000 people. It's not the most popular or the most scenic city, but it's quite diverse with a nice variety of niche cultures, from making craft beers to having a lively punk scene. It's sort of a rough but beautiful city."

He tells the story of LiMu Radio. "It's quite simple. Back then, our university had five distinct campuses, and at that point, the big problem with the student community and also with the staff was that these different facilities didn't really know what the other one was doing. And there was this lack of a sense of community, and unity."

With a couple of colleagues, Ari came up with an interesting plan. "Me and a couple of colleagues were big fans of British and American college radio, and we listened to it online. And we were very fond of the whole, very *upbeat spirit* that was coming out of college radio. And we thought, *hey, why don't we try this at our university?*" It was a simple idea, to "bring in some students to kick off a project where we would start our own campus radio, which would unite all the students from different facilities." That was the plan, and plans are always free and easy to dream. To make the radio station a reality would take some funding, and they knew where to go next.

DOI: 10.4324/9781003263739-10

In Finland, the top person in charge of a university is the Rector. But when Ari shared their plans, "she was *very skeptical* about this, because it's not very common in Finland to have any sort of campus or college radio station. So, the Rector said, 'I think *this is not going to work, but* we'll give you a couple hundred euros, you can do whatever you can with it.'"

Two-hundred euros is about the same as 200 US dollars, or 165 British pounds, and starting a radio station with that would seem impossible; but not to Ari. He was *actually happy* with that result! "I was quite optimistic, because I was certain that she wouldn't buy the idea at all and say, *no, you can't do this.* But she gave us permission!"

Permission to go ahead was far more valuable than the 200 euros, but what a daunting future lay ahead. Looking back, he says: "For me, and for the eight students involved at first … it would have probably ended up being a short-term project if we would have received let's say 10,000 euros and all the equipment ready. But now that we have this huge challenge, we have no money, no experts, nothing, only our crazy ideas and enthusiasm, and people from different backgrounds, then it becomes a challenge."

Against all the odds, they began. "You know the story about David and Goliath? That's what took place at that moment!" says Ari. Short on money but overflowing with enthusiasm, "we had our kickoff meeting, and I told them about the idea and said, *hey, guys, we have an opportunity to make Finnish history here. How about it?* And I told them that we have a budget of 200 euros. They weren't very happy. But nevertheless, it initiated their ideation process. So, if we have no money, what can we do? Since no college radio existed in Finland, they googled 'how to set up a college radio station' and quickly discovered hundreds of college radio stations in the USA.

Interestingly the time seemed right. "We were basically fed up with the mainstream radio that was happening in Finland at that point," remembers Ari. "If you don't get over the mainstream media's threshold of publicity, then you're basically unable to get your voices heard. And that was also one of the key things from day one, that our station could bring light to the diverse cultures, these micro cultures within our area, within our region that don't get any publicity." Ari wanted LiMu Radio, as they were calling it, to champion the unheard and the undiscovered, especially in the area of music. "For example, with underground bands, the story of this music doesn't get heard anywhere. That was also important for us, and still is."

And how did the local community respond when the station finally launched, as an online streaming station? "We had so many listeners coming in from outside of our university that we got a bigger budget, because no one expected it to be such a success." With success comes increased attention. Starting with just eight students, the radio station grew. "We had about 60 or 70 students. And at that point, the university administration and all the faculties also got interested. And they realized that, *hey, we have this unique learning environment, how could we use that?* So, we had all these different courses that were starting to think that maybe we could do part of the course as a radio show or something like that. In 2016, or 2017, we had about 300 students come through the radio station!" Though still without an FM license, and streaming only, it is still having an impact.

As for the students themselves, "First of all, those eight students who initially started the radio, most of them were very shy, very unsure about their abilities to do anything. Most of them were introverts. And when they did radio, most of them did it for three or four years, they started to bloom, their communication abilities grew better. They took agency from doing the radio!" Ari is proud of how the students clearly flourished. "They became pretty proud of what they had accomplished. And that was the light that kept LiMu radio alive. And it's the coolest thing for me, being the initiator, from the perspective of bringing these different disciplines together was to see these students who previously had nothing to do with each other, yet they *really found each other* in this joint project of doing radio. So yeah, I think they grew as professionals and as human beings."

For Ari, finding your voice on the radio is all about being liberated in who you are and being free from judgment and expectations. "This magical medium does not need any superstars. It does not require you to be brave enough to put your face on the screen. You can be as ugly as a human can possibly be and still do good radio. That's the whole philosophy behind radio" (see Figure 7.1).

FIGURE 7.1 Ari Hautaniemi (Photo credit: Hilma Hautaniemi).

The next stages of audio production

I love Ari's story because it conveys such enthusiasm in his commitment to establish radio in unpromising circumstances, and for his particular concern to champion the unheard and the undiscovered. That aim resonates with the signature dish we are creating. Of course, behind the production of all LiMu Radio's programs lies the eight-stage process we are working through.

So far, continuing the analogy of preparing a meal, we have planned a menu with guests in mind, and ensured that the many different ingredients are assembled, with the initial work in the kitchen readying the meal for the oven with review and checking. In the last chapter, the first three stages require effort, as for the cooking process. Now we consider the next three.

When preparing to cook a meal, peeling potatoes and carrots, weighing ingredients to ensure they are the right quantity and quality is essential. For the whole dish to turn out well, each element deserves attention. This is not unlike stage 4 of the production process where we start *editing and preparing your audio to be inserted into a script*. Once completed, you are able to move to stage 5: *write your script*. The script ties together your prepared audio with a framework for your story or piece. It holds the whole project together so that, like a meal cooking in the oven, it browns appropriately, bringing out the flavor, and moving the whole production closer to presentation. Stage 6, *assembling your content* according to your script, comes together very quickly, much like when you turn the gas off, take the meal out of the oven, and plate it for your guests. You are arranging your 'food' for the best presentation.

In the oven, when the cook has prepared the meal properly, it's all about the right amount of heat that produces good results. These next audio stages require continued effort and energy – 'heat' – from the creators *themselves*. While you can leave an oven unattended as it cooks, you will need to stay on top of every second of audio that you want to use. In this chapter, we shall stay with the *Unheard Among Us* project and develop it further. We will focus on the following stages of the production process:

Stage 4. *Edit your audio for your script*
Edit and prepare your audio so it can be inserted into a script

Stage 5. *Write your script*
Write your script, tying together your edited audio with a structure for your story or piece

Stage 6. *Assemble your content*
Put together all your audio, closely following your final script

Stage 4. Edit your audio

Editing can be simply defined as changing something by either *adding* or *removing* parts of it. It's about getting rid of the audio you *do not want*, adding audio that you *need*, and then arranging it all to meet your production goals. You can copy, cut, and paste audio just as you would lines and paragraphs of text. This book's early exercises required content that did not need editing. Recording continuous material once you press *record* obviously avoids the trickier issues of editing since it flows naturally.

Interestingly, the first radio recording of a tragedy in real time was the *Hindenburg* disaster, now considered one of the most famous radio broadcasts in history. Herb Morrison was on his own as presenter and producer when his 1937 eyewitness report captured the explosion and disintegration of the German passenger airship, *Hindenburg*. It's an astonishing moment of time captured in sound. Morrison, a radio reporter, was recording the event to tape, for Chicago radio station WLS, when the airship suddenly exploded into flames, resulting in his famous exclamation, *"Oh the humanity!"* Even though by the time it was broadcast on the radio the event had passed into history, it was the first time anyone had recorded in audio and described a disaster as a first-hand, live witness. The reason it was so impactful was because it was unedited and unfiltered in the moment, authentic communication as he reacted to what he saw.

Typically, most editing-free content involves just your voice, or an interview or discussion with someone else. Some podcasts are mostly composed of this type of audio content. Types of other audio projects that can be done with this mostly editing-free method include:

- A live event such as a wedding or speech
- A movie or book review
- Audio blog/diary
- Commentating sports games and activities
- Cooking recipes in the kitchen
- Creating an audiobook
- Interview of family and friends
- Live performances such as music, theatrical performances, and other prepared pieces
- Poem readings
- Recording soundscapes/different environments
- Travelogs

Mostly, *editing-free* means that even if you just edit or tidy up the very beginning and the very end, you are leaving all the content in between as recorded, without edits. But by even doing this minimal editing, your audio immediately sounds improved.

Yet most audio projects want more than minimal editing. Audiences have limited tolerance for "warts and all" audio, and with so many polished and professional-sounding podcasts and audio content out there, material that includes mistakes causes annoyance. Often such errors are relatively easy to edit out anyway. Sure, raw audio is certainly authentic, but it can be difficult to listen to.

This next stage of the production process assumes that you will have a lot of raw audio which now requires editing. From your careful review of your content (stage 3), you have identified which moments will be included and which parts won't. Editing many different pieces of audio together can create something special, but this requires much more effort and time to produce. The end result could be a complex audio project with dozens, if not hundreds, of edits.

We've already noted in Chapter 3 the types of audio projects that are pre-recorded and will likely require editing:

- Documentary or a feature including multiple people
- Newscast with multiple stories
- Package about a topic or issue of interest
- Panel discussion with multiple speakers
- Podcast episode with an introduction and other sound elements
- Radio drama with multiple characters

The act of editing involves making hard, sometimes uncomfortable decisions about what content stays and what *must go*. When I write "must go" I mean editing it out of this particular audio project. But in this age of digital audio production, nothing is ever really thrown away; you can simply move it to the *Unused Audio* folder. That's what we call *nondestructive* editing because you can store unused material rather than delete it permanently. Occasionally, I have gone back and found some edited audio which ended up being important.

R.E.A.L. Moment

An example of good scriptwriting, brilliant audio editing, and compelling content is the podcast *Ukraine War Diaries* produced by Sky News (Mulhern, 2023). The traumatic experiences of "deadly rocket attacks, displacement, dangerous missions to the front line" are told through the emotionally powerful stories of Ukrainians who have been experiencing the impact of war since 2022. The diaries of Ilyas Verdiev, Oksana Koshel, and her husband Seva Koshel are carefully presented with helpful narration from producer

Robert Mulhern. His voice adds crucial explanation and context for listeners to fully understand what's going on. We feel as if we are listening to a person sitting right next to us, with the intimacy of a close friend or family member. Mulhern provides the details and information that are essential for us to understand the stories we hear and to imagine ourselves in the same position. He presents information with incredible clarity and emotional punch. It's engaging audio at its best.

For creating good audio, editing is where the magic happens. A good *final edit* (the last changes you make before you share or distribute your content) should be flawless, or as good as possible, so that listeners are unaware of the edits. On the other hand, if you can hear the clunky way audio has been edited, that's a bit like finding a fly in your soup.

To achieve editing to the best of our ability we now consider:

- Working with a DAW (an audio editing app or program)
- How audio "looks"
- Gaining experience with a DAW
- Remember timing is everything
- Safety first – being aware of ethical and legal considerations

Working with a DAW

To edit your audio, you will likely need a computer program or phone app known as a DAW, which stands for *Digital Audio Workstation*. Several free audio editing options are available for your smartphone or computer, though paying for software gives more options and professional support. Be aware that, although some apps may be free to use, you may have to make in-app purchases to unlock full features. Investigate and try to use an app to its fullest potential before making any purchase.

Free smartphone audio editing apps:

- Audio Editor (MacOS)
- AudioLab – Audio Editor Recorder & Ringtone Maker (Android)
- EZAudioCut (MacOS)
- Lexis Audio Editor (Android)
- Media Converter (Android)
- MixPad (Android)
- Recording Studio: Audio Editor (MacOS)
- SoundLab Audio Editor (MacOS)
- WavePad Audio/Music Editor (Android & MacOS)

Free computer/PC audio editing apps:

- Audacity (Windows, MacOS, Linux)
- AudioTool (Windows)
- Garageband (MacOS)
- Ocenaudio (Windows, MacOS, Linux)
- WavePad Audio Editing Software (Windows)
- Wavosaur (Windows)

Paid computer/PC audio editing apps:

- Acoustica (Windows, MacOS)
- Adobe Audition (Windows, MacOS)
- Avid ProTools (Windows, MacOS)
- Magix Sound Forge Pro (Windows, MacOS)

You may choose to have an audio editing app on your smartphone and also one on your computer so you can edit quickly on your phone before importing it into your computer for further editing.

Once you have decided on the app(s) you are going to use, experiment and play. The next section shows you how to begin the process. As you work through the steps below, test different options on your app. Find out which suits you best and grow in confidence. If you are going to work between a phone app and desktop computer you should also familiarize yourself with the process of moving files back and forth so you can do so reliably, whilst also maintaining your organizational framework and file management system.

How audio "looks"

When you first import, load, or record audio into a DAW, you can see on the screen the sound you have recorded. A blank file indicates silence, or no audio, so from the start, you will know if the audio you think you have is actually there. Just by seeing the DAW screen displays you will be able to tell a great deal about your audio:

- How long is that particular audio file?
- Is the audio recorded at a good volume, not too quiet and not too loud?
- Is the audio complete, or are there moments where there is an abrupt silence or the audio file stops unexpectedly?
- Is the audio recorded in mono or stereo?

We shall see this as I illustrate the editing process using Adobe Audition, a popular DAW used in many audio classrooms. From Figure 7.2 you can see

FIGURE 7.2   Adobe Audition screen with no audio loaded (top) and with audio loaded (bottom screen) (©2023 with express permission from Adobe).

what a DAW such as Adobe Audition looks like when no audio is loaded (the top screen) versus when your audio is loaded (the bottom screen).

Note that when you first load or import your audio, you will often be presented with a full, zoomed out view of your entire audio file. That's helpful for you to grasp a sense of how long and how well recorded the entire audio file is. At a glance you can see if all your audio is there. But when you start editing you will want to zoom in, and focus on your audio presented in measurements of seconds rather than minutes.

What you are looking at on the screen when audio is loaded is the digital form of your recorded soundwaves. Your DAW will show the length of the recording, as well as its **amplitude** (volume). A low amplitude and your audio is too quiet; too high and you could get distortion. Amplitude is measured in decibels, or **dB**. A good rule of thumb is that you want your audio to peak at **–3 dB** in the DAW, and you can adjust your audio's volume until you are at that level. If you have recorded your audio well in the first place, it should have the right volume which requires minimal volume adjustment. As you gain more experience, you will be able to quickly tell, just from the visual display of your audio, whether you are in good shape as you begin your project.

Gaining experience with a DAW

As you spend more time with a particular DAW, you will soon learn the quickest way to get things done, such as using keyboard shortcuts and program features such as noise and hiss reduction or automatic volume (amplitude) adjustment can increase your efficiency using it.

Earlier (at stage 2) we saw the benefits of organizing your audio into separate digital folders: **RAW Audio/Edited Audio/Other Audio**. To begin with, all your recorded audio will be placed into the **RAW Audio** folder. As you edit it, you will export or save it to your **Edited Audio** folder as a new file. You will start to see the building blocks of your content grow. These audio recordings are also known as *clips*.

When you first load your audio clips, a single clip should look like Figure 7.3. Raw audio is on the chopping board, you have successfully loaded or imported your audio into the program, and after you have reviewed it, it awaits editing.

In addition to recording directly into the DAW, audio can be imported by copying and pasting, or the software itself may open it to *import* it. Most audio will come, depending on how it's recorded, as a file format such as mp3, mp4, WAV, or similar. Most DAWs, such as Adobe Audition, have in-built capabilities to recognize a variety of audio formats.

In the picture above, the audio has now been zoomed in from the entire file, so that just a few seconds fill the screen. Notice the long gaps of silence between the sound waves, between the words recorded. Raw unedited audio looks like this, and you will want to keep many of those gaps of silence in

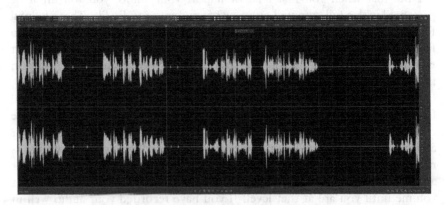

FIGURE 7.3 Adobe Audition showing audio zoomed in for closer inspection (©2023 with express permission from Adobe).

there, or maybe slightly shorten some if they seem too long, as removing them completely can make someone sound unnatural when they are talking.

For your project a number of steps now need to be taken:

- **Step 1:** *Review* all your clips to see which ones can be deleted or discarded right away. Small clips that contain your voice testing the microphone, or bumps and noises should be discarded immediately. All the clips that remain should contain substantive content that will need editing.
- **Step 2:** These remaining clips need to be "topped" and "tailed," which means cropping the audio at the start and at the end, tidying it up for more detailed editing later. Doing this can save you time, as there may be several seconds if not minutes of dead air at the beginning or end of your audio clip. In the clip pictured below there is some off-mic talking before the important audio starts. You can see the difference, as the volume of the audio is clearly quieter than the rest of it. You simply select or highlight that audio (in white) and then delete it.
- **Step 3:** Check whether your recordings are in *mono* or *stereo*. The track edited above is in stereo, with two lines of audio – the top is left channel, and the bottom is right channel. From a glance, it looks as if the audio is duplicated in both channels. Mono recordings have just one, central channel. The DAW will allow you to easily convert all your mono recordings into stereo, providing consistency in your audio project from start to finish. Many producers prefer to work in stereo for added interest. For example, with an interview, you might have the interviewer speaking from the left of the audio spectrum, and the interviewee on the right. This can give a sense to the listener of their different physical spaces. It is always an advantage to make the change to stereo early on. There are only a few circumstances where mono would be preferred, such as broadcasting on an AM radio station, or livestreaming.
- **Step 4:** Check your unedited audio clips for consistency in *volume*. Any DAW program will allow you to adjust the amplitude (volume) to make quiet content louder, and loud content quieter. As a listener, you know how irritating sudden volume changes can be! Be warned though, you may find that some of your audio recordings were recorded too loudly with distortions which we call *clipping*. Unfortunately, loud distorted recordings can rarely be fixed. As technology develops however, we have seen the invention of some add-on tools and plug-ins that can recover distorted files using interpretive algorithms. Some of these repair tools are quite remarkable in what they can fix, but as with all things, there are limits, and it is always best not to rely on after-the-fact fixes to heal mistakes that could have been prevented with more careful execution. When audio is too quiet, the DAW can adjust its volume by increasing its *gain*. In the audio clip below you can clearly see evidence of clipping, where the sound is

obviously too loud and is distorted. *This is evidenced by waveforms that look squared off at the top. Audio running up against a hard ceiling is what causes the unpleasant sound we call clipping.* Many professional audio producers will never consider any audio if it's clipped, even if it might be fixed by a few tricks and clicks. Remember, adjusting your audio's volume to peak at a maximum of −3 dB is a good rule of thumb.

- **Step 5:** Check that all your audio files share the same bitrate and sample rate. Pro TIP: Never record your master files in a lossy or compressed format like MP4 or MP3. These formats save space by throwing away information. Once it's gone it can never be recovered. This can have negative effects further down your production chain. Try to record as an uncompressed WAV file.

A bit or sample rate measures the resolution of the data that is gathered on a sound (measured in *kbps*, kilobits per second). Generally, the higher the bitrate and sample rate, the *higher the quality* of audio. In a simplified sense, you can think of bitrate as affecting the resolution of amplitude data, and sample rate as affecting the resolution of frequency data. Though you can upconvert audio to a higher resolution with a DAW, if something is initially recorded at a low resolution that information is lost forever. You will not be improving sound by upsampling, just making the file larger. You will certainly want to make a deliberate choice of bitrate and sample rate when you *export* or *mixdown* your final audio project to the standard of where you want to share or broadcast it. For example, video or film productions tend to center around 16-bit/48k or 24-bit/96k, whereas radio systems might prefer 16-bit/44.1k or 24-bit/88.2k. You may notice the sample rates are multiples of one another in each case. Mathematically these work better together and allow for more precise up/down conversion. A good baseline is to choose a master format of at least a 16-bit, 44,100 Khz, stereo WAV, or AIFF audio file. This is the quality of a commercial CD. You can record at a higher bitrate, say 48,000 Khz or 96,000 Khz, but the difference in quality is not obviously discernable and will result in your audio files taking up much more space on your hard drive.

The best way to ensure consistency in data rate is to ensure you record all your audio at the same, high setting to begin with and maintain that resolution throughout your production chain. MP3, MP4, and other compressed file types are *distribution* formats. You are intentionally choosing to throw away information for smaller files that are easier to move and store if you record in a compressed format like MP3 or MP4.

- **Step 6:** Ensure that you have all your edited clips in one place (the *Edited Audio* folder) and that you have noted the individual length of each clip, as well as the total running time of the clips all together. This is crucial information as we go into the next stage (see Figures 7.4 and 7.5).

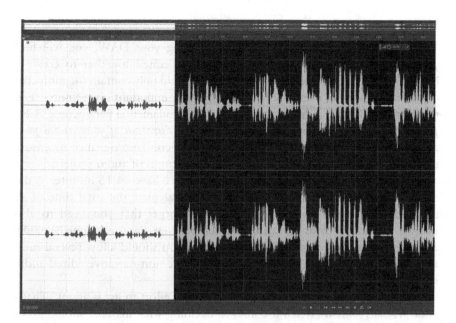

FIGURE 7.4 Adobe Audition showing audio selected (white background), ready for deletion (©2023 with express permission from Adobe).

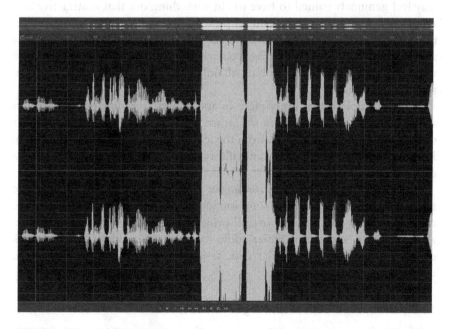

FIGURE 7.5 Adobe Audition showing audio that's too loud/distorted (©2023 with express permission from Adobe).

Timing is everything

After you have gone through these steps using your DAW, you will find yourself with audio clips that are ready to be edited together to create a longer, whole audio piece. Your edited clips should only contain the moments of audio you want to use. One factor is especially important now: timing. The total length of your audio program gives the fundamental parameters. *A key principle is that you should always think of the duration of your audio piece throughout all of the production stages*. It takes constant vigilance to ensure that you are on target to produce the desired length of audio project.

With our *Unheard Among Us* audio project we have set 15 minutes as the desired time duration. An easy mistake is to calculate the total time of all the audio clips you want to use, and then forget that you need to also include the time of your narration! Remember that you speak approximately 3 words per second. For a 15-minute piece, you should allow several minutes for your narration. That could mean all the non-narrative edited audio should not exceed 10, 11, or 12 minutes total.

Editing out content that took much time and effort to get is agony. That's your *precious content*! When it comes to deciding what material should go or stay in a project, you need to look at the requirements and goals of the project itself. That should help clarify your decision-making when you think, *is this audio necessary to include*? Interesting material is not always relevant, and you may feel genuinely pained to have to cut something out that is attractive and appealing yet, in reality, serves no purpose for your project's goal. As you get more experience, you will understand the key difference between *interesting* and *relevant* content. Try to free yourself from attachment to special clips which get their hooks into you but will unbalance or overrun the overall piece if you include them.

A key principle is that every piece of audio, and every line of your written script *needs to justify its place in the larger whole*. Indeed, you can create your own system to rank your audio from the least important (1) to the most (10). Keeping the project's goals in mind allows you to sort out which pieces are as close to 10 as possible!

I suggest that you *start with the longest pieces of audio*, so that you edit the most difficult material first. Your longest audio recordings are likely the most important part of your overall project and, once you've edited these, all that's left is supporting easier audio material. Also, if you become stuck or tired of editing a particular clip, save your progress and move on to editing something else.

Safety first: Heed ethical and legal considerations

Editing audio content, for the most part, *deletes* content. Some deletions are obviously acceptable. In the audio clip below the long "err" between words

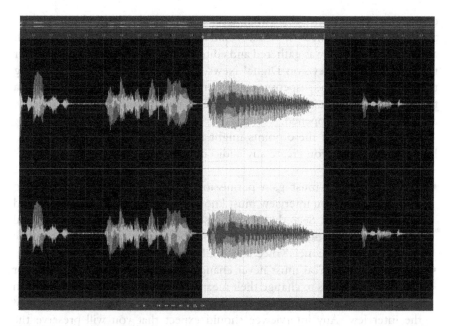

FIGURE 7.6   Adobe Audition showing an "err" selected ready for deletion (©2023 with express permission from Adobe).

(highlighted in white) is rightly deleted. You should do the same for coughs, sneezing, and other noises (see Figure 7.6).

Going through your audio and deleting *ums* and *errs* may not be a fun way to spend a weekend, but it is important work for your listeners' sake. Consider using web-based editors like *Descript* (https://www.descript.com) that edit audio through a word processor-type interface, which makes it incredibly quick and easy to remove words and moments you do not want. Yet, in some circumstances, these ums and errs can reveal much and should be retained. According to J-Source, the Canadian Journalism Project, "It's okay, even expected, that you will **cut out ums, errs, long pauses, and other examples of verbal stalling** – unless the verbal stalling *is a key part of the story*, as in the case of a politician ducking tough questions" (McGuire, 2017, When Editing Interviews).

It is a dangerous step, however, when you delete the words of *other* people, or move them around, placing them in a different order. Doing that changes the context and possible meaning of those words. In essence, again from J-Source, "it's okay to make edits that help someone sound sharper, tighter, clearer. **It's just NEVER okay to change the meaning of what they said**." You run the risk of being legally liable for misrepresentation.

The Radio Television Digital News Association (RTDNA) urges audio editors and producers not to add any sounds or effects that accentuate a story or imply anything other than what actually happened. "A good question to ask in such circumstances is, 'What would audiences say if they knew the truth about how this story was gathered and edited?' Would viewers feel deceived or tricked?" (Radio Television Digital News Association, n.d.) Creative editing that generates drama, suspense, or excitement in your audio piece can be a temptation. But, unfortunately, it could easily end up misleading an audience about what really happened.

Although some of these points might be obvious, bear in mind the following issues when you create any audio content:

- **Permission:** You must gain permission from anyone that you wish to record. Anyone you interview must know that they are being recorded and will be on record. Secretly recording someone could lead you into legal trouble. An exception to this rule would be a press conference or public event, where someone's voice is being broadcast to a mass audience.
- **Ethical editing:** You must never change the order of people's words, or edit their sentences to change their meaning. Think carefully when using an unguarded moment, out of context from what they are saying in the rest of the interview. Any interviewee should expect that you will preserve the meaning and the sequence of their communication, even with edits made for concision.
- **Misrepresenting material:** Be careful not to use audio from another source that can mislead your audience. For example, don't use sound effects to suggest being in a location when you are not. Don't add sounds that create a false picture to the audience.
- **Copyright aware:** You should take great care when using the work of someone else. It's possible to use audio from other sources, as long as you are careful about how much you use, and in what context. This is known as *fair use* and is defined as "limited use of copyrighted material without permission from the copyright holder for purposes such as criticism, parody, news reporting, research and scholarship, and teaching" (Baylor University, 2023, Fair Use section). What that means is that you should first know if the audio you want to use is copyrighted and you should also have obtained it legally. Giving credit to a copyright holder is not the same thing as having permission to use it.

Just how much audio can you use? Using relatively *brief* excerpts is usually no problem, but longer excerpts could be forbidden without consent of the copyright holder. It's a myth that there's a *30-second rule*, and using that much content could be illegal. These rules also apply to using music in your work, although a good solution is to use royalty-free music that has fewer restrictions, or even create your own music if possible! There are plenty of audio materials that you can use that are in the *public domain*, or can be obtained affordably with a *creative commons* license. Always do a thorough check about using any material that you have not created. You should consider using a copyright decision tree like this: https://www.uvu.edu/ogc/docs/1.copyright.decision.tree.flowchart.9.22.2021.pdf

- **Disclaimers matter:** As mentioned earlier, giving legal disclaimers is important. What is a disclaimer? "A media disclaimer is a legal statement accompanying a piece of media such as a video, song, or newspaper article, providing information about how the media can be used and limiting **liability** on the part of the provider" (McMahon, 2023, para. 1). Examples of limiting liability might be stating the limits of how your content should be used, and by stating that you are not to be held responsible if factual errors are made. There are plenty of disclaimers that you can download online and modify for your purpose.

- **Fact checking is important:** Although it can seem impossible to fact check every piece of information in your content, there are times when it can be especially important. You should make every effort to confirm key information brought up by an interviewee or some other source of content that you are using. If you, or someone you are including in your piece, makes dubious or inaccurate factual assertions there can be legal ramifications – as well as a loss of credibility on your part. Be careful to present people's thoughts and assertions as being their own, which provides editorial integrity and protection on your part. Fact checking does not have to be as time consuming as you might expect. With a wealth of information quickly available in an online search, you are looking to confirm information such as dates, numbers, and other events from more than one reputable source.

These are just some legal and ethical considerations to be aware of. It's important to know the legal and ethical boundaries when you start creating audio.

Chapter 7, R.E.A.L. Exercise 1: Wielding the knife for your *Unheard Among Us* project

Let's start editing your *Unheard Among Us* audio. In the last chapter, the last exercise had you reviewing your audio and deciding which audio will be used and edited. Let's now go to the next stage and start editing it. This exercise requires you to upload your unedited audio clips into a DAW program of your choice. Remember, there are lots of DAW options, from Audacity for free, to Adobe Audition for an excellent paid option.

1 **Start with your longest audio clips first. Go through this process with each one.**

2 **If you have not already determined it, you will have to decide what parts of each audio file to keep and what parts you want to edit out, including editing out *ums* or *errs* to flow well.**

3 Remember: It's important not to overwrite the original RAW audio file, but save a copy of your edited audio file in the *Edited Audio* folder with the suffix EDIT as part of the filename. For example, *interviewEDIT, narrationEDIT, IntroEDIT.* It's not a bad idea to get into the habit of appending *_v1 or _v2* to files as soon as you start to edit them.

4 Edit all of the audio clips you intend to use, ensuring they are edited to your satisfaction.

5 Finally, after you have edited your clips, ensure that they are together in the same *Edited Audio* folder, and that you have calculated the total running time of all your clips.

Pro TIP: *make your cuts at zero crossings, where the waveform crosses the center line into silence. This avoids pops and clicks at the edit point.*

After completing this exercise, you are ready to start writing your script, with the confidence that you know you have the audio clips you need to create your audio piece. You now just need a script, and presumably, your voice, to tie it all together. You are getting there!

Stage 5. Write your script, incorporating moments from your recorded audio

You have come a long way in the production process. After initial planning you have gathered recorded material, reviewed it, and now edited it for inclusion in your audio piece. You will return to your DAW once more to assemble your final edit once you have a script to follow.

Edited clips now give you a library of audio content that needs to be threaded together. When you began, you identified *who* you wanted to interview, and *what* you wanted to interview them about. Now you have their edited answers as well as other types of audio such as music, sound effects, and other content. At the beginning of production a content plan was essential for anticipating the kind of audio you need, but writing a *script* uses the actual edited audio.

Your script will sequence your audio into a cohesive, singular piece. There is considerable ongoing debate by audio content creators about which comes first, the edited content you have gathered or the script. Some argue that a script should always come first, and others contend that edited content decides the direction of your script. I prefer the latter practice, writing the script after you have already edited the content. There is a danger, if you write your script before conducting your interviews, that you could steer the content towards your own biases, rather than truly letting the interview go where it does.

Writing a fuller script to bring all the parts together might seem too time-consuming. Some students ask, *does not it slow you down?* It can, but the alternative of trying to structure and sequence your content without a script is likely to be much less successful, and eventually even more time consuming than if you just wrote a script. Even professional broadcasters, who go live on the air without a full script, often have notes that they use as a safety net. It's incredibly difficult to create high-quality content without a script. It becomes your guide and your framework. As a well-thought-out structure, it guides what sound elements you will include, both verbal and non-verbal. Like a safety net, it saves you from losing your way. In short, your script *transforms your edited audio materials, your active words, into a singular piece.*

Writing a script forces you to be realistic. Beforehand, you may have an idea for your ideal audio piece. But do you have the edited materials to achieve and support it? Now you have to create a script around *what you actually have.*

As *Cloudradio* advises, with a careful script (CloudRadio, 2020):

- **You will have more control over the content**
- **You will not forget what you planned to say**
- **You establish structure and maintain the flow**
- **You'll have the drive to research and rehearse**

You will be a more effective communicator when you heed this advice, and your audio will be more engaging for the audience.

The process of writing audio scripts involves three steps: *Select, Generate,* and *Evaluate.*

Step 1: Select – Choose the appropriate type of script

Much depends on the nature of the program you have chosen. In Chapter 6, I described some of the main types of audio programs and mentioned the kinds of scripts that they need. Interviews typically need scripted beginnings and endings, while news stories need to be tied together with a linking script. I mentioned that documentaries are demanding, with scripts that not only hold the audio clips together but provide context and understanding. Commercials and PSA's are short but require many drafts. Drama and comedy require full scripts and are the Everest of content production.

As you have read, there is a world of difference between all the different types of scripts you could write. At one extreme, a spot script lasting a minute or less will be brief on paper and yet probably require many drafts. Scripting a documentary – and even more a comedy script – needs many more words with high creativity. As you develop skills you will find yourself creating several different kinds of scripts.

Deliberately, I chose personal pieces as the starting point for our exercises. Personal pieces are likely to involve scripts for the narrator's voice. In the last chapter's set of exercises for the three stages you should have planned the outline, collected audio, and by review/listen, ensured you have the audio you need.

In my experience, there are two fundamental approaches to scriptwriting when it comes to audio production. The easiest is to sequence your audio in a **linear** sequence, so that one audio clip follows another, with the narrator's voice in between. The other type of script is written to include **multitrack** audio, when more than one audio clip plays at the same time.

Multitracking is when you play more than one audio clip **simultaneously**. Each clip will be assigned its own track, so that you can control the timing and volume of each track in relation to the others. For example, say you want to include music or the sound of a location underneath the opening narrator's voice – that would be achieved by multitracking. We will explore this production technique later, but for now, you need to decide how much audio production detail will be in your script. Keeping it simple is best to begin with.

For many, including myself, writing a linear script is easier to do, and then experimenting with multitracking, adding or "sprinkling" in sound effects, music, and other sound clips after a rough edit of the piece is assembled. After all, it's difficult to imagine and write in your script how you might imagine multitracking something. It's far easier to experiment with your DAW after you have assembled a rough edit or 'cut' of your piece. Often through practical experimentation, you can find exactly what you need.

Step 2: Generate – Fill out links between clips

At this stage, you have the vital task of arranging the order of your audio clips so that the content flows. Also you have the unnerving but exciting freedom to write active words for the ear that will hold it all together. Your voice and style make your approach unique, and the pattern you structure could take any form as you generate material. Keep in mind that your audience must be able to understand and follow what is going on at all times. Think carefully about how you will tell a story that will engage and keep your audience listening. If they like what they hear, they will be interested in what comes next. It's a mistake to undervalue the linking script that ties together your audio clips. It's the links that provide vital context and information!

Several important actions are needed as you develop the script:

- **Order your components chronologically**
- **Write the script**
- **Format the script**

Let's explore these different tasks further.

- **Order components chronologically**

  Stage 4, *Editing Audio,* concludes with filling your *Edited Audio* folder full of edited clippings for your project. These are the essential components around which your script will be written. Depending on the type of script you are writing, you may not need any components beyond just your voice, or someone else's. However, with our project *Unheard Among Us,* these audio clips require a structure to order their sequence and ensure effective usage. They are likely to be disorganized until you sort them. Part of the scriptwriting creative process involves thinking through how these different pieces can best belong together. If you are telling a story you should think carefully about how you present it chronologically throughout your script. You can also experiment with how you use your audio. You may decide to use an interview with someone early in your piece and then return to them before the end. Perhaps you use parts of one interview threaded throughout the piece. You should be creative in how you order your audio content.

  To make this process as easy as possible, make a list of the following audio content that you will be using in your piece. This might include:
- **Narrator's track** - the primary narrator's voice that will be used to tie everything together; it will likely be your voice
- **Interviewees** – all the individual people you will be including in your piece. You may have multiple audio clips from just one person. Make sure you label each one so you don't lose track of them and the order that you want to use them. Interviewees can also be called *sources.* Some audio producers also call these *actualities,* others call them *sound bites.*
- **Sound effects** – all the non-verbal audio such as ambient and environmental sounds, as well as specific sounds such as a phone ringing, door closing, footsteps, etc. Sound effects are either natural in origin, or human made.
- **Sound clips** – audio from movies, television, other podcasts, and radio broadcasts (you will need to be careful here – see the earlier section on legal and ethical considerations)
- **Music** – any music that you will be using in your piece (again see the legal section later)

Think of these different components as different food items on your plate. In what order will they best fit together? Once you have decided on the order of your audio, *you now have the structure or guideline for writing your script.*

Often, the component that best ties these components together is **narration.** Typically that's you *voicing it.* Sometimes a script may comprise only narration if the rest of the audio consists of a series of audio clips. For example:

NARRATOR:	It was in 1972 that the Mayor of Boston decided to promote the city and its attractions to tourists in Europe.
MAYOR OF BOSTON:	[Duration: 00:25]
NARRATOR:	This was followed by more intense efforts the following year.

In this version of the script, you are including a clip of the mayor speaking. Sometimes you will narrate the words from an interview, avoiding a bit of audio editing. However, increasingly, and especially when posting content online, audiences like to hear other voices. So, get the mayor of Boston in the script.

- **Write your script**

  All audio projects share certain fundamentals: an opening, ending, and the sections in between! A strong **introduction** captures listeners' attention from the beginning. Whether it's straightforward spoken words, a montage of audio clip highlights from the whole piece, or some introductory music, those first seconds and minutes are crucially important. Some script writers only firm up their beginning once other parts of the script are written. This ensures a substantial start which trails some of the following story. In journalism, this start is known as the *lede* and is expected to be as strong and interesting as possible. Engaging your audience from the start keeps them listening! The introduction should leave the audience wanting more. They could be intrigued, surprised, or shocked by your introduction.

  Similarly, you need to plan an ending, a **conclusion,** to your piece. A strong ending leaves the listener with a sense of closure and completion. They will feel satisfied that they have learned or experienced something of value. As a young presenter on radio in the UK, I was always told,

  "Tell your audience what you're going to *tell them*, tell people you are telling them *as you tell it*, and then, finish by telling them what *they've just heard!*" The conclusion may include music, credits of those involved in helping make your project, and maybe a preview of your next audio piece or upcoming episode if relevant. A resounding finale can only leave a strong impression.

  What you present to your audience has to be clearly understandable, from the very first second to the very last, with a sense of finality at the end of your script, so that your audience knows that it's come to a natural conclusion. Avoiding confusion is a golden rule. No listener at the end of a piece should usually think *What did I just hear? I need to listen to that again to understand.* Your opening and conclusion should frame what's to come and what's just been. Audiences can recognize good crafting and will continue listening, perhaps even thinking about it long after it has ended.

Between the introduction and the conclusion, you will need structure that we can call **chapters** or **parts**. This "middle" of your piece is the real meat! Audio clips need to be linked by scripted narration that provides important context and explanation. You should be building your story as you progress through the piece. When you approach the midpoint of your piece, it can be challenging to ensure that you and your audience are not overwhelmed by too much information, and that you maintain momentum. That's why having chapters is so helpful. You can pause before providing a recap of the key moments of the story so far, offering a moment for listeners to process and understand.

These three elements – *introduction*, *chapters*, and *conclusion* – require the best of your writing for the ear. As you develop the structure, you may still need to tinker with the chronological sequence. What would your piece sound like if you started with an event that happened at the end of your story, and from there then worked your way from the beginning to the end, where you started? Unpredictability can offer a fresh and intriguing listening experience, so consider offering some twists or surprises in how you present your material.

This book holds the principle that you will develop your voice through audio production, and that includes scriptwriting. So embrace scriptwriting as your opportunity to craft and experiment with finding your voice. After all, it's *another form of your voice*, as you type or write words on the page. If you could say anything, and had the time to pick the perfect way to say it, what would you say?

- **Format your script**
  The cardinal rule for scriptwriting is: *whatever works for you is the best option*. After all, your script will not be seen by your listeners. How you arrive at the final script is what works best for you. But before you start writing/typing anything consider these questions:
- How are you going to read your script? Off a page, a computer, a phone, a tablet?
- Who will be reading your script? Will it be you or someone else, or more than one person?
- If someone else is reading your script, will they know *how best* to read it?
- Will someone be giving you content requirements/information that need to be in the script?
- Is there anyone that you can find to read your script to give feedback?

Being aware about the content of each of the audio clips you are using is crucial. You will always need to be aware of the tone of your content going into and out of a clip so you can avoid any jarring or conflicting mood in your narrated words and the way you deliver them. For example, you would not follow a clip of someone who is describing the death of a family member with a humorous or happy tone, as that would clearly be inappropriate. Use your best judgment to ensure there are no jarring moments in your script, and that your transitions are smoothly handled.

Here are some guidelines for scripting audio content:

- At the very least, you should use *double spacing*, to make it easier to read.
- If printed, your script should use a large font, think size 14 and above.
- Difficult words (names and places for example) can be obvious stumbling blocks when it comes to reading any script. Therefore spell out any potentially tricky words *phonetically* – spell them as you should say them.
- It's OK to simplify for your audience's sake. *Round off figures and numbers.* For example, do not say 1.97 million, say 2 million, or nearly 2 million.
- All instructions (in a live script especially) should be CAPITALIZED, so as to easily show instructions and non-audio information. All spoken lines should be typed normally.
- Include page numbers! Dropped scripts can result in disaster if your pages are not numbered!
- Put ### at the end of a script to indicate that it is finished.
- Put (more) at the bottom of a page if it continues into the next page. That allows the reader to know they will be continuing.
- You may choose to **bold certain words or parts of your script** if you want to remind yourself to emphasize their importance or a particular moment. This is also a good way to stress keywords, to emphasize emotion in certain places in your script.

Remember, you are writing a script in order to be as helpful as possible to yourself and/or other people. Never forget the requirements of the human voice, taking into consideration the need for breathing gaps and moments when the voice needs extra energy or emotion. Formatting a script needs to grasp technical requirements for the active voice.

- Step 3: **Evaluate** – refine your script as you read it aloud

Earlier, when discovering your voice, we learned the vital importance of writing for the ear with an active voice using active words. Now, as the script has come together you need to read it out loud to yourself. Hearing the words with your outside voice puts you in the strategic role of listener. As soon as you hear the words, you need to evaluate how satisfying the audio sounds. Unnecessary or ineffective words likely still clutter up the script. As a rule, *you want your audience to understand what is happening at all times.* Become too complicated, or boring, and you will lose them.

Remember the appeal of R.E.A.L. audio! If you are producing work that is grounded in the reality of the human experience, of *your* experience, you will find an audience that will *relate* and *engage* with what they hear, will recognize your *authenticity,* and experience *liberation* at the end.

This is **the** point at which your own voice should come through powerfully. As we noted earlier, you should really think about keeping the script as naturally conversational as possible. Obviously for news reports and documentaries you will use greater formality, but listeners should recognize they are hearing something that is like normal, natural conversation. Relatable. Authentic. The audience is unlikely to realize just how much work you have done for it to sound and flow as it does!

This refining stage of a script is critical. Certain parts may need clarification or emphasizing. Maybe a section of your script is too repetitive, or frankly rather boring and predictable. More importantly, you may realize that the order of content you have planned can still be improved. Are you getting the most impact out of your audio clips? That all depends on how you are using them. Communicators often stress the importance of "rehearsal," sometimes called "*pre-hearsal.*" Picturing your listener in mind, you should read your script looking for any words or moments that might sound *just not as strong as they could be.* This is your last opportunity to make changes to your words to improve flow and understanding.

Expect changes in your scripts as you work on them and read them through, and keep telling yourself that any changes are not a sign of weakness or failure on your part. Every time you have to change or edit your script, it only strengthens and improves what you have. At some point, you will realize you are likely working on your final version of the script. You will feel a sense of peace about arriving at that moment, which should bolster your confidence too! After hard work with the final script, *you should be satisfied that it's the most effective work you can do at that time.* Of course, with unlimited time, there can be unlimited changes. My audio engineer colleague Greg Mattison has a saying, "No project is complete until it's irrecoverable." That's speaking to the neverending temptation to go back and make changes *just one more time.* But there comes a moment when you need to stop and be satisfied with what you have.

I use the word *evaluate* for this step because a major part of this stage involves ensuring the script is keeping to time. If you decide your *Unheard Among Us* exercise is going to be about 15 minutes long, always check that the script stays within the time bounds. You already know how long each clip lasts, so your script gives a safety margin allowing you to shave off a minute or two, or maybe add more words.

Chapter 7, R.E.A.L. Exercise 2: You call the shots
At this stage, all your *Unheard Among Us* audio clips should be edited, so your task now is to arrange them within a script.

1 Using the content plan you made for your *Unheard Among Us* project, now try to write a script for your piece that uses the edited audio clips that you have ready to go.

2 What components need to go into your introduction?

3 What needs to go in the middle?

4 How do you plan to end the piece?

5 How will you sequence all the sound clips that you want to include, as well as write for your own voice? How will you ensure consistency in the overall structure, so that you don't have too much content in one part, and too little in another?

This exercise is all about you scripting a wholly realized audio piece and working out exactly what you will need in order to do it. At all stages of writing, consider how each section or stage will flow into the next. You can quickly get lost and overwhelmed if you don't take some time to envision your audio project as a whole, before you start writing. If you have a good overall content plan, you will stay on track, even if you are working on a detailed, close-up level.

Stage 6. Assemble your content – Putting it all together

With your final script in hand, or on your screen, you are now ready to assemble your larger audio piece.

You can simply drag and drop your audio clips into your DAW and order them according to your script. I prefer to record the narration script in one audio file, then split it into parts and insert them between the non-narration audio clips. Because you have a completed script, it should go fairly quickly at this point because you have done the hard work.

Once you have ordered your audio clips and have assembled a rough edit or cut of your piece, note the total duration of the piece so far. Are you within the time limits that you have set for yourself? If not, you may need to go back to your script to see if you can find areas to shorten or edit out. Or you might be able to edit some of your audio clips to make them shorter.

If all is good, you should be looking at a screen containing your rough cut. Now you can consider what could be added. This is where it's fun to imagine the possibilities of enhancing your audio. Here are some sound ideas to consider adding to your audio piece before you are finished:

- **Montages and soundscapes**
  How about putting together a collection of important moments from your audio clips, like a highlight/sizzle reel? That could go at the beginning as

an exciting preview of what's to come. Or how about including a few seconds of a location before you add any other sounds or voices? For example, you could have a few seconds of a forest, or busy city, before you introduce voice or music. That kind of ambience provides a rich sense of atmosphere to your piece.

- **Vox pops**
  Vox pops (from the Latin phrase *Vox Populi* – voice of the people) are soundbites of people responding to the same question, like very short interviews. They are often edited to have a variety of different voices in quick succession and can provide an energizing burst of content.

- **Using music effectively**
  From using introductory music at the start, and at the end, consider using music to transition, or *segue,* from one chapter or moment in your audio piece to another. Music can provide a mental break or change in mood if used well. Music can also add serious emotional power to your content. Just make sure you use music that you have permission for!

- **Using the stereo field**
  Using the stereo field to add space to your audio can add interest and increase engagement with your piece. What if you had the sound of running footsteps go from your left ear to the right before fading out? What about placing sounds like music and sound effects in certain sound spaces? Using the space between left and right, not forgetting the center, will add interest to your piece.

  Spatial audio is all about giving a precise location to sounds for the listener, so they feel as if they are in the same physical space as what they are hearing. 3D audio used in movie soundtracks is deeply involved with spatial audio and sound design and utilizes all spaces around the listener (front, back, sides, above, and below) to provide a sense of immersion.

- **Audio tools and effects**
  Most DAWs offer a suite of tools and processes that can add a variety of effects to your audio. Consider adding *reverberation* if you want to give the impression of being inside a large space or cavernous location. Perhaps even using some *echo* might also work. You can experiment with effects such as *delay* and *pitch adjustment* to alter the sounds you have recorded.

Mixing and mastering your project

When you are mixing your piece you are ensuring that the volume levels of all the pieces are well handled, and that nothing is too quiet or too loud from what it should be. Mastering is the final process before you declare your piece is ready to be shared. That's when you make sure that the overall sound of your piece is consistent, within good volume ranges, and well edited. You will need to have an overview of your piece as well as be able to know that every second from start to finish has been looked at and adjusted accordingly.

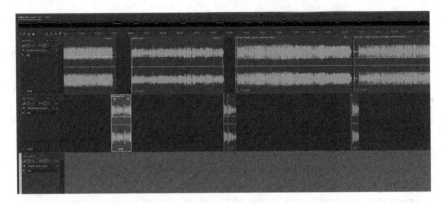

FIGURE 7.7 What a Multitrack Editor session in Adobe Audition looks like (©2023 with express permission from Adobe).

For ensuring a professional and consistent sound to your finished audio there are a set of specific tools that you can use in your DAW to help master your project. For example, *dynamic compression* essentially lowers the volume of the loud moments in your audio, and amplifies the quiet moments. That provides an overall consistency in your audio. Another option is to *equalize* your audio – to use an EQ process to ensure that certain audio frequencies, such as treble or bass, are not too powerful or not too quiet. An EQ function can boost, lower, or isolate certain frequencies if needed.

When you start creating audio content, it's easy to become overwhelmed with all the options and technical information, so the best way is to keep it simple at first, and as you grow in confidence, experiment with your audio to see if there are more effective ways of moving your audience. A key principle is that *all the elements you use in your audio should be used to support the overall purpose of your piece, and should be mixed with no detectable problems* (see Figure 7.7).

Chapter 7, R.E.A.L. Exercise 3: You call the shots (part two)
Having completed Exercise 2, you now work in greater detail on your *Unheard Among Us* project. Now that you have written a script, it's time to assemble your piece using your DAW. Most people write the host narration when they write the script, so don't forget to record and edit the narration so it is ready to go like your other edited audio.

1 **Carefully following your script, now import and arrange your audio into your DAW. It should be relatively easy, just importing and then dragging and moving your audio into place/sequence.**

2 **Don't forget to include the narration track too!**

3 **Once you have assembled the entire piece, check the total time to ensure it's not too long.**

4 **Listen back to the entire piece and take notes of any problems with the audio.**

5 **From those notes, use the DAW tools to fix those problems or adjust the audio until you are satisfied (use amplitude adjustment if it's too loud or quiet for example).**

After this stage you should go back yet again and listen to the whole piece, ensuring that you have resolved all audio problems. Common problems at this stage are that certain audio clips are either too loud or too quiet compared to other parts, especially audio clips next to each other. Most DAWs allow you to individually adjust the volume of each audio clip to resolve this problem. You will also want to leave some silence (perhaps 0.5–1.0 seconds) between audio clips, so that you retain a natural sense of human conversation and rhythm, and the clips don't breathlessly and unnaturally run into each other without natural pauses.

This is also an opportunity for you to imagine what other types of audio content or techniques you can use – music, sound effects, etc. – to further enhance your piece. But at this stage, good is good enough. Be careful of becoming a perfectionist! It's possible to stuff too much into your piece so your audience can become overwhelmed.

When you are finally ready to create a single audio file that contains all your mixed and edited work, then you *mixdown* your audio session into an audio file. A project is considered "cooked" after the final mixdown. The cake is baked, the meal is ready, and at that point you cannot add more ingredients. At best, you can add some icing or salt on top with *mastering*, but essentially your project is complete and ready to be shared or distributed.

What is the difference between mixing and mastering? Professional audio engineer Venia explains the key difference: "Mixing is focused on individual tracks and the relationships between them, while mastering is focused on the overall sound of the finished product. Another difference is that mixing is typically done during the production phase of a project, while mastering is done after the mix is complete" (Venia, 2022, para. 2). A good example is realizing when you listen back to your audio project that there is too much bass, or not enough treble, or that there are significant differences in volume throughout the piece, going from too low to too high. Mastering can help compress the audio to ensure that there is a consistency throughout, and adjust the EQ (*equalization*) of the piece to make it sound better. You really do not want your listeners having to adjust their stereo or headphones when they hear your work!

If you have followed all these exercises carefully, at this point you should have a fifteen-minute or so audio file that is your *Unheard Among Us* project! You have worked hard to get to this point; now it's time to share it.

Moving on

These last two chapters have so far detailed the first six stages of the production process and completes this book's second role of *developer,* having started as a *discoverer.* It's time to move on to the last two roles of *deliverer* and *decoder* to finish the production process:

Stage 7. *Broadcast/Distribute*
Share your content with an audience.

Stage 8. *Don't forget feedback*
Reflect upon your work with feedback from yourself and others.

As we reach the *Broadcast/Share* stage, note that distributing your content to an audience can take two main forms. First, by *podcast* distribution, and second, by *live radio* and/or streaming. All the work in the kitchen, behind the scenes, creating the meal now comes out into the open, as guests see it and taste it.

Final thoughts: *Waking the dead:* How one audio artist and professor creates innovative and powerful sound art to change lives and challenge perspectives

As we have been discussing how to write a script in this chapter, this interview is presented in scripted style for a radio program, where the narrator is italicized, the actuality (Professor Obadike) is in bold, and my questions are in regular font.

INTERVIEW WITH PROFESSOR KEITH OBADIKE BY ROB QUICKE
[Duration: 00:15] «<<INTRO MUSIC: Fades in and finishes cold»>>

Narrator:	*Rob Quicke is talking with Professor Keith Obadike, internationally renowned sound artist and professor who teaches at Cornell University. Keith was a former faculty colleague at William Paterson University for 16 years. With an MFA in Sound Design from Yale University, Keith and his wife Mendi work together on projects using sound in radical and experimental ways. Rob Quicke interviewed Obadike to find out more.*
Rob Quicke:	So, can you explain how you use sound in your work?
Keith Obadike:	**Sometimes we use a sound to tell stories. Other times we're using sound to shape space. And I mean that**

	literally to make a room that we're working in seem bigger or smaller.
Narrator:	*Experiencing one of their projects can often entail being in a space with an object in the room and being immersed with sounds that are unfamiliar and unexpected. The result is that you will feel and also think about what you are experiencing and seeing.*
Keith Obadike:	Part of what we're used to people doing in the visual arts is directing the eye. How can you use sound to direct the eye? Well, we're always looking for sound to confirm what we're seeing with our eyes.
Rob Quicke:	What do you mean? Can you explain that further?
Keith Obadike:	Well, I'm looking at you. And I'm confirming that I'm looking at Rob because I'm like, "hey, that's Rob's voice, and that's Rob's face. That's Rob." And then if I'm looking at you, and I heard some voice that I didn't expect, I might say, "oh, is that actually Rob?" Right? So, we're always looking for sound to confirm what we're seeing with our eyes.
Rob Quicke:	I get it. Sound can be used to make us question the reality of what we're seeing.
Keith Obadike:	And so that's part of how you can use sound to destabilize an image, to stabilize an image, to direct vision somewhere else. Sometimes we start out by stabilizing what you see, and then we destabilize it to make you question what you're looking at.
Narrator:	*Quicke then asked Obadike about the larger purpose of their work.*
Rob Quicke:	Are there recurring themes that run through your projects?
Keith Obadike:	I would say that, overall, the projects are about freedom. That's the overall thing that we're exploring. The projects vary a lot, we use language, we use images, we do performances, all of those things, but they're exploring freedom in different ways.
Narrator:	*Obadike then describes one of their projects: Stereo Helix for Sally Hemings (2012). The inspiration for the project was a small antique bell with a significant history, as Obadike explains.*
Keith Obadike:	Thomas Jefferson was a President of the United States and Sally Hemings was a woman who was enslaved by Jefferson. She was also related to his wife's half-sister. Anyway, one object that belonged to Sally Hemings was this bell – a servant's bell. We got permission to ring the bell.

Narrator:	*The recording of the bell was then manipulated ...*
Keith Obadike:	... in order to derive multiple textures, pitches, colors, and effects.
Narrator:	*Let's hear some of Stereo Helix for Sally Hemings:*

[**Duration: 00:23**] «<<SOUND EXCERPT: Mendi + Keith Obadike – American Cypher: Stereo Helix for Sally Hemings, fades out»>>

Rob Quicke:	What was your purpose in doing that?
Keith Obadike:	We really wanted to center people's attention on this bell, and we made a soundscape from the bell, but as a way of having you look at this object and think about the relationship between these people and their families interwoven, and in a kind of interesting way. But we think of them as different because of how we think of race in America. Right? When you hear the bell, you are hearing something that has not been heard for 200 years. I think it's listening to history. You could get really spiritual and say, okay, you're ringing the bell, you're sort of waking the dead, you know, bringing these ghosts into the room. But another way, you're just sort of listening to the stories that have been obscured at different moments and buried in history.
Narrator:	*The result is emotionally powerful and thought provoking for all who experience it.*
Rob Quicke:	So, what advice would you give to those who want to experiment with audio in a similar way?
Keith Obadike:	I would say for somebody who's getting started, who hasn't done this kind of thing before, first start by just collecting the stories of families and friends. Because the stories are more interesting than any technical thing that you might do. Surprising things come out!
Narrator:	*Obadike believes that people can be a source of unexpected and valuable content.*
Keith Obadike:	People are infinitely interesting. And so, can we capture something about the magic of people in audio and bring that back to other listeners in a kind of visceral and meaningful way? I mean, that's what it's all about.
Rob Quicke:	Professor Obadike, thanks for joining me today!

[Duration: 00:15] «<<OUTRO MUSIC: Fades in and finishes cold»>>

References

Baylor University. (2023, January 5). *Copyright.* https://libguides.baylor.edu/copyright/fairuse

CloudRadio. (2020, August 14). *8 tips on how to write a radio script.* https://www.cloudrad.io/8-tips-on-how-to-write-a-radio-script

McGuire, M. (2017, August 17). *Ethical guidelines for editing audio.* J-Source. https://j-source.ca/ethical-guidelines-for-editing-audio/

McMahon, M. (2023, June 29). *What is a media disclaimer?* My Law Questions. https://www.mylawquestions.com/what-is-a-media-disclaimer.htm

Mulhern, R. (2023, February 25). One year, three lives & our stories of war (No. 68) [Audio podcast episode]. In *Ukraine War Diaries.* Sky News. https://news.sky.com/story/ukraine-war-diaries-documenting-one-year-of-life-in-a-war-zone-12818818

Radio Television Digital News Association. (n.d.). *Video & audio editing.* Retrieved July 3, 2023, from https://www.rtdna.org/video-and-audio-editing

Venia, M. (2022, December 1). What is the difference between mixing and mastering? *Venia Mastering.* https://veniamastering.studio/blogs/learn/difference-mixing-mastering

PART III

Deliverer

Part III moves on from the process of *developing* audio into its *delivery*. I divide this section about broadcasting our projects into two parts. This chapter describes creating and delivering podcasts, which are an exciting possibility. Podcasts can be created by anyone working in audio, but for those who do not have opportunities for going live with all the potential that a radio station provides, they offer a golden opportunity. Chapter 9 assumes that for those of you fortunate enough to access a radio station you have the chance to experience the exhilaration of going live! Whatever your toolkit and circumstances, delivery is wide open for you, as you shall see.

DOI: 10.4324/9781003263739-11

8

FASTER, SOONER, MORE

The insatiable audience for podcasts

First thoughts: *The Heartbeat of a Snake:* **How one Indian nature educator created a unique podcast that captured the imagination of her listeners and brought nature stories to Indian urbanites**

Picture this: In front of you is a Russell's viper snake. It is such a venomous snake that it causes up to 25,000 deaths in India every year. Recognizable by its flattened triangular-shaped head, its brown body has three series of dark brown spots that run its length. Known for its aggressive behavior, it has the reputation of being one of the deadliest snakes in the world. Luckily this snake is under anesthesia, which allows our interviewee to get close enough to feel its heartbeat.

Sara Mohan (personal communication, July 28, 2022), 36, born and raised in Chennai in the south of India, is no stranger to the animal kingdom. Growing up, she had strong ideas about her future. "I was convinced that I wanted to be a marine biologist. So, I started with my undergrad studies in biology here in Chennai." Once she graduated, her life took an unexpected turn, because her father identified her as a natural communicator. Secretly, her father did something that would change Sara's life.

"My father, somebody who knows me very well, decided that I couldn't give up on this whole side of communication and using the English language, which I do have a great passion for. So, he went ahead and put in my application to the Asian College of Journalism (ACJ) *without checking with me,*" she remembers. Was Sara upset that he did that? "I'm so glad he did!" she immediately replies. Sara got accepted into the prestigious postgraduate program and was accepted into the radio journalism track.

DOI: 10.4324/9781003263739-12

"After the ACJ, I also worked in broadcasting for a while. I then went and did my Master's in Biodiversity and Conservation. And while doing that course, towards the very end of it, I was thinking about how science communication is just so important." But Sara felt that scientists struggle to communicate effectively. "Scientists don't get it right at all most of the time. I think we tend to get caught up in the semantics and the technical jargon so much that it takes away from what your actual gut-wrenching message should be. But I do think it's getting better," she says optimistically.

It was while doing her master's project in Leeds, UK, that Sara realized she wanted to tell the human stories behind the data. "I was interested because it was all data in terms of numbers and biodiversity coming up. But I was so interested in the voices of the people who were talking about why they were doing it. So that's when the idea sort of sparked. I was just thinking, it would be amazing to get stories like this."

Back in India, Sara decided in 2021 she should bring together her love of nature, science, and radio. The problem was, there were so few podcasters in India that were focusing on these topics, that it was hard to find inspiration. Then, life also got in the way, and Sara went through some difficult times in her personal life. It must have seemed at one point that the idea would never happen, and she seemed to doubt the sound of her voice. "It took me a while to really, really get going. And honestly, more than anything else, I think it was the lack of confidence because I hadn't done much with radio, or sound per se, or audio production after graduating from the ACJ."

Knowing of people's natural wariness and cynicism about science and nature shows, Sara thought she'd try to entice an audience to her podcast with curiosity. "I didn't want people to know what the heck the show was about, at least in the beginning. Like I wanted them to be drawn to the title, be amused by it. I wanted it to sound a little bit whimsical," she laughs.

The enticing title she came up with for her podcast was *Tigress on Tuk-Tuk*. "The idea was to think about what was very quintessentially Indian in terms of wild India and in terms of urban India. I mean, everybody knows about India's tiger conservation, the numbers going up, everybody in India knows about how important an animal it is to us. And the auto rickshaw (or tuk-tuk), I don't think there's anything more typically urban India than the rickshaw. So, I thought we should marry these things together." Hence *Tigress on Tuk-Tuk*!

Despite lacking confidence, Sara found a quiet place in her house to record, and she went for it. "So, I just stuck myself in my cupboard and just did the damn thing and then just put it out. And, there's been no looking back ever since."

During the course of season one, Sara would fearlessly investigate the lives of frogs, toads, sea-life, bats, and spiders. But was there a particular moment doing her first season that really stood out? "One time when I was doing this episode on snakes. I was talking to Gerry Martin, who was one of the leading experts in the country. And we were looking at a Russell's viper, which is one of the big four venomous snakes in this part of the country. And it had been knocked out. It was under anesthesia. He was doing basic weighing and measuring, and he was getting into the details and then he just said, *okay, hold on a second, give me like just two fingers*," inviting Sara to touch the snake.

Sara had no idea what was to come next, but she trusted Gerry. After all, he's one of India's leading herpetologists. "So, then he guided my hand underneath the snake. Not under the snake's belly, about a quarter of the way down from its mouth or a little more than that, I think. And I wasn't expecting it at all! I thought he was just getting me to feel the snake and get a better idea for how it felt." Instead of just feeling the texture of the snake's skin, Sara felt something else. A heartbeat. "I felt its heartbeat and in the audio, I gasp *oh! a snake's heartbeat!* It sort of hit me somewhere in the middle, between my gut and my heart."

This small moment had massive implications for Sara. "The whole story had been addressing the issue of snakebites, which is such a big deal in India, and on how to deal with these creatures and how we always get it wrong and how people like Gerry are sort of really fighting to get the right messages out." But feeling the heartbeat of this creature made Sara realize its own fight for survival too. "So, here is this other creature which also has a heartbeat *just like you* and is probably just living its life *just like you*, and probably just wants to go home *just like you*," Sara says powerfully. "Feeling its heartbeat peacefully was something so moving for me, and I really wanted to tell the story. At that moment I was completely Team Snake and wanted to tell the story right!"

Now that Sara has finished the first season of her podcast, with 13 episodes, the response and reaction has been massive. She's been featured in Indian media and has made an impact on social media. "Now that I've done it, there's so much positive response and it's making a difference and people care about it almost as much as I do!" she says. These days Sara receives messages and emails asking when season two is coming out.

I asked Sara, has creating a podcast helped her find her voice? She answers without hesitation. "With each episode, I think I've grown in confidence. And I've grown to like the sound of my own voice and to understand that there was nothing wrong with it in the first place!" (see Figure 8.1).

FIGURE 8.1 Sara Mohan (Photo credit: Suriya Narayanan).

The rise of podcasting as a popular medium: It's radio but not as we know it

I wanted to begin with Sara's story because it illustrates how someone who clearly has a love of audio and knows its power to connect with people found herself without the resources of a radio station and yet was able to create and share compelling audio. I love her down-to-earth honesty, when she told us how she found a quiet place in her house to record, and she went for it: "So, I just stuck myself in my cupboard and just did the damn thing and then just put it out. And, there's been no looking back ever since." That takes us right back to the early soundproofing methods with the basic audio toolbox in Chapter 2. It also reinforces the determination needed to create a worthwhile podcast.

The idea of podcasting has its roots in the 1980s when computers were first used to record sound, but it only emerged as a medium in its own right about 2004. Siobhan McHugh in *The Power of Podcasting* writes, "Radio's flirty first cousin, podcasting, arrived quietly as a tech innovation in 2001 and as a term in 2004, then exploded as a pop-culture phenomenon in 2014" (McHugh, 2022, Prologue). These last 15 years have seen dramatic changes to the way we access media. Streaming has taken off in a massive way, with platforms like YouTube and Spotify also investing heavily into podcasting.

One of the reasons podcasts have become so successful is because of the invention of the RSS feed. RSS stands for *Really Simple Syndication*. The need for RSS emerged after Adam Curry (a former MTV VJ) and Dave Winer (a software developer and coder) wanted to find a way that audio content would automatically be downloaded to their iPods when it came available. The two are widely credited with inventing podcasting. Podcasts were set to explode in popularity when in 2005, Apple CEO Steve Jobs introduced an update to Apple's iTunes software that would allow users to easily subscribe to podcasts that would then be downloaded to their laptops and iPods. The RSS feed is instrumental in making that possible, as it contains all the information about the podcast, and when it's updated with new episodes or content, lets subscribers know and automatically access that content.

Back in the early 2000s, before smartphones established themselves, we accessed media very differently. Creating any type of audio content was usually done at home on physical formats like cassette tapes and CDs, using basic microphones, to be shared with limited audiences. I have childhood memories of scrambling to record an interview or musical performance that was broadcasting live on the radio to a cassette tape. Sometimes my stereo antenna needed orientation for a clearer sound, which would require me standing on a chair holding my radio aloft like some offering to the gods. I knew that if it failed to record, the opportunity was forever gone!

Podcasting could not be more different. You are in control of the sound and when you hear it. People listen to podcasts on the move – they *pick, play,* and *pause* whatever they want from their mobile phones. That's a double-edged sword. It's so easy to start listening to a podcast, and it's also easy to switch to something else if your podcast doesn't keep your attention.

Though similar to radio, it works on different principles. As a creator, you can record a podcast about anything you like, for as long as you like, and share it with whomever you like. That sense of creative freedom can be exhilarating. At their best, podcasts can seem to come from deep within their creators with all the benefits of intimacy within personal conversation. Podcasts have an extra performative aspect. You have audience expectations in spades. And meeting those expectations is truly thrilling, though, as we shall see, it is also demanding. Podcasts really push self-development forward, especially if you are doing one alone and responsible for producing every second. That's intensive but satisfying!

Podcasts have allowed almost anyone the opportunity to express themselves and to invite experimentation with ideas and artistic innovation. Living in an age of convenience, we can now access media on a whim and satisfy any interest or passion we have. Think of a limitless canvas for painting pictures with words. More than any other medium, podcasting can genuinely help you *find your voice*, as it can be as expansive and deep as you want it, with only the boundaries you set yourself defining the space to work in.

The advent of podcasts owes a great deal to radio. As Todd Richards (personal communication, July 18, 2022), who broadcasts on WBWC in Cleveland, believes: "Radio is primarily live, even if it turns into a podcast after the fact. If you like a podcast, then the only reason you like a podcast is because radio *shaped it first*. There's an opening, there are credits. It's almost like the curtain goes up and there's an established thing. All that was radio in the first place. Theater of the mind has not changed, it's just changed its delivery."

Because of their similarities with radio, much that is involved in the creation of podcasts is found in the previous chapters. The *discoverer* stage remains essential with vital issues such as using appropriate audio equipment. *Developers* engage in the process of creating audio, first creating content for themselves as an audience of one, and then developing confidence by preparing a feast for others. Podcasts are an extension of this process. Writing for the ear and assessing audiences with the eight stages of audio production are still indispensable here. All that you have read and worked on through this book applies to the creation of podcasts.

Though I believe that podcasts are a *form* of radio and its creation follows many of the same requirements as radio, they do have distinctive and important elements.

Live vs. on-demand

Several times in this book we have contrasted live audio with pre-recorded. Obviously, radio transmits programs at specific times, requiring audiences to tune in or miss them (though many stations offer replays on demand). In contrast, podcasts are pre-recorded and available for listeners to hear at their convenience. Streaming, especially on smartphones, has made on-demand audio hugely popular. There are many live podcasts that are essentially video streams on YouTube, Twitch, Twitter, and Facebook that are broadcast live but are then uploaded as an episode to a podcast platform for listening on-demand at the audience's convenience. That's made possible with websites like StreamYard (https://streamyard.com), where you can "interview guests anywhere in the world, on any device, in perfect quality." With separate audio and video tracks, you can edit your content to your requirements.

Edison Research reveals striking data. The Infinite Dial Report found that in 2022, US weekly podcast listeners averaged listening to eight podcasts *per week*! That follows other milestones that over half the US population said they listened to podcasts in 2019, and in 2020 more than a third of Americans listened to podcasts regularly (Edison Research, 2022a). Back in 2012 Edison Research calculated that 29 million Americans listened to podcasts, but by 2022 the figure would rise to 62 million (Edison Research, 2022b). These trends are likely true for many other countries too.

This extraordinary rise of podcasting means that a whole new generation of young people have discovered an audio-only format that can fit into their busy lives and meet them where they are, in ways that radio cannot do so easily. Podcasts are here to stay, as an easily accessible way of delivering audio content.

Mass audience content vs. nicely niche

Radio is much more likely for economic viability to focus on mass audiences with mainstream content, while podcasts are free to explore niche and obscure topics and content. For creating R.E.A.L. audio, podcasts are fruitful ground to be both *authentic* and also *liberating*.

This sheer range of podcast content reminds Sean Ross from *Radio Insight* of an earlier time in broadcast history: "Podcasts are a lot like the early days of cable television in America. … There is a podcast for every hobby, giving a glimpse into somebody else's world, which is also one of the attractions of radio – a sense of place" (personal communication, February 18, 2022). Inevitably, the downside to this massive array of content that can make it difficult for any new podcast to find an audience. Audiences also find it difficult to find the most appropriate podcast in an overwhelming tidal wave of content.

Yet, when you recognize that creating audio develops your self-identity and finds your voice, then podcasts give unparalleled opportunity. They can help *you* grow in personal style and confidence, which lies at the heart of building an audience who keep listening because of who *you* are and what *you* are creating. Nicely niche allows you *to be you!*

More relaxed regulations, so you can be unfiltered

Coming next, Chapter 9 explores radio broadcasting in more detail and gives rules and regulations about transmission. As you might expect, there are many do's and don'ts about what's legally permissible. While certain podcast hosting companies will have their own clear editorial guidelines, outside these companies, you have complete freedom of expression. That's a tremendous advantage for podcasters.

Yet, with great freedom comes great responsibility. Including swear words and mature content does not necessarily improve your podcast or make it more popular. Producing substantive, quality content while respecting your audience's sensibilities still remains the wise and successful approach.

Creating a podcast can be a thrilling and life-changing experience, and assist you in your quest to find your own voice. It always helps to listen to other podcasts, particularly ones that appeal to you. This first exercise asks you to benefit from some careful listening. Be warned though, when you start listening to podcasts in this way, you are not hearing it as a casual listener, but analyzing it critically as an audio producer and creator. That process can strip away some of the magic that a typical listener gets from a podcast! Yet, you can still thrill to the best emotional moments even as you work out how they move you technically.

Unheard Among Us – *The next step*

As you enter the *deliverer* stage, you have to decide what you want to do with your *Unheard Among Us* audio project. As a standalone audio piece, if you want an audience to hear it, you may well decide to upload it to an online platform such as Soundcloud, Mixcloud, or YouTube and then share its URL with friends and family. I also encourage you to submit the work to my website so other people can hear it too: www.unheardamongus.com

Remember, a standalone audio piece is not typically considered a podcast, which is accepted as an *episodic* audio form. In the next chapter you will explore the medium of radio, and that might be a good outlet to share your *Unheard Among Us* content too.

After learning about podcasting in the next few pages, perhaps you will use Exercise 2 in this chapter to develop the *Unheard Among Us* idea further. However, before that, let's explore and understand the unique audio format of a podcast.

Chapter 8, R.E.A.L. Exercise 1: Take it apart
What makes a great podcast? Why are they so interesting? In this exercise you will deconstruct a podcast to learn what techniques you can adopt for your own benefit.

1 Choose a podcast that seems interesting to you.

2 Listen to the first episode of the podcast and take notes. Consider how they start and how they finish the episode.

3 What types of content did they have in the episode? Music, sound effects, and atmosphere? Interviewees and sound clips? Make a list of all the different types of audio used.

4 Take into consideration the amount of time spent on each section. Was the introduction longer than the outro or end credits? What type of audio content took up the most time during the episode?

5 What type of sound editing techniques did they use? Was there multitracking, with voice-over music? How did the podcast flow? How long did they allow soundbites to run for? Was there a *technical style* to the episode?

6 Considering all that information, can you make an educated guess as to why the podcast is successful in the way that it works?

Careful analysis of how something works is a vital way of learning lessons from other people's work *that we can apply to our own*. There is no shame in wanting to understand exactly why a podcast works so well. By doing so, you will unlock the secrets of its success. Of course, you can conduct the same experiment on more than one podcast, so you really understand different approaches.

How to plan a podcast

A podcast starts with a vision or an idea of what that podcast could be. Inspiration can strike you at any moment. You might be driving your car, sitting at the dentist, or watching a film when you have an idea that seems perfect for a podcast. In fact, you might be surprised that there are even podcasts created by dentists! (Farran, 2014–Present) From that initial spark of excitement will come a broad intention to create a podcast about *that thing*. You might first think of a name for the podcast as your initial starting point and go from there, or the idea comes first and the name much later on. Either way, you must seize on that exciting spark of inspiration.

How you go from that initial idea to something that an audience can listen to needs careful planning. It starts by thinking about your core reasons for doing the podcast: *why, who, what, how,* and *who with*.

Why to start: Identifying your mission and goal

Your audience needs to know *why* you have chosen this subject for your podcast. Answering *why* requires you to have a *mission* and a *goal*. These two words describe different aspects. A *mission* could be, for example, to explore how your local community helps homeless people, but your *goal* may be to encourage listeners to donate to a cause or become more involved as volunteers. Another example of a *mission* might be to talk about playing certain video games, with the *goal* that your listeners become better gamers and achieve higher scores. You perhaps might be discussing a popular television series, with the goal of giving your listeners inside information or secrets about the show.

Every time, a goal attached to a mission should be an invitation for listeners, at the very least, *to increase their knowledge* about a topic or issue. So, once you know your primary mission and your goal, you should make every effort to ensure the content you create sticks closely to them. Straying from your central mission and goal loses an audience, although an occasional surprise foray into related or similar topics can help keep your content fresh and unexpected. Sometimes interesting secondary goals arise from your core mission.

If someone asks you the simple question, *what's your podcast all about?* you should be able to answer them in a single sentence. Only by knowing exactly what your mission and goal are can you give a succinct answer. For example, *my podcast is about how soccer fans celebrate the game around the world, and*

I want my audience to learn about different fan cultures. From advice-giving shows, travelogs, game shows, and quizzes to serious documentaries and investigations, the sky's the limit for choice! But the audience needs to know *why* you have chosen this subject. What is its value to them? Why should they keep listening?

Who: *Identifying your target audience*

Who is your podcast for? Who do you hope will listen? Podcasts, by definition, are for specific audiences. Thinking about who you want to listen to your podcast gives focus and accompanies the task of setting out its mission and goal. It's difficult to do a podcast about something that you know little about (although that journey of discovery could make for an interesting podcast)! After all, you have expertise in who *you are* and will have confidence in your knowledge about the specific topic for the podcast. So, is your target audience likely to be people similar to yourself?

Compared with your earlier task of identifying an audio audience (Chapter 3), your questions about who your podcast audience will be are narrower, beginning with its specific focus:

- **Who will be interested in the particular topic of your podcast?**
- **Are they similar in age, or work in the same industry?**
- **What else might they have in common with each other and you?**
- **What other podcasts or social media does this audience already like and follow?**
- **What do you want your audience to take away from your podcast?**

These questions should greatly help identify the *core* group of listeners. Hopefully, as your podcast gains traction, you will encourage direct contact with this core whose feedback will then reveal the accuracy of your audience identification!

What *podcasting format: What's right for you?*

The question *what?* involves, first, choosing the best *format* and second (in the next section), what *form* should the episodes take?

Chapter 7 included a section on the variety of scripts possible for audio projects. Podcasting has a similar range, with each script type having different requirements. Think carefully about which format seems best suited to you and your podcast's focus:

- **Interview podcasts** – The typical interviewer/host and interviewee/s – a great majority of podcasts are in this category. Although such podcasts require research for any interview (see Chapter 5), interviews generate content easily. All the rules of the "dance" need heeding, but when interviewees share the same focus as the podcast it should stir enthusiasm and make for good listening. For example:

The Joe Rogan Experience – With an audience of millions, this US-based podcast features plenty of interviews about subject matter that's not afraid to be controversial.

WTF with Marc Maron – One of the very first podcasters, who still brilliantly interviews celebrities, authors, musicians, and people from all walks of life. Easy to get hooked.

On the Contrary – An Indian podcast about "listening to those who are different from us. Every episode features a dialogue between the presenter and guests as they discuss a topic such as gender, climate change, caste, mental health, and more."

- **Conversational podcasts** – Less formal in tone than an interview podcast, these likely have more than one host, perhaps a friend or friends, who can easily play off each other to create interesting, free-flowing conversation. Be warned though, what may seem interesting to you and your friends might have limited appeal for your audience, but a panel, or roundtable, conversation can be very lively and engaging if done well. A popular topic of conversational podcasts is sports and athletics. As most people follow professional and local sports teams, there is always something new to talk about. For example:

Talking Sopranos – By Michael Imperioli and Steve Schirripa, two former cast members of the US TV series *The Sopranos* is compelling with stories from behind the scenes.

Not Your African Cliche – A 2019 podcast series that fought back against many narratives about Africa by four young Nigerian women speaking powerfully from their experiences.

The Frank Skinner Show – A UK-based podcast featuring legendary British comedian Frank Skinner and his co-hosts Emily and Alun. A very funny and conversational listen.

- **"How to"/Educational podcasts** – Offering guidance and instruction on a particular topic or issue, these podcasts can vary from helping you with plumbing to finding your spiritual purpose in life. Typically the host or producer is an expert in one thing, and that drives the focus and content of the podcast. The value in these podcasts is that they provide specific information that can be used by the listener. For example:

Fix It 101 Podcast – "Do you have a leaky faucet? Would you like to put a ceiling fan in your bedroom? Welcome to Fix It 101!" This US-based podcast is hosted by Jason, Pam, and Jeff, who answer listeners' questions about plumbing, electrical work, and other household issues.

The Doorstep Kitchen – This British podcast offers tips and tricks for cooking from cook and author Kat Holbrook, as well as guests including chefs, farmers, and producers.

Let's Talk Yoga – "Hi, I'm Arundhati, Indian immigrant yoga teacher in the US having powerful conversations about teaching yoga, cultural appropriation, merging yoga & business, and much more." Learn about yoga and about how to teach it to others!

- **Storytelling/investigative podcasts** – Offering immersive and deeply detailed non-fiction stories that draw listeners in. Compared with interviews, creating content for this podcast type is immensely time-consuming to create. However, audiences rate this type of podcast as one of the most satisfying and popular. As we noted before, being caught up in a story has a powerful dynamic. Many podcasters who are journalists are particularly at home creating this type of content. For example:

Serial – When this US podcast launched, it changed the history of podcasting with its massive audience riveted to learn the latest twists and turns every week in the true murder case of Hae Min Lee.

Casefile True Crime Podcast – An Australian weekly podcast offering absorbing real-life stories that are essential listening for true crime newbies and hardcore fans alike.

UK True Crime Podcast – Since 2016, host Adam Lloyd has served up weekly episodes on lesser- and well-known UK crime cases.

- **Monologue podcasts** – This is you alone. By definition, the most intimate podcast format when you open a window to your soul. As with storytelling, creating interesting content is demanding. It must not have too narrow a focus, otherwise it exhausts content too quickly. Putting yourself at the center needs creative energy to write the script and ensure you use the time well. Certainly, it gives you independence, but it is also relentlessly hard work. Other types of podcasts more easily involve others, which makes generating content easier.

Latina For Real – as authentic as it gets. Liz is "an Argentinian woman in her late 20 s experiencing life and using her voice."

Have You Heard George's Podcast? – Although it finished in 2021, this BBC podcast is from George the Poet and "delivers a fresh take on inner-city life through a mix of storytelling, music, and fiction." A tour-de-force of personal communication.

Timesuck with Dan Cummins – Easy to get pulled into binge listening to this weekly podcast that "enthusiastically dives into time sucks about everything from Charles Manson to the Lizard Illuminati, absurdly and sarcastically sharing the best of what he uncovers with you."

- **Theatre/comedy podcasts** – Thrilling for audiences who enjoy comedy or drama. Because these are highly performative in nature they demand even more time, energy, and skill than storytelling. They have a distinct advantage that audiences like a dose of fiction compared to the well-worn reality of most podcasts.

The Sarah Silverman Podcast – A hilarious podcast by the US comedian, actress, and author; there is never a dull moment. Be warned, there can be some strong language!

RHLSTP with Richard Herring – A UK podcast in which Richard Herring chats with some of the biggest names in British comedy. "Stephen Fry, Steve Coogan, Russell Brand, Sarah Millican, David Mitchell are amongst the many comedy stars to have been interviewed."

The Debaters with Steve Patterson – A Canadian podcast "where comedians go toe-to-toe in a battle of laughs and logic." Hosted by Steve Patterson, the program is a "combustible combination of sharply crafted comedic rants and hilarious ad libs." Very entertaining!

- **Music podcasts** – Where it's all about new and undiscovered music, or perhaps obscure and forgotten artists and recordings. These podcasts discuss the creation, history, and future of the medium of music.

  Song Exploder – This is a "music-driven podcast, where new music artists arrive every week to answer questions and dissect the meanings and histories of a song." Hosted and produced by Hrishikesh Hirway.

  All Songs Considered – This weekly NPR podcast from the US has become legendary for its role in exposing audiences to new music. Hosted by Bob Boilen and Robin Hilton and "dedicated to finding music you'll fall in love with and change your life!"

  Tsubaki FM – Coming from Japan, this weekly podcast is broadcast live at the weekends and "focuses on DJs across Japan, with broadcasts from places including Tokyo, Nagoya, and Kyoto." If you want the latest from the Japanese underground music scene, here it is.

- **News/sports podcasts** – Containing the very latest news or sports stories, including analysis and information. These podcasts contain the latest information and typically are listened to once and once only because of their limited timeliness. For example:

  The News Agents – Three of the UK's best journalists – Emily Maitlis, Jon Sopel, and Lewis Goodall – got together for this daily podcast delivering the latest news and analysis.

  Sweden in Focus – A weekly look from Stockholm at the biggest news stories happening in Sweden with the journalists who know them best.

  The Bill Simmons Podcast – the most downloaded sports podcast of all time, according to Apple Podcasts. Has interviews with athletes, celebrities, and experts. Based in the US.

- **Sound art podcasts** – These are more unusual audio experiments that utilize sound design. Typically these types of podcasts are exercises in artistic expression, aiming to provoke emotional responses. Less conventional, they can be liberating to make and listen to, surprising their listeners. For example:

stopGOstop: field recordings, sound collage, and sound art – This is a podcast that "explores the idea that sound recordings can act as sediment – an accumulation of recorded cultural material – distributed via RSS feed, and listened to on headphones. Each episode is a new sonic layer, incorporating field recordings, plunderphonics, and electroacoustic sound." Definitely something to stretch your imagination.

The Institute Of Spectra-Sonic Sound – Prepare for something completely different! A podcast that describes itself simply as: "New experimental/noise/drone/sound art from all over the world. Headphones on."

Sound + Image Lab: The Dolby Institute Podcast – A podcast where Dolby Institute director Glenn Kiser talks with "the artists who are using image and sound technologies creatively in some of your favorite films, TV shows, video games, and songs."

These are some of the predominant forms of podcast out there, with a few examples of each, but the wonder of audio is that you can conjure up your own vision for making R.E.A.L. impact with what you create. You might even invent a hybrid format that utilizes some of these. You should never stick with a podcast format if you discover that it does not fit your unique style of communication.

What *form: Deciding episode form, length, and release schedules*

Audiences assume that podcasts will have more than one episode. Options include a **limited series** of episodes, an **ongoing** regular production, or even a **recurring** podcast that returns at a **certain time every year** for a period of time (Halloween anyone?). The choice is yours, but you must beware of taking on more than you can handle. Creating podcast episodes requires more time and effort than you think.

To start with, set your sights on an achievable number of episodes, and then consider how long each episode should be. Bear in mind that it's absolutely fine to adjust your podcast as you go, based on audience feedback. For example, you may be excited to offer an hour per episode, but if your audience is suggesting that it's good content but too long per episode, definitely make changes to shorten it. Audiences will be attracted to content that is well written and extends interestingly so that they have a sense of satisfaction that their time was well invested.

How long should each episode be? Podcaster Matthew McLean argues that aiming for 20 minutes is a good start: "If your episode contains a solid 20 minutes of good content that delivers on its title and serves your audience, then 20 minutes is the perfect podcast episode length. Why stretch that out to an hour, or cut it down to 15 minutes? That's just putting artificial roadblocks in front of you in your quest to make the best content you're capable of" (Mclean, 2023, para. 5).

Creating a pilot episode first will give you direct experience as to how hard or easy it is to meet the time requirement you are setting for yourself. Based on your pilot episode, and any feedback, you should gain a good idea what length works best for you.

Should all the episodes be the exact same length? If you are producing your podcasts for another organization or media entity, they may well have length requirements. Otherwise, it's a lot easier and more organic to achieve an approximate time for each episode. Try to let the content determine the running time, and not the other way round. That puts your audience first.

In practice, audiences are flexible in their listening habits, and many will listen to podcasts when and wherever they can. Often audiences will listen to a single episode over a period of hours or days, listening to a few minutes at a time, like reading a few pages from a book. Being available on-demand offers listeners that convenience.

When planning the number of episodes, a keyword is *sustainability*. In the interview at the end of this chapter Hannah rightly emphasizes the need for sustainability when searching for a model to help students create podcasts. This is an important difference between radio and podcasts. Nothing is worse than *podfade* – the burning out and ending of a podcast after a period of time! (see R.E.A.L. Moment for a personal example).

R.E.A.L. Moment

In the early days of podcasting, from 2005 to 2009, I created a weekly radio show which was also a podcast. Called *Britsound,* it was an hour in duration. At first it was fun to make the week's hour of content. I would start prepping on a Tuesday and by Saturday I would be ready to go. As the podcast grew, and was even highlighted in *Time Out Chicago* magazine, the problems multiplied. Twenty-eight radio stations picked up the show. Everyone was having a good time, except me.

What began as a passion project quickly became an all-consuming commitment. The pressure to have weekly interviews with famous British artists and then editing and uploading to the website all added up to cumulative crushing pressure. In the end, I was spending about twenty hours per week on a one-hour show. Add to that my full-time job and being a new parent, it was too much. I kept going as long as I could, but the process of creating that one hour of content every single week was relentless. I stubbornly held on for four long years (!) before one day collapsing due to total exhaustion. I had found myself working all hours of the day, never having a day off. I was taken to the hospital and told that something must change. Sadly, but with great relief, *Britsound* was one of the things in my life to go. It took a doctor's order for me to finally stop.

How *will you present your podcast: Branding and sound imaging*

Perhaps, like Sara, the idea for your podcast started with a catchy title, and you thought, *that would make a great name for my podcast.* Yet, that is merely the starting point for what comes next, as you think through other necessary choices.

- The **name** of the podcast – Will it be catchy, funny, serious, or mysterious? Always consider your target audience when deciding a name, and consider the appropriateness of any cultural reference or language. Be careful not to use any copyrighted name or work, which can lead to legal problems.
- The **titles for each episode** – Attractive titles will intrigue audiences and keep them listening. They can be numbered to give sequence such as: *Episode 3: The Plot Thickens.* Think of episode titles like chapters in a book.
- **Intro and Outro** – Will you use music or a montage of sounds? If using music, remember not to use copyrighted music. Maybe you can create a montage of sounds by editing together the most exciting moments of your podcast series, to intrigue the audience. How will you handle the outro, the method by which you conclude each podcast episode? Could that also include a brief montage of clips from the following episode – "on the next episode …" – to entice the listeners to keep listening?
- **Sound effects and music** – Will you use sound effects (sfx) to enrich your audio atmosphere? Music "beds" that play underneath the voices in your podcast can add excitement and energy. How do you intend pacing your podcast? Fast with rapid exits or calm with slow, deliberate pacing throughout? Will there be music interludes to give your audience mental breaks?
- What kind of **artwork** or **logo** will your podcast have? Once you have established a name and an identity, you will need a visual identity for social media, websites, and streaming platforms. Will your logo attract attention? Many people *do* judge a book by its cover, so you will need to present enticing and striking visual images to promote your podcast.

All these elements are *stylistic choices* that need to hook the listener beyond the first few cursory seconds and minutes. You want them to be sufficiently interested that they keep on listening.

Who with: *Collaborating as part of a creative team*

While some may start podcasts on their own, many choose to work with others. Never be reluctant to work with other people, knowing that you can learn from them as much as they can from you. We have already emphasized the many advantages of working in teams in Chapter 4. Let's restate the general positives about team working: first, they develop the art of problem-solving; second, they nurture creative energy; and third, they share the workload.

According to Corey Mosely, a blogger who focuses on employee engagement, "Collaboration ought to inform the way your team works – it should be baked in. The more eyes on a given project from the get-go, the easier it becomes to spot problems (and solve them)" (Moseley, n.d, para. 8). Working on your own can so easily miss something that another person sees. Of course, they may have strong differing opinions, but good team building always seeks genuine compromise between points of view, with the shared aim of improving your audio content together. Being realistic about the need to compromise and to understand that your voice will perhaps be one of several expressing thoughts and opinions is essential for good results.

The second particularly valuable aspect of working in a team versus working on your own is the sense of renewed energy and morale-boosting that teams can inspire during times when the project is flagging or entering a difficult phase. It's hard to sustain energy and creativity when you are working solo, and the sense of camaraderie when a team completes a project successfully gives a great adrenaline rush. Nothing beats celebrating with others!

Third, and the most obvious advantage of belonging to a team, comes from its ability to divide up tasks among the members, completing them in a much quicker timeframe. You may only be responsible for a part of the project, such as the writing or the editing. Much depends on how large the team becomes. At the beginning, within a small group, informal responsibilities can be agreed among friends. More ambitious projects need more formal allocation of responsibilities when appointed team leaders assign roles that suit members' skills so they complement each other.

Also consider aligning your podcast with a *podcast network*. A podcast network is a collection of many different podcasts on a plethora of topics that are united by being on a network owned by a single company. There are advantages to that. For example, through sheer volume of content, you could end up making money through advertising spots if your podcast gains enough listeners, and you may find that certain networks have the same type of content as your show, which enables them to sell advertising on the network's podcasts. Either way, being part of a podcast network can bring you into contact with other people who are creating similar content, and you can learn and share from each other. Being part of a network can also help with promotion on social media, as other podcasts on the network can cross-promote each other, resulting in more listeners, and more followers for you.

Chapter 8, R.E.A.L. Exercise 2: The plan, the vision

Now that you have completed your *Unheard Among Us* audio piece, you could use this exercise to develop a podcast series based on that work.

This exercise asks you to put together a *plan* for your own podcast. You decide the content that you will include and how to produce it. What decisions will you make? Who will you be involved with?

1 Come up with an idea for a podcast, and decide what its primary mission and goals will be. It's good to create a Word document for your plan.

2 If you can suggest a name for the podcast, that's great, but not essential.

3 Decide how you would structure the podcast. What format would you use? For example, would you use an interview or solo format, or a panel discussion format?

4 Once you have decided the format, think about the content focus of each episode and decide on how many episodes you would create. Approximately, how long would each episode last?

5 How much are *you* in the podcast? Are you the narrator? How much would need to be scripted?

6 What other aspects would you need to incorporate into your podcast? Music, sound effects, other people?

7 Once you have completed this plan, read through carefully what you have come up with. Consider the total podcast from the first to last episode. Is there anything missing that should be included?

Taking time to plan a podcast series like this, several aspects will strike you as essential before you get down to the practicalities of creating one. What would you need to include, at the very least, for your podcast to be successful? Creating a plan offers key reality checks to keep you on track through the creation process.

The podcast production process – Similarities and a big difference

This short section is highly significant. As you have already seen, planning a podcast shares much in common with planning other types of audio. In fact, the section earlier about asking leading questions is equivalent to stage 1 of the eight-stage production process (see Fig 6.2, Chapter 6). As you engaged with Exercise 2 you were working through the necessary early planning part of the process.

The first six stages of the production process apply to audio in general. *Plan, gather/record, review/listen, edit audio, write script,* and *assemble* are the key to successful projects. Sara, whose resources were so limited that she had to record in a cupboard, followed these steps to make *Tigress on Tuk-Tuk*.

But, at stage 7, podcasts differ dramatically in their needs for *broadcast/distribute*. This explains why I needed to include the making of podcasts in this *deliverer* section. *Broadcast/share* for podcasts raises distinctive new issues of distribution platforms and website, RSS and social media upkeep, and artwork.

Promotion: Using social media and tools to get your podcast out there

Once you have reached stage 7 of the production process, you will want as many people as possible to hear your hard work. David Hooper, author of *Big Podcast* (2019), writes, "Why not own the fact that you want … to reach as many people as possible? There's no shame in that" (Hooper, 2019, Introduction). Let's explore the next steps for getting your podcast out there.

Distribution platforms and websites for podcasts

When you are ready to deliver your podcast, you need to decide whether you will distribute it via your own website or use a hosting platform.

Using your own website seems the most straightforward choice. It gives you complete control over your podcast's presentation with freedom to make any changes. This independence allows you to engage with listeners through an online forum and perhaps even a shop.

However, most podcasters choose to use a hosting *platform*. As we shall see, various hosting programs provide platforms where you upload your podcast episodes for them to facilitate downloading by your audience. Their storage and bandwidth capabilities are likely to be far greater than yours, with facilities to store your podcast episodes for distribution. Platforms will also likely offer analytics features, so you can see how many people have downloaded or listened to your podcast. That's important information to have!

When choosing a podcasting platform be aware that while some platforms are free, others will cost, because they offer advantages like more storage, bandwidth, and audio-enhancing tools. They also submit your podcast to various directories and search engines, so it can be found easily. And, importantly, they can also assist with monetization should you get to that level of popularity. These are considerable benefits.

Depending on your budget, there are a variety of options available. Here's just a few examples of popular platforms to consider:

- Blubrry – https://blubrry.com
- Buzzsprout – www.buzzsprout.com
- Captivate – https://www.captivate.fm

- Castos.com – www.castos.com
- Libsyn – https://libsyn.com
- Podbean – www.podbean.com
- Resonate – https://resonaterecordings.com/hosting
- Spotify for Podcasters – https://podcasters.spotify.com
- Soundcloud – www.soundcloud.com
- Transistor – https://transistor.fm

Check which platform best suits your location and country and make sure you investigate thoroughly its details before signing up. Some companies are ready to start charging you a monthly fee for their services before you have a single listener! At a basic level, you do not need to pay anything to dip your toe into the podcasting platform experience. When you decide which platform, you will need to take your podcast as a completed mp3 audio file (make sure it's not WAV which is larger) and upload it onto what will serve as your online base.

RSS, social media upkeep, what needs to be done and when

If you choose your website to host your podcast, audiences will only discover you through direct access to your website. That's clearly limiting your range. At the beginning of this chapter, I mentioned the role that RSS (*Really Simple Syndication*) played in the emergence of podcasts. An RSS feed is vital for expanding distribution, and you can subscribe to one from an online web-page. Containing essential information about your podcast such as its title, its creator, its duration, and a summary of updates, RSS will reach a range of websites and platforms. It's a well-tested way of putting your podcast in front of many eyes and ears.

If you choose a hosting platform, many of them will offer tools such as helping you generate and update your RSS feed. That is clearly more efficient than manually setting one up on your website. Some platforms will distribute your podcast to all the main podcasting channels such as Apple Podcasts, Spotify, iHeartRadio, and Stitcher using the RSS feed. Since podcasts began with Apple, it is absolutely essential to ensure that your RSS feed is compatible with Apple Podcasts. RSS readers can pick up your content automatically whenever it's updated with fresh material. Some platforms may also assist in generating transcripts of your audio to help those who are hard of hearing. Transcripts can be valuable for promoting content on social media or your own website.

Alongside working with RSS, promote your podcast on social media. Using short audio clips or highlighting moments from your podcast with accompanying video effectively attracts attention on platforms such as Twitter, Instagram, Facebook, YouTube, and TikTok. For a podcast to be successful, try to utilize all forms of social media platforms to promote your content. You may even want to generate a QR code so that people can use their phones to easily locate your podcast. Pepper QR codes on business cards, social media pages, or printed on flyers and posters. Grab any chance to promote your podcast.

Artwork and images associated with your podcast

I mentioned earlier the misleading saying, *never judge a book by its cover.* Again, let me assure you, many will judge your podcast by its artwork! How you visually represent your podcast makes it distinctive or not! Take time to check out other podcasts' artwork, so you get an idea of what works and what does not. If your artwork looks unprofessional, people may well draw the same conclusion about the podcast content. That seems unfair, but in a culture that so often values image highly, some people's first look will turn them off from trying you. Harsh but true.

So, work to make a positive impact. Create artwork that makes a good first impression. Don't be sloppy. Work with others if you have little confidence in this area. Ensure that the image or artwork you use is related to the content matter of your podcast. Do you have a distinctive logo or lettering for the title? Is it colorful and eye-catching? At a basic level, is it mistake-free and can be clearly read on a small screen such as a phone?

You don't need to purchase Adobe Illustrator or Photoshop to create your podcast artwork, for plenty of free tools can do the job. Websites like Canva are free to use, with payment required to unlock advanced features. Alternatives to Canva include Artboard Studio, Crello, Fotoroam, Pixlr, Snappa, to name a few. Just ensure that your work meets the size requirements of your podcast platform. For example, Apple Podcasts accept "show cover artwork ranging from 1400 × 1400 × 1400 to 3000 × 3000 × 3000 pixels" ("Artwork Requirements," n.d.). Ensure also that you are uploading your artwork in the correct image format – such as JPEG or PNG – and have the correct dpi as well (the standard is 72 dpi).

Further, you can create a promotional trailer for your podcast to capture people's interest. Always keep thinking how best to make arresting content. Often this is the very last stage to getting your podcast distributed, but don't make the mistake of rushing through your artwork. Hasty work can let you down. Poor artwork can actually make or break your podcast's future.

As mentioned earlier in this chapter, some podcasts are essentially video streams that are edited into episodes just like you would audio content. Whilst this is another option, consider carefully the extra cost of buying video cameras, the software it would take to edit your video, and the extra time involved in putting it all together. These are new skills that require investment in more than one sense. As this book serves as an introduction to audio production, this next level of adding a visual element is a step that you can explore, but this book's focus is primarily on audio-only content, created with the lowest possible technological entry barrier.

What's next? Keeping up with the podcast after it has launched

Once you upload and distribute your podcast, how will you *grow* your audience? Depending on what type of podcast you are launching, you have decisions to make beyond uploading new podcast episodes. After you have created a trailer for your podcast, what about creating highlight clips to promote individual episodes? Using keywords in your podcast description improves your SEO (search engine optimization) ranking with search engines like Google. Post about your podcast on social media and encourage the audience to do the same. If you have a guest on your podcast, ask them to promote the episode they are on.

Second, it is essential to build a community that connects through listening to your podcast. Always try to interact with your audience, inviting questions and opinions, and welcoming feedback. Invite them to post reviews of your podcast and share it with friends. Social media channels provide a readily accessible way of posting exclusive content not originally heard on the podcast. They also help listeners engage with each other around your content. Establishing a forum or discussion board on your website can similarly encourage community participation. Create a sense of being an "insider" for those that engage with you regularly. Who knows, perhaps even have competitions and award prizes such as t-shirts and stickers with your podcast logo on them. Try to get the attention of other podcasters, who will perhaps invite you on their show, and you can reciprocate when appropriate.

There is no shortcut to massive success when it comes to building an audience. If you are consistent, deliver great podcasts, and meet your audience expectations, typically your audience will grow over time. That can be measured by the number of listens or downloads your podcast receives. As I mentioned earlier, most podcast-hosting platforms will give you that valuable data to let you know how you are connecting with an audience, and what episodes and moments in those episodes attracted the most attention. All of this is information you can build upon as you grow your podcast.

Other ideas to promote your podcast

Once your podcast episode is completed, that's not the end of your work. There is still much that can be done to promote your podcast using the audio content you have recorded and edited. Consider the following ideas:

- **Use clips or snippets from your audio**, the best bits/highlights, as the basis to create quick 30/45-second **videos** on TikTok or social media like

Facebook, Twitter, and Instagram. Use these video teasers to get people to check out and listen to the whole podcast episode.

- **Send your completed podcast to any guest/s that appeared on that episode and ask them to promote it.** Many guests do not think about doing any promotional work themselves, but if you provide them with the information about where people can find out more, they can assist in growing your audience through sharing your podcast on their social media posts and engaging with their followers.

- **Don't be afraid to reuse or replay older audio content** from previous episodes in your latest episode as a flashback, as your audience will likely not be aware of previous guests and content. If you have some big names in the past, you can get continued traction if you remind your audience of a moment in your podcast's history, and find a way to tie that into your current episode. The same goes for issues and topics – if you find you are covering something that you've previously covered, you can incorporate clips from older podcasts.

- If your guest or content from a particular podcast episode is relevant to a particular community, say on Facebook or Reddit, **don't be afraid to actively post a link to your content in these online communities**. You don't have to write a press release, but if you let people know that your podcast is covering something of genuine interest to them, you will be able to build an audience. Perhaps consider creating your own subreddit page where you can share content and engage with your audience.

- **Try to make guest appearances on other people's podcasts!** If there are similar podcasts to yours in terms of content, don't be afraid to introduce yourself and offer yourself as a guest for their podcast. That can lead to mutual promotion for both of you.

You will soon realize that if you have gone to the trouble of creating a podcast, you will want as many people as possible to hear it! For this next exercise, let's put some of that promotional spirit into action.

Chapter 8, R.E.A.L. Exercise 3: First impressions matter

Record a 30-second promo for your imagined podcast. How will you grab your audience's attention and communicate your podcast's mission? This exercise asks you to put together, from initial idea to recorded piece, a proper introduction for your imagined podcast in Exercise 2. As it's only 30 seconds, it's not too arduous a task and encourages you to be creative.

1 **Brainstorm an idea for promoting your podcast (Exercise 2) within 30 seconds of audio.**

2 **Consider that you would have to include the podcast title and explain the main focus of the podcast to the audience.**

3 How would you write your short script?

4 What audio elements would you include – such as music and sound effects?

5 Once you are happy with your script, go ahead and record it and put it together. Aim for exactly 30 seconds in length.

6 Listen back to the finished audio. Does it excite you? Do you feel that it would interest an audience?

Of course, there's only one direct way to find out if your promo connects to the listener, and that's by playing it to friends and family and getting feedback from them. As always, this feedback is crucial. You may think that the podcast's focus comes across brilliantly only to find your family has a different view! We will visit the crucial topic of feedback in Chapter 10, but it's important that you can get engagement from the start, and even 30 seconds of audio can provide that.

Final Thoughts: *Learning Without Trying:* How one woman took her passion for podcasting all the way to her dream job.

Picture this: A huge boombox stereo system, ubiquitous in the 1980s with CD player, cassette player, and of course, radio. But this is 2011! Such music systems are rare, but for this American student, Hannah Copeland, it is a beloved possession.

"I remember, in my sophomore year of college, I had a big, chunky, 80s stereo I carted around just because *I loved it*. None of my friends had big chunky radios." At college in Missouri, USA, her boombox fired her imagination for radio and audio, particularly National Public Radio (NPR). "I remember lying on the floor and listening to NPR in my apartment. And it just kind of dawned on me like, *oh, this is an employer. I could work for them*" (H. Copeland, personal communication, July 26, 2022).

Later, she moved to Truman State University. "This was really influential because there I met someone who was opening a very small arts and music venue in downtown Kirksville, Missouri." Named *The Aquadome*, it might sound impressive, but initially she thought, "You can't get more DIY than this! The rent was $600 a month. And it was a huge, super dilapidated building ... bats upstairs, and dirty. And it was *gross*. But it was awesome!"

"I was just like, *this is the coolest thing ever*. How can I get involved? So, I started working with her. And long story short, she eventually moved on. And I stayed." Hannah was suddenly responsible for running the entire venue – a baptism by fire for any college student. Before long Hannah had dreams of opening up a similar venue in Kansas City. With a bigger city came bigger challenges. "I realized that a lot of the success of *The Aquadome* hinged on the fact we had very cheap rent. And it just wasn't possible in a bigger city to rent out a tiny little venue and charge $5 a person and make no money. So, the music venue idea, I put it in a box and thought, *Okay, I need to get a job.* And that's kind of when the NPR idea revived itself."

She started working at KCUR in Kansas City, an NPR affiliate, and then moved to KCSU radio at Colorado State University in 2016. At that point, podcasts were becoming increasingly popular. "At that point, I really understood the importance of podcasting as a sustainable, essential element of a radio station, especially a public radio station. And I just see, honestly, all college radio stations, all public radio stations need to have podcasts, need to have *good* sustainable podcasts to be viable for their future."

Hannah worked on developing podcast programs from scratch. "If you say, 'I have a podcast', it means that you have a series of episodes about a topic. The topic can be big, or the topic can be small. But a podcast is not a single audio file just sitting on the internet somewhere. KCSU had some single audio files sitting on the internet, but they did not have podcast shows."

Working with the students, Hannah set up a model to create sustainable podcasts. "I wanted to keep the rules easy to follow," she explains. "You have to have a minimum of five episodes per semester. Those episodes have to be 30 minutes or less and be FCC clean." A further rule was crucial. "You produce the episodes by *yourself*, we will help you and we will train you, but *you* have to do it." Importantly, Hannah also adds, "I think a huge thing that people skip over all the time, is that *podcasting is about writing*."

Underlying her podcast model was the need for sustainability. "I'm all about sustainability and I try to be sustainable in everything that I do. And when I say *sustainable,* I'm talking in a business sense. I don't like to start projects that I know will fail. So, I was just kind of racking my brains thinking, if I'm going to put effort into podcasting, I want this to work. I want this to be good for the students who come here."

Over her six years at KCSU, the podcasts that the students produced were creative and interesting. But Hannah sensed a change in her life was coming and started to look for another audio challenge. And then she found a job listed at NPR, helping edit podcasts and other technical production responsibilities. "I remember specifically reading about this job called Broadcast Recording Technician. It seemed like a huge, massive challenge for me. And I remember feeling a tingle down my spine reading this just thinking, *wow, this is so intense*." This was her dream job imagined all those years before as a student listening to NPR on her old stereo. "I was just like, *I must conquer!*" she laughs.

It took three months, two audio tests, one personality interview, a day-long visit with eight interviews back-to-back, and Hannah got the job. "It was just nuts. And then they picked me, and I moved." The job title would be changed

FIGURE 8.2 Hannah Copeland (Photo: Tony Villalobos May).

to Audio Engineer, and Hannah was officially working at NPR in Washington, DC, producing podcasts and other audio content for a national audience.

So, what advice would Hannah give anyone exploring the idea of creating a podcast? "Whatever you want your mission to be, just know why you're doing the podcast," she says. "What is your *why*? You start with the why and then, what is your *mission?*" She continues, "It doesn't have to be perfect, but, you know, let's at least shoot for something sustainable. That makes somewhat of an impact!"

And why does Hannah love podcasts? "If you're plugged into a good radio show or a good podcast, you can just learn so much. And you don't have to take the time to sit down and read a book or read an article." She pauses before continuing. "It's multitasking that I like. I love driving or doing my laundry or cooking dinner or mowing my lawn and listening to something great. And I just love with audio how much I can learn in a day *without even trying*" (see Figure 8.2).

References

Artwork requirements. (n.d.). Apple Podcasts for Creators. Retrieved July 3, 2023, from https://podcasters.apple.com/support/896-artwork-requirements

Edison Research. (2022a, March 23). *The infinite dial 2022.* http://www.edisonresearch.com/wp-content/uploads/2022/03/Infinite-Dial-2022-Webinar-revised.pdf

Edison Research. (2022b, March 30). *Podcasting's key statistics for 2022.* https://www.edisonresearch.com/podcastings-key-statistics-for-2022/

Farran, H. (2014–Present). *Dentistry uncensored with Howard Farran* [Audio podcast]. Dental Town. https://www.dentaltown.com/blog/54/dentistry-uncensored-with-howard-farran

Hooper, D. (2019). *Big podcast: Grow your podcast audience, build listener loyalty, and get everybody talking about your show.* Big Podcast.

McHugh, S. (2022). *The power of podcasting: Telling stories through sound.* Columbia University Press.

Mclean, M. (2023, June 12). *How long should a podcast be? Data, examples, & tips.* The Podcast Host. https://www.thepodcasthost.com/planning/podcast-episode-length/

9

GOING LIVE! THE THRILL OF LIVE RADIO

First thoughts: *"Audition ka lang nang audition!"* **How one girl saw a vision of her future on the radio and fought hard to make it reality**

Picture this: Inside a house in San Juan City, Metro Manila, Philippines, a 10-year-old girl stands with her mother listening to the radio. The next moment will change the girl's life and set in motion an extraordinary journey.

"I have a vivid memory of that moment," says Gayle Resubal, who is now 21. "I was listening to one of my mom's favorite radio stations here in the Philippines, Monster RX 93.1, an FM station. And they had a popular morning program. My mom sent in greetings via Facebook asking that they say hello to her daughters." When one of the female DJs read their names on the air, with millions of people listening, it made an immediate emotional impact. "I remember crying because, *oh my gosh, she said our names on the radio, on air!*" At that moment, her 10-year-old mind registered the power of radio to connect with listeners. "That's the turning point of my life that, okay, I want to be just like her. I want to be a radio jock" (G. Resubal, personal communication, January 17, 2022).

This childhood wish stayed. At 18, she enrolled as a communication student at the University of Santo Tomas in Manila. With over 40,000 students, a great variety of programs were offered, but to her only one activity mattered – the campus radio outlet, UST Tiger Radio. An online, web-streaming station, it was the perfect fit – a pop radio station that played music and broadcast programming that resonated with Gayle.

Unfortunately, it did not begin well. Because no trainer was available, she was left on her own to do a show. Unsurprisingly, she found being on air intimidating and nerve-wracking. Desperately she responded: *"What am I supposed*

DOI: 10.4324/9781003263739-13

to do? So, I wrote *everything* down. And for a while, for a few months, that's how it went. I was writing everything that I was going to say."

Imagine the amount of time and effort involved. Eventually, she was paired with another student jock for training, who couldn't believe Gayle's workload. "At first, they were shocked! Like, *that's how you're doing it?* And then they taught me how to do bullet points so that I won't have to write everything down. They were pretty nice about it and they gave me pointers on what I could do better. It allowed me to be more creative and freer with how I express myself."

During that first year at university, she discovered that the hugely successful commercial radio station Monster RX 93.1 FM had a student jock training program. The very same station that provided that magical moment when she was 10 years old. To her great disappointment, her application to join the hugely competitive program was rejected. So, she doubled down in giving her best to her student station, UST Tiger Radio. When given the opportunity to be part of the morning show, she jumped at the chance. "You were freer to talk about anything. And I mostly talked about fashion because I'm a fashion gal … . I was super interested about models, about fashion, pop culture, so I felt like I had more creative freedom on that show." Later, an afternoon show racked up more radio experience.

A year later, Gayle applied again for the Monster RX 93.1 student training program and this time was accepted. She explains: "To clarify, the student jock program of Monster RX 93.1 is not really for you to be a radio jock *at that station*, they just offered it like a program for you to explore radio. You get to train with the actual radio jocks of the station. But you're not really considered as one of them." She was benefitting from professional radio experience, but her big dream still felt far away.

Some students might have settled for this prestigious jock training program as the best they could reach. But not Gayle. In December 2021, she heard that one of the professional jocks was leaving, opening up a rare spot at the station. "One of my trainers that I was close to at Monster RX told me that, 'hey, we need a new jock. Tell them that you want to audition.' So, I messaged them and sent my resume." She figured she had nothing to lose.

"The next day, the bosses called me: 'Okay, *you're going to start tomorrow as an actual radio jock!*' I was talking to my parents when I received that call. And then when the call ended, I cried," remembers Gayle. "The moment felt like a full circle for me. At 10 years old, I was crying with my mom. And now, I was crying again with my mom." The impossible dream had become reality. All her involvement with radio over the years had helped Gayle find her voice, develop her confidence and communication skills, and change her life.

What words of advice would Gayle give to someone who dreams of working in radio? Her reply is short and emphatic, *"Audition ka lang nang audition!"*

FIGURE 9.1 Gayle Resubal (Photo credit: Gayle Resubal).

she says in Filipino. I ask her how that translates in English. "Simple. *Just audition*. If you're interested in doing something, *go do it!*" (Figure 9.1).

Radio station opportunities – Seize them if you can

While Chapter 8 concentrates on creating and delivering podcasts, this chapter assumes that you are fortunate enough to have access to a radio station, whether that's college, hospital, community, internet-only, or professional. Gayle's enthusiastic story emphasizes the bonus of experiencing live radio in a station. You sense her excitement! True, her journey suffered some bumps on the road, but what triumph when she achieved her dream.

I realize how seizing the opportunity to be involved with on-air radio is easier for some. Gayle was fortunate that this happened at school and later at college. She was able to access equipment that would not be available otherwise and, most importantly, encounter others on the same journey of audio self-discovery. Sharing information and knowledge makes all the difference to audio production, and accelerates your own development. I will describe two possible tracks: one, the more traditional non-professional route of college and community radio; and two, setting up your own radio "station."

College and community radio

As you can tell from this book, and especially Chapter 3, I am a great believer in the power of college radio. It's central to my own audio journey. College radio is known as student radio or campus radio in countries all over the world. I have already extolled some of its values in Chapter 3. Its mission is to provide a training ground for learning about radio and broadcasting while creating unique programming that serves the community. Because it is non-professional, it is more forgiving and less pressurizing. Here ideas are welcome, mistakes (more likely to be) forgiven, with a flexibility that enables students to find their voice. You can quickly become part of a team that feels more like a family with genuine acceptance and belonging. Depending on your age and eligibility (some stations are limited to currently enrolled students only), college radio is a splendid place to learn about producing audio content and going live.

R.E.A.L. Moment

In 2007, I arrived as general manager of WPSC FM at William Paterson University of New Jersey. Frankly, the station was in serious decline. I was told that I had two years to turn it around, otherwise *the university might shut it down*. No pressure, then. But, from past experience, I was convinced that college radio stations can be places of vibrant creativity and engagement, creating brilliant, unique programming. Close to New York City and its no. 1 market in the country, I could see potential for a *no guts, no glory* approach.

We made several changes, including relaunching ourselves as *Brave New Radio,* and soon became very popular on campus. In the almost 15 years I was general manager of the station, we won over 20 national awards, including the prestigious Marconi Award for Best Non-Commercial Radio Station (2018) and Best College Radio Station (2021). The Marconi Award is presented by the National Association of Broadcasters and is the highest award in the US radio industry. How did we make this happen? By harnessing the passion of the students and unleashing their creativity on the air. Let the voices of the students be heard! We encouraged students to experiment and try new experiences.

My experiences in college radio directly informed my R.E.A.L. approach. Students were interested to hear other students discuss things that were *relatable* to them. They were thoroughly *engaged* by the *authenticity* of fellow student broadcasters, who felt *liberated* to talk about topics that no one else was. In short, college radio was both empowering and transformative. I witnessed many students finding their voices while at college radio.

Community radio shares similarities with college radio. Both serve their local community in distinctive ways, providing a platform for voices that represent different local groups and constituents. Yet, community radio probably has more funding, with a stronger broadcast range, if it's on the FM/AM dial. College radio has always struggled to achieve enough transmitter power, but community radio stations seem to have an advantage in this respect.

While college radio is more likely to have some restrictions, community radio can invite much wider involvement. Perhaps there are volunteer vacancies or internships or even jobs that you can apply for that might not be available in college radio. Often involvement requires serious commitment, since it is a form of service to the community. Dr. Shuchi Srivastava, writing about community radio, affirms that it "plays an important role in the communication of a certain community and is a form of public service broadcasting. It reflects the culture, ideology, ideas, norms, and values of a particular community" (Srivastava, 2022, p. 66). This rings true for community radio stations in the USA. For example, Brad Savage is program director and radio specialist at WAPS-FM "The Summit" at Akron Public Schools in Ohio. Savage, like Srivastava, accurately describes community radio's mission: "Community radio is really unique, and one primary difference is this: Community radio in general can cut out the commercial pressures of casting the widest (lowest common denominator) net to reach everyone. So in the case of an eclectic music station, the selections can be more broad and true to a focus on music (as opposed to a tight format)" (personal communication, April 20, 2022).

Remember that college and community radio stations offer a range of roles too. Being on-air personalities is only one role among many. Other important roles include: producing content (music and talk-based), music, news, program planning and scheduling, promoting the radio station, selling commercial airtime, equipment maintenance, and engineering. You do not need to have an on-air role to have opportunities to help you find your voice. These roles provide experience of working with other people, discussing and brainstorming ideas, experimenting, troubleshooting, and playing around with possibilities – all of which inform your understanding of how content is produced, from the initial idea to the finished product. Sharing in that creative process where different ideas are thrashed out, compromises made, and surprises pop up, provides invaluable learning. Often messy and complicated, always hidden from the audience, this is the stuff of R.E.A.L. radio. You can discover so much about yourself.

Gaining an internship, or work experience, can make so much difference to you, and in some cases it can lead to eventual employment at the radio station. Though it's unrealistic to expect that working in these other roles would result in on-air experience, just being in such an environment and learning how radio stations operate gives such useful information. That's the benefit of non-professional radio.

For those who have no access to a college or community radio station, the two options of using smartphone apps or creating your own radio station give some freedom and experience in choosing formats and kinds of shows.

Setting up your own radio station

Earlier in this book we explored the many options available for those wanting to set up their own radio station online. To show you how creating your own station can happen, I shared in Chapter 7 an inspiring interview with Ari about the founding of LiMu Radio in Finland. Working with very little money, he was able to set up an internet radio station that was an effective outlet for the students' voices. As we come to our first exercise, let's consider how a radio station presents its programming and those people on it.

Chapter 9, R.E.A.L. Exercise 1: The answer is right there

This exercise illuminates the issue of live radio because many of my students ask the question: how good do I have to be if I want to do radio professionally? I reply, *just turn on the radio and listen; the answer is right there*. But, do more than that. Analyzing how someone practices their craft informs you about developing your own style.

Choose a radio station that you listen to or pick one that seems interesting to you.

1 Listen to the first 30 minutes and take notes as you listen. You are *actively* listening now, not just being a passive listener.

2 Consider how the host or presenter speaks. What do they talk about? Do you notice any patterns or techniques they use when speaking? Certain words or phrases?

3 What types of content did they have in the segment you heard? Was it just music or was there talk and guests? Make a list of all the different types of audio content they included, and keep track of how much time was spent on each.

4 After taking into consideration the amount of time spent on each type of content, at the end of the 30 minutes, can you sum up how many talk breaks there were, or how much of the show was just music, or talk? Look at how the time was spent.

Considering all that information, can you make an educated guess as to why the radio show is successful in the way that it works? Can you understand why the on-air presenter is good at their job? Is there anything that makes them unique? With this exercise, you will be able to understand how those on radio are delivering a performance and practicing their craft. You will not listen to the radio the same again! I find that many students are surprised after they have completed this exercise. They never really 'listened' to radio before this exercise, and now have a whole new level of understanding.

Live radio – Things you need to know

Clearly, there is a fundamental difference between pre-recorded content and broadcasting live radio. Adrenaline and energy requirements are very different. Live radio gives an adrenaline rush like few other experiences. Scientists have yet to invent a way that fast-forwards time, but after doing a live radio show, you will think they have! A three-hour radio show can feel like 30 minutes! Delivering live radio shifts gears dramatically.

While live broadcast can be thrilling, it can also be anxiety inducing. Accompanying the exhilaration of performing live radio, technical duties keep you busy. Whether your nerves respond well to the experience will likely determine your future commitment to it. Both pre-recorded audio and live radio can definitely help you find your own voice, but as we shall see, live radio stretches you in new ways.

A former student of mine, Nick Gomez, flourished at the campus radio station. After interning at the legendary Z100 station in New York, he got his big break into a professional career as an overnight host. He has gone on from strength to strength. I asked Nick how he found his voice on the radio, and how he felt comfortable with who he was. "I will, while I'm alone, find a comfortable way to be saying things on the radio. I'm sure other people who are insane, like me, probably do it." Nick recognizes how important the *discoverer* stage remains. It is a safe space for him, without the presence of an audience, to experiment and try things.

Nick continues: "I think a big part of me finding my temperament and attitude and energy on the radio was when I was in the running for my first part-time job. I had sent in a demo and they brought me in for an interview. One of the notes they gave me from the demo was that they really liked how laid back and casual I sounded, but not *checked out*. And that was a starting point for me – *oh, this is how I can kind of be different from everybody else*. But also be comfortable!"

That was a key realization for Nick, as it can be for you. As he says: "Taking that advice, and then leaning into it and finding the best way to be comfortable and sound like yourself on the radio, I think can eliminate any jitters because you're not worrying about putting on a voice because that's what you think radio is supposed to sound like. When somebody tells you you sound good being yourself, then it's easier to do that without having to worry."

With his encouragement in mind, this section will describe some essential principles and practices for live radio. As you will see, along with the advantages there are significant limitations and choices. I shall concentrate on four main areas of focus:

- The significance of station formats – understanding these signature marks that make stations different from each other is essential for grasping opportunities of live radio
- The range of radio shows that are represented by different formats
- Essential prepping needed for a comfortable studio experience
- Critical rules for broadcasting

Learning a station's particular format and what must be played on the air

It's helpful in Gayle's story at the start of this chapter to see that she experienced different sorts of station *formats*. Essentially, a radio station's format expresses its identity. In the USA since the 1950s, radio stations have increasingly developed distinct formats to serve as templates for their programming. Stations use their formats as their best marketing tools, to describe their specific type of content with the aim of attracting an audience that seeks exactly that sort of programming. Names such as Hot FM, Z100, Reprezent Radio, X-RAY FM, and Brave New Radio all conjure ideas of how a station may sound before you have even heard them. That's the point of the format.

And what a range of formats are out there! According to News Generation (n.d.), there are at least 40 different radio formats, which include (a not exhaustive list):

- 80's Hits
- Active Rock
- Adult Contemporary
- Adult Hits
- Adult Standards/Middle of the Road
- Album Adult Alternative
- Album Oriented Rock
- All News
- All Sports
- Alternative
- Children's Radio
- Christian Adult Contemporary

- Classic Country
- Classic Rock
- Classical
- College
- Comedy
- Country
- Dance
- Easy Listening
- Educational
- Gospel
- Hot Adult Contemporary
- Jazz
- Lite Adult Contemporary
- Mainstream Rock
- Modern Adult Contemporary
- New Country
- News Talk Information
- Nostalgia
- Oldies
- Pop Contemporary Hit Radio
- Religious
- Rhythmic
- Smooth AC
- Soft Adult Contemporary
- Southern Gospel
- Spanish
- Talk/Personality
- Top 40
- Urban Adult Contemporary
- Urban Contemporary
- Urban Oldies
- Variety
- World Ethnic

Different countries and cultures have radio formats that reflect their tastes and music. That's the beauty of radio. There's always another radio station on the dial that delivers what you are looking for. The audio world is now immersed with music, talk, and audio programming that represents groups and communities from around the globe. That means plenty of surprises, like The Lot Radio (www.thelotradio.com), a not-for-profit, independent radio station broadcasting from a shipping container in NYC. You can watch their DJs spin records live from Brooklyn with passion and energy that is contagious. And yes, they are broadcasting live from a small metal box!

Note too that formats can change. Plenty of radio stations have changed beloved formats when their audience declined. At the radio station that I managed, WPSC at William Paterson University, we changed formats in 2021 because we recognized that we were no longer reaching the student body, our core listeners. Instead of being an alternative rock music college radio station, we realized that the majority of students on campus preferred to listen to hip-hop music. Program director and student Vont Leak remembers, "The initial idea was brought up after the few students who stuck around during the pandemic school year favored the alternative hip-hop music we were playing" (personal communication, August 12, 2022).

So, we changed to become the first Alt Hip-Hop college radio station in the USA, and we instantly attracted more listeners and engagement. You could feel the improved engagement. Leak says this is because they "took the time to learn and implement new clock structures, music libraries, imaging pieces, and overall a new vibe to the station that hasn't been seen in college radio anywhere else." The new format was *Brave New Radio*. Sometimes you need to make brave changes to stay fresh and reach new audiences.

For anyone who hopes to gain live radio experience working at a radio station, understanding the parameters and rules of its specific format is crucial. The station lives or dies according to the size of its listening numbers, and that depends on the appeal of their particular format. A whole industry of radio consultants are involved in researching listeners' interests to help successful radio stations fine-tune their formats to keep their audiences listening.

Commercial pressure adds to the mix. Generating advertising revenue for commercial stations, or listener/supporter donations and underwriting for non-commercial stations, is the lifeblood for success. Formats therefore target certain demographics. For example, an advertiser seeking to reach a primarily male audience in the 25–50 age range would likely prefer a sports radio station as a likely outlet. Or, an advertiser seeking a young audience would likely target a top 40, urban contemporary station. Obviously, thinking about business models for sustaining radio stations goes way beyond the scope of this book. What is essential is that your approach to gaining on-air experience at a radio station pays rigorous attention to the station's format. That's where and how you must fit in.

Different types of radio shows

Just as you need to have a clear picture of a radio station's format, so you must also be aware how the format determines its programs' or shows' content. Each involves different on-air tasks as shown in these essential types of radio show:

- *Music shows*
  Your task will be to play music on the air along with talk breaks and other programming content. You may be expected to mix, crossfade, or fade out the music yourself, as well as take listener calls and have interviews, commercial stop sets, and other content.
- *News bulletins and broadcasts*
  Your responsibility may be to read the news live on the air, to play prerecorded news content, or to monitor a live news feed coming from somewhere else (like a press conference). You may have to handle breaking or emergency news and be adaptable in communicating that news to your audience, especially when requiring sensitivity with serious issues and disasters.
- *Phone-ins and talk shows*
  These programs require considerable responsibility, where you present conversational topics that resonate and engage with your audience. you will have to handle debate between callers and in-studio guests, and stay in control of what happens. That could involve the delicate task of ensuring guests stay on topic and avoid distractions. You may work with a producer whose job is to screen callers before they make it to the air, but this is not always the case. You will be expected to maintain control of a show where anything can happen, and there is always the possibility of an unexpected moment that can change the course of a show. This is some of the most intensive radio work you can do.
- *Live sports*
  You are either involved with broadcasting a sports game as a play-by-play commentator or as a color commentator (someone who gives analysis and other insight into a game). Always, you will need to keep track of the clock, to ensure that you include all your show requirements such as commercials, PSAs, station imaging, and announcements. Live sports can be thrilling to broadcast, especially when you are present at the game experiencing first-hand the crowd's energy and enthusiasm.

These are just some examples of radio programming that you may be involved with at a radio station. Each has unique requirements and challenges, but they all have one thing in common: *they require preparation for you to do them well.*

Preparing properly – The materials you will need

As we saw at the *developer* stage, all radio shows require preparation, or "prep," as the industry calls it. Going live requires extra care. Your plan for your show needs not only an order of content but also a clear idea how the program will sound from start to finish. Prep is essential for success.

I mentioned Nick Gomez earlier. As I write in 2023, Nick at the age of 25 has joined Hot 99.5 FM in Washington, DC as host. I asked him how he preps for his radio show. "A lot of people think prepping for a show is like sitting down for half an hour, an hour, 90 minutes and looking for what happened during the day and writing down notes and having your top stories. I think that's definitely part of it," he smiles, "but a lot of the prepping for a show is *living* the content and the lifestyle of the show that you're doing." For him, prep involves a kind of distilling process, where you get to live in the content. Otherwise you can lose the sense of being in-formed and sounding as though you are on top of the content. As he sums up: "Sitting down for 90 minutes before your show starts is not going to adequately prepare you to sound like you're in touch. So you have to really live whatever the content is. If you're not informed, you're gonna sound like an idiot."

The authenticity of the R.E.A.L. approach is about communicating something truthfully. Nick knows that if he is not immersed in the music and the culture of his show and radio station format, he will not authen-tically communicate with his audience. Prepping for a radio show is so much more than just sharing topical stories, information, and personal observa-tions. It's about seizing time to communicate the essence of who you are because you are feeling the real-time experience of the music and content alongside the listener. Sincerity and interest are evident when you take time to prep.

In my experience, I have seen radio professionals forgo prepping for a show, believing that they can improvise or "wing it" in the moment. Some may get away with it, but their content will rarely match the quality of communication that has been thought about and considered beforehand. Audiences recognize the ring of authenticity when content is well-considered and crafted by thought and intention.

Remember the rules

In addition to understanding the format, different types of radio shows, and the essential art of prep, you should do your due diligence with regard to broadcasting rules and regulations. Every culture has unspoken and spoken rules of good taste, decency, and appropriate behavior. Just because you can say something, it does not mean that you should! Generally, swear words and words that are commonly considered to be offensive, such as racist and sexist language, will be prohibited from being broadcast. Earlier in this book we considered the freedom that unregulated content online can provide but noted how content that is controversial or provocative always stirs up, sometimes negative, repercussions.

Every country therefore has regulations about what can and cannot be said on the air. Massive fines, along with swift career terminations, can result from failing to follow these rules, even when what was said was accidental. In the USA, the Federal Communications Commission (FCC) oversees all terrestrial radio broadcasts. Their rules about on-air content and conduct apply to all radio stations that broadcast on FM, AM, and HD radio. Whichever country you are in will have similar guidelines and rules. For example, in the UK, the authority is Ofcom, who regulate all radio, TV, video, and on-demand content.

Nick Gomez (personal communication, November 7, 2022) responds to these rules in a positive way. "When it comes to restrictions, I think it's a very minimal impact, because we know the line that we can't cross. But when it comes to fulfilling our obligations as someone who's supposed to be there for the community, I think that's kind of the most impact on the show. That's something that in addition to living the content of your show, for 24/7 something that's in the back of your mind is, *well, what's happening in the community right now? How can I tie this in? Or should I maybe not talk about this?*" Those are valid questions to ask if you are thoughtfully considering how best to serve your audience and community.

Always maintain a level of professional conduct when you are broadcasting. This advice might not apply in the same way when it comes to podcasting. So much depends on your podcast's platform, which may have guidelines for content. Always remember, with freedom of content comes great responsibility!

Unheard among us on radio?

The *deliverer* stage is all about sharing your content with an audience. There are at least a couple of ways for you to share or develop your *Unheard Among Us* content on the radio. First, you might appear as a guest on a radio show to play and talk about your content, if the issue is of interest to your local radio station. Second, you might find that your *Unheard Among Us* content is merely the starting point for a series of radio features or even a radio show in its own right. Something to consider!

The second exercise is one that my students enjoy tremendously, as they get to decide what music they will share.

Chapter 9, R.E.A.L. Exercise 2: My Top 10

With this exercise, you will be putting together a musical top 10 list of your favorite music. You may choose a theme for your list, such as best holiday music, or best love songs, etc. The aim is for you to experience what it's like to arrange and assemble a complete radio feature and to engage in radio prep.

1 Decide your theme for your Top 10 list. Then pick 10 songs that you wish to include.

2 You may also decide to do a countdown from 10 to 1, based on what you consider your favorites, or other criteria. Decide how you will order the songs.

3 For each song, write an intro that does not exceed 30 seconds. In that time, explain not only why you have chosen that song but also try to include some interesting information and trivia that perhaps your audience would not know.

4 After you have recorded your song intros, piece together in a digital audio editor your voice tracks along with the music, and then listen to the entire piece.

Prepping the process of sequencing audio and voice tracks, and then hearing the final piece from start to finish, gives you an understanding of how radio shows are the summation of *lots of different pieces* into a total whole. By getting to grips with the mechanics of producing radio content, you will understand the efforts of those who do it professionally, and be able to listen and learn from them too. The students in my class are usually enthusiastic about this exercise, especially because they hear the choices of their peers as well as share their own music passions.

R.E.A.L. Moment

The COVID-19 pandemic was a unique moment in global history. Many people around the world suddenly found themselves at home for many hours of the day. In May 2020, writing in the *New York Times*, journalist Kate Murphy wrote that "confined as most of us still are and with our normal routines disrupted, we are literally captive audiences" (Murphy, 2020, para. 3). It was an important moment for radio, as *Radio Insight's* Sean Ross explains, "What people wanted from radio used to be something to talk about at the water cooler; now radio has to be the conversation at the water cooler" (personal communication, July 17, 2022). During peak quarantine when many people were at home under lockdown, radio was like a co-worker when you no longer had actual co-workers to physically be with. Radio was a connection to the outside world that offered information and programming that kept people going. It was a unique moment that reminded everyone of the powerful role that radio plays in bringing essential information and comfort to those that listen.

Ensuring all goes well – Some troubleshooting

I hope that by discovering more of your voice, gaining experience on air, and listening carefully to feedback, you will grow in confidence for on-air broadcasting. But, even with the best of preparation, you cannot count on everything going perfectly, especially in the early days. In *discoverer* mode nobody hears your mistakes, and our exercises in the first part of this book were for an audience of one. Using pre-recorded material gives the luxury of review and editing. Once you press play on pre-recorded content, your only concern is that it is not interrupted by equipment failure. Nearly always, you can relax, knowing the hard work has been done and, after editing, your content is as you want your audience to hear it. Inevitably, going live exposes any mistakes and technical problems *in the moment*, which brings a different kind of stress. Sometimes in the shock of an unexpected problem you can panic.

From first-hand experience working in live radio professionally, I can testify that several things can go wrong. But being aware of these potential mishaps means they are less likely to be unexpected. And you are less likely to panic. Here are some of the ways that live radio can fail to go according to plan.

Missing audio content

Among panic-inducing moments on a live radio show, few are worse than when you hit the button to play something and it does not play! We call that moment or period of unintended silence "dead air." *Oh, the panic of dead air!* Despite excellent preparation and technical expertise, it is the dreaded possibility of going live. It can be an immediate turnoff for your audience, although some might be fascinated by hearing something going wrong! But the longer it continues the more excruciating it can be. Seconds can feel like minutes and minutes like a slow death. For live radio, dead air is to be avoided at all costs!

It may be caused by a missing pre-recorded story or clip, or a caller whose line suddenly fails. Or the next song disappears because a digital file has become corrupted. You expected to play something and it wasn't there. Fortunately, many radio stations have technology that recognizes a dead-air problem and after a period of silence, say 15 seconds, will switch to music or another form of automated programming to ensure the silence no longer continues. Of course, you will need to be in the studio when that happens. One famous incident took place in 1977, when WPFM in Panama City, Florida, played the ABC Radio News at the top of the hour, which was then followed by four long minutes of pure silence. Eventually music came on. After the song the DJ returned to the air and said, "If there's one thing I've learned, it's never go to the bathroom during ABC News" ("Dead Air," n.d.).

If you do not have such technological contingencies available, you should ensure that you have prepped backup material or content that is ready to go as a safety net. Sometimes when a digital music file is not working, or your automation goes down, the radio station has CDs, or another computer program that you can use until the problem is fixed. There may be a line input to the board where you can plug in another audio device to play music or audio, such as a smartphone.

If no substitute audio is available, perhaps you can skip to the next part of your show, though you will need to deal with the shortfall before the end of the station clock/hour – that is, the time you have to fill because of the missing content. At least if you move into the next thing, you will have some time to figure out how to cover the missing audio.

The goal in dead-air situations is therefore two-fold. First, *stop the continuing silence*. Second, *resolve the problem* that caused the dead air in the first place. The tricky part can be filling the silence while you figure out how to fix the problem. It's a rare talent to have the ability to talk for several minutes without preparation. But you can help yourself by the quality of your prep. That should give you some talking points where you have confidence with the content. An experienced professional smoothly moves on when they are confronted with missing audio. You too should not let it derail you, but take it in stride. You may be fortunate to have an engineer or producer at the radio station to help with any such eventuality.

Nick Gomez shares his advice for moments like these. "When slipping up on something or something not coming out the way that you wanted it to, first, no one can tell. *No one knows.* You're the only person who knew what you wanted to say. Everybody else thinks that what you said is exactly what you wanted to say. So even though you might turn your microphone off and be like, *that didn't come out the way that I wanted to*, no one knows that. And the second part of that is, you're literally a human, it's fine. That's how people talk. We trip over words."

Nick shares one final piece of advice. "Something that I learned from the same person who told me not to worry about tripping over yourself – anytime he would air something that was pre-recorded with his voice, he would keep his mic *on* so that he would be there to save it if something needed to be saved." Being alert and ready is vital in moments like this.

Microphone mishaps

Microphones can be the best of friends and the worst. Fantastic when they work, useless and embarrassing when they don't. In my own on-air work I have been upset by microphones that have suddenly stopped working due to a loose wire or broken mic cable, or have developed strange sounds like buzzing or humming, usually caused by a broken or failing cable or connection. Occasionally a microphone has suddenly distorted what was said into it, even when the levels were set low. I've also had a microphone fall to the floor when I was speaking into it because the mic arm decided to collapse. And scariest of all, I've also received an electric shock from a microphone! So, from personal experience, you can see why I need to mention microphone mishaps.

The solution obviously involves taking time beforehand to check equipment in basic ways like ensuring the mic arm is firmly fixed and you have run checks on loose wires, failing cables, or poor connections. When problems still occur, there should be unused microphones already plugged into the board nearby. Sometimes a replacement microphone may not be so easily accessible, but you do need to be prepared. In the worst of situations when there is total microphone failure, some pre-prepared substitute audio should give immediate cover. That's when the role of an engineer or producer earns their weight in gold.

Unpredictable in-studio guests

Going live on-air with in-studio guests can present another imponderable situation. All the issues we saw in Chapter 5 about engaging in the interview dance are exposed. Generally, interaction will work well if preparation has effectively laid the ground. Sometimes, however, your guest can be much less interesting than you hoped. Especially when interviewing less experienced guests, the act of being live with the surrounding studio paraphernalia can freeze them. They can feel pressure in the moment. Hoped-for flashes of brilliance may dry up in nervousness. Of course, sometimes the opposite happens, when nervousness releases garrulous enthusiasm. Finding encouragement for the nervous guest and control for the over-exuberant guest is a skill to be cultivated. This is where experience counts.

Worse, when going live, is the guest who says something they shouldn't, such as swearing or using discriminatory language. Such a mishap has legal repercussions. Remember earlier the need to heed broadcasting rules. Fortunately, such happenings are rare, but when a guest has performed an on-air protest, you may have to bring the program to a swift finish.

You need to be vigilant from the first minute your guest enters the studio, explaining what is expected of them. Emphasizing the positives, you should also alert them to any negatives you foresee, especially if early conversation alerts you to a potential problem. Live interviews involve engagement with guests right from the beginning until *after* they have left the station. If you are doing a radio show by yourself, having backup with other people present from the radio station offers some security should it be needed.

Phoners that go wrong

For many radio stations, call-ins are a vital way to engage with listeners. Talk-based shows discussing local news and politics thrive when phoners take to air. Their participation helps the community hear different members express themselves. And, bluntly, in financial terms, many radio stations rely upon the participation of callers to make shows viable.

But, just as we considered with unpredictable studio guests, callers need to be handled carefully. So much is unknown about the caller unless they have become one of the regulars. You are even assuming that they are who they say they are. While their contribution can really perk up discussion, it can also prove highly disruptive. Even though you may have a producer that screens the callers and conducts a quick pre-interview, once a caller is on the air you have no idea of what could happen next.

Some stations employ techniques to try and safeguard against such problems. Some pre-record their live callers, to ensure they can edit out or catch offensive or unwanted content. Others press a finger on the 'dump' button in the on-air studio to catch something potentially problematic. Typically a radio station will have a buffer of several seconds of delay before content airs on the radio, so that if something offensive is said, the radio presenter can simply hit the "dump" button and those seconds of objectionable content never make it to air. When I worked in commercial radio in the UK, hitting the button meant going straight into the next song. As you grow in experience you will develop techniques when it comes to handling difficult callers.

One final word about having expectations of your callers. A radio presenter may expect great and exciting radio when they tell a winning caller that they have won tickets to a concert or a prize. Surely, there will be joyous emotion? Strangely, I have found that quite often their response is flat and underwhelming. Of course, once in a while, you will get a fantastic caller who is wildly enthusiastic, who will restore your faith in humanity and the power of live radio! But you never know exactly what may happen. That's all part of coping with phoners!

What's that noise? Sounds outside of your control

Remember back in Chapter 2 when we explored how the microphone can pick up sounds of your environment? That can happen on live radio too. Consider the following potential unwanted sources of noise:

- Conversational noise outside the studio
- Telephones ringing inside and outside the studio
- Noise from above and below the studio
- Environmental noise from outside such as traffic and vehicular sirens

- Flushing toilets in the building!
- Doors being slammed in the building
- Animals outside the building such as barking dogs

So many unwanted sounds can make their way into your studio. Though most studios are soundproofed, mistakes can happen. In London, England, one radio station had professional soundproofing that was rendered useless when someone opened the studio window to the outside noise because it was too hot inside.

When noise interrupts and is genuinely out of your control, you must do your best to find a way to work in that environment by explaining it to your listeners. Try not to let the environment distract you from doing your best.

Your ability to handle stressful situations and communicate effectively despite them will build up your resilience and flexibility so that you flourish as a radio broadcaster. If you can survive the adrenaline requirements of live radio, then you can handle a lot! From discoverer to developer, you finally are a *deliverer,* and there is great satisfaction in creating and delivering radio content to an audience.

Outside live remote broadcasting

You may have an opportunity to participate in a live radio broadcast at an outside location. *Outside* can mean a lot of things, from being in a field with animals, to being in a restaurant or local bar. Regardless of where you are set up, you will be outside your normal studio environment and need to be especially aware of any potential problems.

First and foremost, you will need to ensure that you have electrical power and internet connectivity. Both are essential and can be unreliable when in an outside location. The internet connection is crucial if you are then broadcasting your content over the internet, or connecting your equipment to equipment at the radio station. An unreliable internet connection can easily lead to dead air.

Second, consider the weather! Are you set up in an area that is safe and dry, and if rain were to occur, would you be sheltered? This is more than just comfort, this is about safety, as you will likely have cables and wires running on the ground. Consider having covers or tarpaulins available if needed.

Again, give thought to the impact of the sounds around you. Always consider the sounds of your location, such as from animals, traffic, and overhead airplanes and helicopters, which could intrude on your live broadcast. If you are in a busy place, is it too loud? Is a crowd there shouting words unsuitable for broadcast? Consider the origin of the *Let's Go Brandon* phrase in the USA. In October 2021, NBC Sports reporter Kelli Stavast was interviewing race car driver Brandon Brown, who had just won an important race.

During the live interview, the crowd behind them were chanting, which a reporter thought was positive. She suggested they were chanting "Let's Go Brandon!" Unfortunately, the audience could clearly hear them shout "F*** Joe Biden!" instead. The moment went viral and entered the meme mainstream, with the phrase being used as an insulting substitute.

Finally, the best thing about remote broadcasts are the people. You get to experience the immediacy of your audience and interact with them. The worst thing about remote broadcasts are also people. From overly interested onlookers, to vocal disruptors, an audience can be rowdy and uncontrollable. That can make for a wild ride. My friend Nicholas from Chicago was doing a live broadcast in a record shop and in the middle of a live segment was interrupted by a customer asking where the Rolling Stones albums were. Once I had an interested onlooker wanting to fiddle with my mixer, and I had to restrain myself from slapping his sweaty hands.

All these factors can make live remote broadcasting not only exhilarating but also full of potential pitfalls.

Chapter 9, R.E.A.L. Exercise 3: Promo this!

With this exercise, you will create a 60-second promo for your radio show. You will not need to put together the actual radio show, but rather a promo that conveys to your audience the uniqueness of you and your show.

1 Imagine you have your own radio show. What would you call it? What would the show be about? Music? Talk? Sports? Decide on the name and format of your show.

2 If you wanted to give the audience a preview of what that show would be, how would you describe and promote it to them? Write a script that tells your audience what your show is about and why they should listen. Is it funny or serious in tone?

3 Are there speech soundbites or music in the promo?

4 Record and produce the finished promo, listening back to the final result. Are you happy with what you have produced?

This exercise has all the enjoyment of coming up with a radio show, without having to produce an entire show, just the promo. Listening back to your finished promo, consider whether it successfully captures the *essence of who you are and what your show is all about.* This is a valuable exercise to see if you can distill the quintessence of what you are all about into just 60 seconds.

Our "Final Thoughts" for this chapter tells the inspiring story of a radio station that lives the mission of providing a spotlight for the unheard and untold in their community.

Final thoughts: *The Heart of Ireland:* **How one student radio station tackled core issues of its local community with their unique radio programming**

Picture this: The Irish city of Limerick. Population 100,000. A lively city of contrasts situated on the west coast of Ireland. Its creative energy attracts people like Ray Burke.

"It was June 2014 when I came to Limerick," says Ray. At 33 years old, he was starting a new job as station manager at a community college radio station, jointly operated by two different educational colleges in the city. "When the job came up, it was perfect for me. I wanted to work in the community sector over the commercial sector because it suited me not to be answerable to shareholders and to be able to do programming that was just more interesting and more inventive" (R. Burke, personal communication, March 1, 2022).

He describes the city he found. "It's a very, very complex city. It's a college town, and it's extremely vibrant with an influx of maybe 40,000 students during the college semesters. They bring in important revenue and jobs, but when they leave, Limerick suffers economically. Severely. There's been a lot of programs and initiatives, like regeneration programs and projects, to combat severe poverty. I would have been unaware of (this) until I moved here."

Working at Wired 99.9FM meant coping with many limitations. "Some elements of the station were just hanging by a thread," remembers Ray. "I was a little bit surprised about the quality of equipment, and one of the desks blew up, actually went on fire!" But Ray felt this was an opportunity to tap into the local culture and energy of Limerick. He realized, for example, how the city was bursting with musical talent. Hip-hop was hugely popular. Ray wanted hip-hop to be showcased widely on his station.

In fact, much happened. A well-known hip-hop music label found its beginnings at the radio station. "There's a music label that's in Limerick that's kind of thriving, and their genesis is in the station. One of the guys that formed the label was a student in the second year. He took some convincing to do a hip-hop show. And I was like, *we have to have a show playing all this music.* So, a lot of the bands that are on his label now he met through interviewing them for his show on Wired 99.9FM." That show has continued to grow in its influence and audience, partly because it's unlike any other show. "You're never going to hear a show like our hip-hop show on FM Irish radio, that gives as much space over to the artists that we do."

Ray sees his mission as creating programming that truly serves the community, and not just with music. "There's large areas, communities and neighborhoods, that are kind of forgotten about. So, in terms of our approach, it's like radio activism or radio advocacy. We're not just trying to cover stories and relay information. It's like, who could actually effect some change here? Who can we interview who can maybe get something done for us, rather than just doing a diluted version of commercial radio, or public service broadcasting. We're trying to do it in an innovative and creative way that might actually remedy some situation." The result is a radio station that offers "a different alternative listening experience to what you can find anywhere else, certainly in this locality."

I asked Ray if he can provide a specific story of how Wired 99.9FM changed someone who became involved in it. He pauses before continuing. "We do a lot of work with members of marginalized communities. So, we work a lot with the Traveler and Minceiri community in Ireland. We do these short training programs that are accredited. We give people the tools and the skills to create these types of programs. That's normally not explored on conventional radio."

Wired 99.9FM wanted to change perceptions of these often misunderstood and maligned communities. "So, we made this great program that was just about celebrating the art and culture of the Traveler community, that was not talking about negative things, but celebrating the art and culture and music." It was in that program that Ray remembers a moment of transformation. "A couple of years ago I was working with a group of people who were from marginalized communities, like former offenders, members of the migrant community, and others. And one of the guys involved with the course talked about leaving. He was questioning himself all the time. He'd had addiction problems for a very long time, and he was coming out of that and working through it. Sometimes you can get quite intimidated by other people in the course."

The man was going to quit, but Ray talked him into staying. One of the main parts of the program was a live panel discussion, in front of an invited studio audience of over 40 people. It was a nerve-wracking prospect. "And he went from nearly leaving, never thinking he would present anything at all, to *chairing the panel* with four invited guests!" Ray saw that he had found something inside and had come alive. "He was amazing! And he went on to do fantastic things in terms of contributing to the station, but also in his own life, he's doing really well. But I knew that what it takes sometimes to get people to go a little bit further is unbridled enthusiasm and encouragement. That was one of those moments where I was so delighted that I had taken the time to talk him into staying, and every time that I've experienced that now, on this program, or with a student volunteer who's getting overwhelmed with college work and stuff like that, I can make them aware that it's always about having fun and doing something to the best of your ability."

That transformative power of radio is why Ray continues to do his job. "There's a sort of madness in wanting to manage a college radio station, because of the hundreds of times where I'm facing obstacles and barriers. And then sometimes I'll hear a program, or somebody will do something, and I'll be like, *this is totally working!* All it takes is just coming in one morning and hearing a student do something that's really good" (see Figure 9.2).

FIGURE 9.2 Ray Burke (Photo credit: Caleb Purcell).

References

Dead air. (n.d.). TV Tropes. Retrieved July 2, 2023, from https://tvtropes.org/pmwiki/pmwiki.php/Main/DeadAir

Murphy, K. (2020, May 5). Listening during a pandemic. *New York Times*. https://www.nytimes.com/2020/05/05/well/family/listening-coronavirus.html

News Generation. (n.d.). *Guide to Radio station formats*. Retrieved July 2, 2023, from https://newsgeneration.com/broadcast-resources/guide-to-radio-station-formats/

Srivastava, S. (2022). Community radio: An emerging platform for awareness and empowerment. *South Asian Research Journal of Humanities and Social Sciences*, *4*(1), 66–70. 10.36346/sarjhss.2022.v04i01.007

PART IV

Decoder

If you have followed this book's path, from *discoverer*, to *developer*, and then to *deliverer*, you will already have an understanding of what areas you consider your strengths and your weaknesses.

When you enter the *developer* and especially *deliverer* spaces, there will be feedback and reaction to what you are offering because your work is for an audience. If you have already been through the process in this book, like using the black book (Chapter 2), you now have the added dimension of receiving feedback from others. This may tackle areas of your communication that you have never considered before. Such feedback can obviously be unsettling, and listening to sharp, honest criticism can be difficult. Yet, it can prove vital to your future success. That's why this final stage is called *decoder*.

DOI: 10.4324/9781003263739-14

10

FEEDBACK

The best way to keep improving

First thoughts: *Facing the mirror:* **How one legendary radio professional teaches others to become better**

Picture this: You are standing naked in front of a full-length mirror. As you see your reflection you no doubt have many thoughts on what you see!

I'm talking with Valerie Geller, an international broadcast consultant and president of Geller Media International. Geller is an in-demand speaker, and she also coaches radio and podcasting talent throughout the world. I know her from her groundbreaking book *Creating Powerful Radio* (1996), and the excellent follow up *Beyond Powerful Radio* (2011). She is known for her coaching expertise, and I figured she would be an excellent person to talk to about the importance of receiving feedback.

What I did not expect was to be talking about being naked. "Looking naked in a mirror is never a comfortable experience!" says Geller. "Unless you're a bodybuilder and you spend your whole life doing that. When you look at yourself naked in a mirror, you can see the good bits and the bad bits and everything in between." The truth of what the mirror shows can be a reality check for most people, but a necessary one. The solution for improving in audio and radio production is much the same for improving your reflection in the mirror. "Hard work is the only way out of this. Okay? Practice, making mistakes, hard work, and understanding. And then you can make choices, you can enhance the positive, you can really look to minimize the negative, and work hard to enhance the things that can get better."

Geller continues the mirror metaphor, but this time with clothes on. "Look in a mirror with a friend next to you. Let's say, for example, Rob, you're picking out a tuxedo and you bring a friend. And you look at the tuxedo and

DOI: 10.4324/9781003263739-15

you are looking at certain parts in the mirror, but you are prejudiced by knowing your own image. And so, it becomes important to understand how you are *perceived by others*. And that's the beauty of having a guide, a Sherpa, an air-checker, a director. Every writer needs an editor, every actor needs a director, and every broadcaster can improve with *feedback*," asserts Geller.

In many ways, this is Geller's core mission. "My work is giving feedback to people to help them engage, and to be better and more powerful storytellers and communicators." Geller believes that everyone is unique, and they should embrace and accept that. "There are things people can't do anything about. You can change the sound of your voice a little bit. But you're given the gift of *your* voice." In her coaching Geller deliberately focuses on the positives. "You have to look at each person's strengths and *strengthen the strengths!* If you have a soprano, why make them a baritone?" Getting feedback will help you to find and develop your strengths. You will also be able to identify weaknesses. That's important knowledge to have.

Geller has so far written five books, but she has never forgotten the beginning of her career. "I wrote these books because I wish someone had taught me the things in the books. I had to learn them the hard way! In the beginning of my career, I lived in 13 cities, I had 13 different jobs. And what I learned was, if you made mistakes, *you got fired*. And if you did well, you got better offers for bigger cities. And so, I moved a lot. And every time I moved, I took all the things I learned. And I would either write an article, or I kept a journal and put them in that book."

But what about the pain of failure, the moments that are not successful? What would Geller say to those who are just starting out in their audio and radio experiences? "A baby learns how to walk by falling on their bum a million times, and then they pick themselves up and figure it out. And failing is as much a part of success." Geller smiles as she recalls a song lyric. "There's a line from Bob Dylan, *'there's no success like failure.'* You fail, and then you learn. And then you get up and you do it again. You try again. The beauty of radio and podcasting is that tomorrow's another day and you get another blank canvas, and you can try something else. And the reality is, you must take risks, and not all risks are going to pay off, some risks fail. But some risks are successful."

In closing, I ask Geller how feedback translates into becoming a more effective audio content creator. Geller replies that it's far more than just about the voice. "Learn all the technical parts of this so that you can have many skills and many uses." She continues, "As well as creating content, understanding production, understanding the power of silence, as well as the power of words and music, understand the power of visual descriptions that you can make a movie in the mind of an audience member and put them in the movie. And when you do that, it becomes so powerful. The bottom line is, your entire audience is made up of story junkies. And when you can storytell powerfully, it's golden, and you will own your audience" (see Figure 10.1).

FIGURE 10.1   Valerie Geller (Photo credit: Valerie Geller).

What critiques you only makes you stronger

Valerie Geller makes the whole issue of receiving feedback sound so very positive, doesn't she? But, we know that the phrase "what critiques you only makes you stronger" is much easier to say than to experience. Of course, we want to appear receptive to critique, mature enough to take constructive criticism, and thick-skinned enough to shrug off destructive criticism. We know that by listening carefully to others we can improve. In reality, it's tough to receive feedback. Having your work decoded is hard on the psyche. But it's necessary for the journey of finding your voice.

I asked a recent audio production class how they approach the experience of receiving critical evaluation. "What about taking ownership of mistakes? Do you do that? Let's be honest, admitting you're wrong is really hard. So how do we take ownership of our mistakes?" A flurry of hands shot up. Their eagerness about receiving critical feedback surprised me. One student was emphatic, "*Don't ever lie.* Just swallow it and own it. It's so much less painful than we think it's gonna be, in my experience." Another student nodded in agreement, "I'm prepared to fail as many times as it takes, because each time I'm learning something. Even though it hurts to fail, each time we learn something *new*."

Then I asked perhaps the toughest question of them all, "How many of you would like to hear the truth about your performance, even if the answer was devastating to you?" Out of the 16 students present, all but one hand was raised. One student insisted, "How else are we going to improve, Professor, if no one is going to *tell us the truth* of how we're doing?"

I think those 15 students were genuine, and they impressed me with their eagerness! But I also know that when this class records something they are proud of (and I hope that happens), not one of them will really find it easy to hear a critique of their performance. But *every* piece of communication can be improved. So many students, especially at the start of their careers, do not have enough self-confidence, and receiving criticism from others may swiftly knock their morale and affect the performance in their work. But you can learn valuable lessons in the lows as much as you can during the highs. In fact, it's precisely during those difficult times that you really find out who you are, and discover how you want to use your voice.

The R.E.A.L. approach to finding your voice means embracing who you are, flaws included. We know it is difficult, but we also recognize that it is essential to become more effective and authentic communicators. As US President Franklin D. Roosevelt said, there is nothing to fear but fear itself!

So let's recognize that getting feedback about your work is crucially important. Nicole Lindsay from TheMuse.com writes that the benefits of getting feedback are numerous, "namely, to improve your skills, work product, and relationships, and to help you meet the expectations" of others in the professional industry (Lindsay, 2020, para. 5). Few of us enjoy personal comments directed at us, but ouches can teach us far more than bland applause.

Following this book's path, from *discoverer* to *developer* and then to *deliverer*, should already give you greater personal understanding of what areas you consider your strengths and your weaknesses. We now need to develop this with a focus on self-assessment, and go much further by adding a dimension of receiving feedback from others. This important fourth stage is called the *decoder* stage. I called it this because it sums up the necessary experience of discerning how your audio works, unpacking the many facets of any one audio project. Good decoding leads to better encoding in what you create!

You may argue that you are only producing audio for yourself, or that you are not at a level where feedback is to be taken seriously. But, I believe passionately that anyone interested in finding their voice in audio should build in the use of feedback. That's why I advised using a black book right from the beginning. I described its use: *Every time I created some audio that worked, I noted it down. Similarly, every time I did something that didn't work, or was a downright mistake, I chronicled that too. Keeping track of the mistakes, and making a note of the triumphs.*

The black book is already an exercise in *decoding*. Hopefully, throughout the exercises you have done in this book, your black book contains notes on your successes and also areas for improvement. Shortly, we shall encounter a formal checklist of items for decoding, but for personal self-assessment you need to develop a system that works for you. In Chapter 2, I described using two columns to record positive and negative findings. Of course, you may note down positives and negatives in a different way.

Any reader who is creating audio content that is not going to be shared could perhaps assume they can skip this chapter because they'll not be seeking feedback about their work from anyone else. No, as we saw at the beginning using the black book, you should always give *yourself* feedback on your work by following a simple process:

- **Take a break, then listen.** After you have created your work, allow some time to pass. It might be a day or two, or much longer. Giving yourself a break enables you to return with "fresh ears." Some students find it difficult to hear themselves and wish they could delay or skip this step. But this step is essential. It is surprising how giving yourself some distance from the first creation can not only allow fresh appreciation of some parts but also spark new thoughts. When you clear the audio from your mental space a second listen is always an ear and eye opener.
- **Take notes of the good and bad.** On your second listen, engage in the serious task of noting the most effective parts (such as how you expressed your thoughts, edited some sound or audio, or structured your work). Be as specific as possible. When you note down the weaker parts that could be improved, seek to be honest. Some may be smaller issues such as how you expressed yourself at some stage, perhaps, or a habit of repeating an expression, such as "like." Did you express something clumsily, or leave it open when it needed to be closed? Bigger issues might also come to light such as the quality of audio, or cleanness of editing.
- **Consider the lessons.** After you have made your notes, reflect carefully. Temperamentally, some of us tend to be perfectionist and too self-critical with our observations. Others may veer toward self-congratulation. Is there balance between the more positive and negative elements of feedback? You might need to be kinder to yourself if you end up with mostly negative feedback. Or more self-aware if you only congratulate yourself. Overall, how significant are the points you observed and how can they lead to practical action? Positive aspects will encourage you to do even better. Negative aspects should be addressed to improve future communication. Only you will read these comments, but acting on them is vital for improving your audio.

Self-decoding needs personal integrity. I believe it is essential to help establish some measure of self-confidence, and that's why I include this rather different exercise. I once did this exercise with a class of students, one of whom said that there is not a day that goes by where she didn't think of how she scored the winning basket at her high school championship basketball game. Hopefully, each of us carries moments when we succeeded and achieved something memorable. Probably, we rarely take the time to write them down and identify them. This exercise, which recalls past achievements, should help establish an unshakeable foundation to strengthen you to weather tough times in life. Others might not know what you are capable of, but as you reflect on your list of achievements, *you* know, and that's an important realization. That inner core of self-confidence is important for dealing with the process of receiving feedback.

Chapter 10, R.E.A.L. Exercise 1: An unshakeable foundation

Create a short list of your proudest life achievements. This will serve as a bulwark reminder of your past successes for when you experience difficult times in the future.

1 **Consider at least three moments in your life that you would consider your greatest life achievements so far. Hopefully you can identify three!**

2 **Write them down, and then consider the question: how often do you think of these moments in your everyday life? How much do they mean to you?**

3 **Recognize that these achievements are part of your history, and can never be taken away. They are part of your essential life story.**

I used my black book not only to keep track of my own audio work but also to make notes of other people's work too: *Every time you hear some audio or radio that impresses you from someone else, make a note and try to analyze why it worked and what you could learn from it. You can learn so much from other people's production techniques and the way they prepare content. Equally, others' mistakes can serve as cautionary reminders of what you should avoid doing.*

Reading, listening, hearing about other people's experiences, good and bad, can be useful information. We don't need to experience mistakes first-hand to learn what *not to do*. If you really want to understand how to create compelling audio content, listen to others who have produced powerful content. Understand their techniques, narrative structure, and production approaches by analyzing how they have constructed their work. The downside to that is it can reduce a listening experience from being an emotional one to a technical exercise. However, that's why I always listen to something more than once, so I can appreciate it as a listener first before I hear it as an audio content creator.

Experience will also give you a discerning mind about what works and what does not, when it comes to other people's work. As you become more experienced, you will be able to detect mistakes or inefficiencies in other people's work that they are perhaps not aware of. You are now developing a *critical ear*, to really process and understand the best methods to produce audio content.

R.E.A.L. Moment

I am sitting in a busy restaurant in New York City having a conversation with Lance Liguez, advisor for UTA Radio, at the University of Texas in Arlington. He's in town because his radio station has been nominated for a prestigious Radio Mercury Award. We are talking about audio and radio production textbooks and what they don't cover. His passion is palpable! "Here's writing, here's how to operate Adobe Audition, here's ... but nothing about performance. There's *nothing* about performance!" I ask him to go on. "So I created my own PowerPoints that go over, based on what I think is the way to develop a broadcast voice, what I've heard from former bosses and former colleagues at a radio station, just how to use your voice for broadcasts, how to tune it for performance" (personal communication, June 20, 2022).

For Lance, developing your broadcasting voice is absolutely necessary. Enunciation, inflection, energy, attitude are all essential, and most textbooks don't cover that. Lance continues, "You have to have interest in your voice to communicate a message, to be a DJ, to be a news person. You have to have that in there. It's not inauthentic, because what you're doing requires it. If you're a music DJ, you need to have energy in your voice to sell the music. If you're reading news, you have to have a certain tone in your voice, along with the inflection and the enunciation to make sure the story is clear."

Lance wants to help his students as much as possible, and giving honest feedback is essential to do that. "I tell them, they're going to get feedback from me and I'm going to be very honest with them." Lance says that when he gives feedback it's all because of a desire to provide a solution to a problem that perhaps the students do not know about. "I give them the bad news first, and say, 'that wasn't good, and here's why'. Then I suggest a better way to do it. I don't want to get out there and go, 'you're terrible', and then leave the room right? So you've got to give feedback truthfully, but then you have to give them a solution." I agree with Lance. The most valuable feedback of all is information that can positively shape your future!

Structured decoding – What do you need detailed feedback on?

Personal decoding is rarely enough on its own. Self-decoding will never be sufficiently distant from your work to enable the kind of rigorous questions that are required. This section describes two much more detailed ways of assessing any audio project. One involves using a checklist, and the other takes the form of an aircheck.

Ideally, you need friends (in the first instance) to share in this more structured process. If you are in a classroom situation it may be that alongside your teacher's assessment, others in the class can share. In the next section, I mention the opportunity for a mentoring role to assist in the process of finding your best voice. The more advanced your work the more critical is the need for the views of constructive outsiders.

Audio checklist

Although not exhaustive, when I evaluate my students' audio projects, I use an audio checklist. I typically assess them in the following areas:

TECHNICAL ASPECTS:

- **Audio Quality:** Is the audio clean, crisp, and well recorded throughout the piece? I've stressed the principle that *the highest quality audio possible should always be your goal whatever level of equipment you use*. In Chapter 2, I provided a full checklist of basic issues about ensuring your equipment and the surroundings are in order for you to record great-sounding audio. Remember, it's always harder to fix bad audio than to record it well in the first place.
- **Editing:** Is the editing done so well that we cannot hear it? In Chapter 6, I stressed the principle that *good editing should be undetectable by the audience*. Poor editing means your audience will be distracted by the mistakes and errors, rather than focus on what you want them to hear. Audiences do notice errors and bad edits, and it immediately diminishes your perceived professionalism and breaks their concentration.
- **Technical Competency:** Is the piece mixed well, using fades, music, and other sound elements appropriately and effectively? Remember the key principle at the end of Chapter 7? *All the elements you use in your audio should be used to support the purpose of your piece, and should be mixed as perfectly as possible, with no detectable problems.* Technical competency is brought to attention mostly when there are mistakes or problems, otherwise your audience should not be concerned with this aspect.

DESIGN

- **Structure & Design:** Is the piece well structured with a clear sense of purpose throughout? Remember the list in Chapter 6 of the many different types of content that you can choose from. Remember the key principle that *the type of audio content you create significantly impacts the required structure and design you'll need.*
- **Writing:** Is the script of the piece well written and without obvious flaws and inconsistencies? Were the introduction, ending, and stories effective? Is your writing written for the ear, to be heard? Remember the key point in Chapter 4, the secret to writing for the ear is *to test your writing by sounding its words out loud to yourself as you write them.* Ensuring that your piece is well understood by the audience, words need to be clear and concise to help them think concretely and precisely when listening to your words.
- **Creativity:** Is the piece creatively presented? Is it imaginative and interesting for the listener? In Chapter 6, we explored how preparing the meal means giving the audience audio content that surprises, emotionally moves and engages them. If something is creatively presented, the audience will be much more engaged.
- **Time:** Does the piece meet the duration requirements? Is it too long or too short? In Chapter 6, I shared the key principle *that you should always be thinking of the duration of your audio piece throughout all the production stages.* It takes constant vigilance to ensure that you are on target to produce the desired length of your audio project.

VOICE

- **Use of Voice:** How is the voice used? Is there a narrator or host? Is it too slow or too fast? Is it an effective voice in delivering *relatable, engaging, authentic,* and *liberating* content? Remember, in Chapter 1, the key principle is *understanding just how many options there are for using your voice to communicate powerfully and effectively.* There is always more than one way to read a script and use your voice.

TAKEAWAYS

- **The takeaway for the AUDIENCE:** What does the audience feel at the end of the piece? What have they learned? What kind of journey do you want them to have experienced?
- **The takeaway for the CREATOR:** Identify one thing the student does really well, and another that they can work on to improve. Constructive criticism is crucial here, as there is always room for improvement, while also recognizing the strengths and successes of the piece.

Airchecking

Another format for decoding involves editing clips of your best work into an audio file. Usually, this focuses on your voice so editing removes music and other elements. If you work in radio, airchecking is something that is regularly done. According to CloudRadio, "The acceptable length of an aircheck is two to five minutes, and if someone wants a taste of more content, they can always reach out and ask for it" (CloudRadio, 2021, Keep it Short section). The idea is to quickly give someone a sample of who you are.

This clearly is a different way of receiving feedback, but its use is widespread and invaluable for those who really want to improve. Audience research analyst Steve Olsen (2016) writes that airechecking can identify problems such as "sloppy announcing breaks, poor ad-libbing skills, badly organized stopsets (announcing breaks), or announcers who are going through the motions on autopilot" (Olson, 2016, para. 9). According to Olsen, all your audience knows "is what they hear. If you don't interest or engage them in a few seconds, they tune you out. And these days, they have more media options than ever." Remember the precision that Nick Gomez described in Chapter 9? How every word when he speaks is chosen carefully for maximum effectiveness? That is a result of being airchecked and having full awareness of what you want to communicate in the moment.

Chapter 10. R.E.A.L. Exercise 2: *The Aircheck* – **time to get feedback**

1 Revisit the assignments you did in Chapter 9. Take your *Top 10* or *Going Live* assignments and seek feedback from someone working in the radio or audio industry.

2 Does their opinion/assessment match your own earlier self-assessment? What advice and points do they make that you never would have thought of yourself?

3 Are there parts of your audio work that are exceptional and you can be proud of?

4 Overall, how do you feel after the aircheck experience? Do you feel encouraged or deflated?

A positive aircheck experience is not just about learning what could be improved, but identifying moments in order to create a voiceover demo or showcase of your best work for your website and future employers. You shouldn't come away from an aircheck experience feeling beaten up and demoralized, but rather with new ideas and the knowledge you are discovering yet more of your voice.

As you accumulate experience and a collection of your best audio moments, you will be able to then use that real work in an online demo, to demonstrate your range and abilities. A demo is a collection of your best radio or audio moments, compiled into one audio file, so that it plays through all your content seamlessly. A demo is especially helpful if you are seeking voiceover work. To begin with, there is nothing wrong with creating a two-minute demo "reel" of your voice, even if you haven't had any clients yet. Having no demo at all means there is no way that any potential client can evaluate your voice. So you will *need* to have a demo that people can listen to. Creating one is easier than you might think.

Jason McCoy from VoiceActing101.com says "you should be able to understand how to make your own demo by carefully listening and analyzing the demos of others. Take notes on how they speak the words, and how they write the script." If you do this a few times, you will be able to produce a voiceover demo from what you have learned, even if you have not yet been professionally hired. "Remember the point of a voiceover demo is to show prospects exactly what you're capable of," adds McCoy. Keeping track of your best audio moments is always a good idea, as you never know how they may come in useful in the future.

Responding to feedback given to you

I wrote that you should not feel beaten up and demoralized when you receive feedback. Undoubtedly this whole section on assessment asks many questions about your character. I once assigned a three-minute audio piece to my class, with the explicit instruction that the length of the piece must be three minutes exactly. One student turned in a piece that exceeded eight minutes. As the class listened, there was a sense that something had gone very wrong in the student's interpretation of the assignment. When I questioned the student why it was so long past the three minutes required, the student replied adamantly that their piece was 'perfect' as it was and could not be edited down. "It's not possible to make it shorter, everything in there is *essential*." Needless to say, listening through with the class, I could, on that first listen, easily identify several minutes of ineffective or repetitious material that could have been edited out. The student receiving the feedback was indignant. It perhaps comes down to experience. If the person receiving feedback is not used to the experience, they can easily react defensively to what's being said to them.

Jim Bolt started in college radio, and was one of the founders of KSSU at California State University-Sacramento at the start of the 1990s. He is currently a global marketing executive with a Notre Dame University MBA, with cross-industry experience driving rapid growth for startups and Fortune 500 companies ranging from pre-revenue to $13B. So, when it comes to working with people and getting the best out of them, Bolt has extensive experience.

"If you're giving someone feedback, and especially students and those who are just starting out in their career, the personal offense aspect of it is probably going to be more prominent," says Bolt (personal communication, December 16, 2022). Students and young professionals can easily interpret feedback as personal criticism. That's because "you're not used to it. You're getting into a situation where you are receiving critiques, you are potentially receiving suggestions on how to improve, and you're young. So you don't know at this point that life is a constant process of reinvention, refocusing, and introspection, looking back on your decisions and saying, 'what could I have done better?'" His advice for anyone receiving criticism or negative feedback about their work is to separate the work from the person. "You're going to have to work harder to understand that it's not about you, *as a person*, it's about your *performance*, which you can directly control," says Bolt.

Scholars have studied the variety of responses to criticism (Hattie & Timperley, 2007). *Constructive feedback* is "when criticism is perceived to be constructive, students see it as simultaneously identifying gaps in understanding and providing specific directions for improvement" (Fong et al., 2018, p. 42). Negative criticism can be considered constructive if it offers specific guidance on how improvements can be achieved and if it's communicated in a compassionate manner.

Feedback valence is the term used to refer to the amount of positivity or negativity upon a person or creative team as a result of the feedback being received. It's complicated how we process feedback. Too much positivity can result in a decrease in motivation, or effort. Too much negativity can result in the same outcome because morale has been diminished and hopelessness can be disabling. Some students have a very low threshold for receiving feedback of any kind. "When students receive criticism, they often interpret the feedback as an indication of failure" (Fong et al., 2018, p. 42).

Yet, researchers have found that generally speaking, "feedback indicating a low success (or high failure) rate was better at driving learning than feedback indicating a high success rate. While positive feedback resulted in better learning than negative feedback, the only condition producing successful learning was training with 10% positive feedback" (Amitay et al., 2015, p. 7). That suggests that while we appreciate positive feedback, we actually learn more when we are told what does not work, what needs to be improved, or what we have failed at. We want to know how we can improve, if we have the stomach to hear it. That level of honesty is required because "learning does not occur when the feedback informs learners that they are doing better than they should be given the task's difficulty" (Amitay et al., 2015, p. 9).

Others will be able to see things that you *cannot*. They will have opinions! If they are willing to spend constructive time in assessing your work, you are the beneficiary of their time and attention as (hopefully) they provide thoughtful analysis of your work. You should expect *lightbulb* moments when you understand the critique and, more importantly, commit to fixing your performance in that area.

Ideally you should take ownership of your mistakes and flaws, looking at it as something to be addressed head on, rather than ignored or denied. Robert Taylor, a radio professional for nearly four decades in the New York and New Jersey area, is spot on when he says "accepting feedback, and being *teachable* is going to be the key to success in your career" (personal communication, March 17, 2023). With extensive experience in the radio industry, Taylor knows that you always need to be open to learning and improving. Regardless of what you hear, "the person receiving the feedback should be very thankful that someone wants to offer feedback!" says Taylor.

But what about the fear of failure? Many people fear failure as being a reflection of themselves personally. Jim Bolt smiles and makes a provocative suggestion: "If you're going to fail, then *fail spectacularly!* Go learn through the process, right? I mean, there are a multitude of things you can take on that will not work out, and never go into it with the idea that *it will fail,* but know that it is not always the end result, it is the *journey.*" It's that journey that informs your development as a person, a process made up of individual moments and phases in life. Bolt gives some final, practical advice, "It's back to you and what you make of it, and your passions and your desires will help guide you to what you'll find most attractive and most rewarding in a career. But the advice to follow your passion is not always right, you can be the most passionate guitar player in the world, and you can still be awful, that doesn't mean you're ever going to be successful at it!"

Not knowing what your passion is, is OK too. As writer Mark Manson asserts, "Life is all about *not knowing,* and then doing something anyway. *All of life* is like this" (Manson, n.d., para. 7). Yet, it might be easier than you think to identify what you are passionate about. "If you're passionate about something, it will already feel like such an ingrained part of your life that you will have to be reminded by people that it's not normal, that other people aren't like that." Follow that instinct. The important thing is to try and give life your best shot because even in failure, there are lessons to be learned, and no one has all the answers to life anyway.

One final aspect of receiving feedback is that it also develops our ability to *listen* to other people. When we listen to what other people have to say, we can learn from them. When we quiet our own voice, we allow space for the voices of others, and what they have to say may well be far more insightful than what we have on our own.

Find a mentor if you can, but a friend will do at first

Ideally, a mentor is someone who is in the same career field that you are starting in and is willing to spend time to support you on your journey.

A mentor should offer honest feedback and take the time to carefully consider your goals and whether you are progressing toward them. They should also be active listeners as you express your feelings and opinions too.

Those with no access to a radio station and who know no one who works in audio will still need to find a mentor who can, broadly, keep you on track and give you feedback about your approach. A parent or family member who is older will likely have learned many lessons along the way that could prove useful to your situation. A similarly aged friend could also help provide encouragement, honest feedback, and keep you accountable. It's about being accompanied on the journey by someone who gives vital feedback from another point of view. There is no shame in having such a mentor, especially if the alternative is having no mentor at all.

Obviously, there is a contrast between setting out on our own and having the advantage of learning in a radio station. *The Washington Post's* Steven Weidinger (2020) emphasizes numerous benefits to having a workplace mentor:

A workplace mentor will:

- Help guide you toward reaching your goals
- Provide encouragement
- Offer honest feedback
- Hold you accountable
- Introduce you to new contacts
- Increase your chances of getting a raise/promotion

Notice that this list, in addition to the fundamental mentoring tasks of encouraging with honest feedback and some level of accountability, includes that a knowledgeable mentor will have the advantages of guiding you toward your goals, introducing you to new contacts, and increasing your career prospects.

Finding someone who works in the career field you want to be in, and is happy to give you advice and feedback even though you are just starting out, is the ideal scenario. Inside knowledge from someone who is actively working in the industry can provide crucial information about what is really happening and what you need to know. The opinion of an insider or expert has credibility because "people are inclined to trust evaluations of their capabilities by those who are themselves skilled in the activity, have access to some objective predictors of performance capability, or possess a rich fund of knowledge gained from observing and comparing many different aspirants and their later accomplishments" (Bandura, 1997, p. 105). Unsurprisingly, researchers have found that the impact of feedback is directly related to the perceived credibility of who is giving that feedback (Poulos & Mahony, 2008).

As you advance you can also benefit from being a member of an organization that provides services such as aircheck feedback and other forms of audio production training. In the USA, being a member of College Broadcasters, Inc., Intercollegiate Broadcasting System, or the Broadcast Education Association, for example, provides contact with professionals and broadcast talent that can give you insights that you won't find anywhere else. Investigate what organizations do the same in your country. A further benefit from belonging to such an organization is that you will connect with others in the same position as you, and you can learn from each other, forming friendships along the way.

Chapter 10. R.E.A.L. Exercise 3: Assessing your highlights

As you are coming to the end of this book, it's time to assess your work when it comes to audio and radio production.

1 From listening to all the work you have produced for the exercises in this book so far, make a list of your favorite pieces.

2 Identify *why* you prefer those pieces to others. Is it the type of content? Is it the way you edited or structured the piece? Is it because of what you had to say, and how you said it?

3 Make a list of areas that you consider your strengths, and areas of weakness.

For this exercise, you should not be too hard on yourself. Some students come up with a one-sided list with many more negatives than positives. It's perhaps easier to identify something you feel needs improvement than the things you got right. Once a student, after doing this exercise said, "I know that I need to work on my voice. I seem to be hesitant to express my own opinions, and you can hear that." Another student concluded, "I have really great content, I just need to edit it better and do it justice when it comes to production." Whether it's about the content or the technical performance, if you can identify the areas that need improvement, when you ask for feedback from someone else, your self-analysis will either be confirmed or challenged.

You may even be surprised by feedback that identifies your greatest weakness as being your biggest asset. For example, a student in my class worried that they sounded too rambling in their narration, but the class disagreed and said that it sounded more authentic and emotionally powerful that way. That illustrates the power of receiving feedback, as it can shift our own opinions and perspectives in dramatic ways.

Keeping the faith: Looking ahead

I know that the majority of my readers may have no intention of developing a professional audio career, but a few may. The previous section covered the territory of mentors helping us enter career paths, so I need to mention two important aspects. First, most of us starting an audio career need to develop *resilience*. Second, it's helpful to develop a *personal motto*.

Feedback with a different dimension

When you are ready to start your career, you need to treat your search as a campaign. That means sending off your resume and cover letter to several jobs every week, making phone calls and emails to follow up opportunities and possibilities, and keeping track of all your efforts. That takes time, and the campaign will end and be considered successful when just one of your applications is accepted, and you are officially hired. It just takes one person to say *yes*.

But, when applying for a position in your campaign, often the only feedback received from the potential employer is in the form of a rejection letter or email. Bluntly, it informs us that there is no future with that particular company or opportunity. Sadly such a rejection is no help, giving no assistance about what we need to improve or change.

The effects of rejection can also compound more damage. Marlo Lyons (2022), writing for the *Harvard Business Review*, says that "rejection stings, and not knowing why you were rejected can cause you to engage in negative self-talk about your skills and capabilities (para. 8)." Worryingly, it does not take many rejections for people to feel doubt about themselves. In a 2022 survey of over 1,000 job applicants, *Joblist* found that "on average, job seekers started losing confidence in themselves after five rejections" ("Almost Half of Job Seekers," 2022, Key Points). It's easy to take rejection personally, but try not to. Jeffrey Kudish (2017) in the *Los Angeles Times* writes that, "If you don't get a 'yes', mentally reframe it in a positive way. Consider the possibilities that you didn't hear back because the company decided not to fill the position. Or maybe that position wouldn't have been the right job for you. There are countless reasons why you might not have gotten the job, so try to keep a positive mental perspective" (para. 3).

It is vital to grow in resilience. Lyons argues that "the more you're rejected, the more resilient you'll become as you learn to recover from the disappointment. ... Knowing how you feel in that moment and what it takes to move forward will give you a formula you can apply when faced with any failure." *Joblist* also found supporting evidence that "part of what helps an applicant to land a new job, even after facing multiple rejections, is not losing confidence" ("Almost Half of Job Seekers," 2022, Presumed Reasons for Rejection section). You must find a way to keep going, despite the *temporary* disappointment of rejection.

Creating a personal motto to live by

One afternoon in my audio production class, I asked the students if they have a personal creed, motto, or mantra by which they live. Hands shot up in the air. "*Try anything once!*" says one. "*Never let anyone tell you what you cannot do!*" says another. "*The only thing we have to fear is fear itself!*" says a student with passion. That afternoon I shared with them my own creed of "*no guts, no glory!*" I told them they should go for their dreams because they should not fear failure and don't want to regret in the future that they did not pursue their dreams. Every student in the classroom shared a piece of wisdom, except a student sitting in the back row, who sat with her head in her hands, avoiding eye contact.

At the very end of the semester, at the very end of the final class, the student who had said nothing in class on that earlier occasion stayed late to talk to me. "I'm graduating and this was my last class. I just wanted to let you know that because of you I decided to apply for my dream job in New York City. I wasn't going to, but you urged us to go for it, *no guts, no glory!* and so I applied, not expecting anything. I can't believe that I just got it and I start next week!"

There is value in having a creed, motto, or mantra by which you live. Something that can be used in times of stress, fear, and uncertainty. It can propel you forward. I have found that failure is not as bad as we fear it is, and so you have nothing to lose by doing your best and following your dreams. By doing so, you are pledging a commitment to personal excellence, to taking a journey where you will try, even if there is no safety net and no guarantee of success. No guts, no glory!

Final thoughts: *We walk on through the ring of fire.* How one professor considers the important lessons from a successful career in the radio industry

I am talking with my former mentor and distinguished professor, Dr. Tim Crook, and I am taken aback when he describes his own professional experiences. "I know what it's like to feel as though every iota of confidence has been driven out of me, like every molecule of confidence has gone, *to be crushed*, to be humiliated, to feel like rubbish" (personal communication, July 29, 2022). I am stunned to hear someone who has been so successful in their career talk like this.

"What actually happened was decades ago, but that was the kind of behavior you got from editors and management, and senior journalists. Absolutely appalling. I had to put up with people shouting and screaming at me and yelling and swearing." Working in the media in the UK of the 1970s and 1980s could be a mercilessly unforgiving environment, where the loudest voices dominated newsrooms and offices, and mistakes were punished severely. Crook remembers that feeling well. "When you're at your lowest and you feel at your most useless, there is the time to say, *Well, there's only one way up, and I'm going up, because you can't go down anymore!* So you just do it. And the other thing is that feeling doesn't go away, even from people like myself."

Over time you build resilience from your mistakes and from the lessons you learn. "What the professionals learn in all different fields is *this is it, this is the way it is, we walk on – through the ring of fire,*" says Crook.

Crook remembers how he assigned a story to a reporter who made a mistake. As the reporter's manager, he took full responsibility for the reporter's error. "I had to go to one of the most important news organizations in the country, one certainly respected in the world, and I had to stand up, while two editors just basically tore me apart, humiliated me, threatening, and warning. So I just had to grovel, apologize, say it will never happen again. But I took full responsibility."

Decades later, in the late 1990s, I met Professor Crook as a student, taking classes in his MA Radio courses at Goldsmiths College, London. By then he was an accomplished author, radio broadcaster, and of course, professor. "I know how *not* to communicate in a teaching environment or a leadership environment, or a mentoring environment or a professional environment. Because, you know, what I see is so awful and destructive. I could never do that to somebody else," explains Crook.

I tell him that I remember his teaching style was supportive and encouraging, that there was an essential *kindness* in the way he taught and interacted with the students. "Well, that's the essence, the raison d'etre, the *whole purpose*, the only way you can make the world a better place. All of the students you have or colleagues you have, you're not going to expect them to like you, or that you'll necessarily like them. But, if you turn the word *love* into *respect*, you have to respect them, and you have to also treat them all equally. And what's also very important, there has to be a capacity for *forgiveness*. You've got to have an open assumption that people can change and get better, because that's the only way the world will get better and be less horrible."

So, what advice would Professor Crook give to someone to help them find their voice when it comes to audio and radio production? "The biggest harm that can ever happen to you is the harm you do to yourself." He pauses and speaks warmly, "I know it's an odd thing to say, but take pleasure in getting things *wrong*, things not necessarily being good. Try not to give yourself too many pressures that then become destructive. Give yourself time to repair. It's like there are certain creatures that can regrow limbs. And so give yourself time to do that. The most important thing is, if it's what you really want to do, whatever other people are saying, however cruel they are, how competitive and deliberately destructive they are, *maintain belief in yourself and stay with it* ... and find people who are really good for you!"

Crook offers one last piece of advice: "You can learn the skills, you can work hard. But the extra factor is *confidence*. Confidence to be able to believe in yourself, to know when you've done something well, to know when it might not be quite right, and to be able to receive constructive feedback to make it better, and to learn from other people." Finding a mentor who can give you that feedback is crucial. You do not want to be alone on this journey.

But it's also been a journey for Crook too, and he surprises me when he talks of his own continued process of self-improvement. "The fact of the matter is, I haven't stopped learning. And I've decided to continue learning and continue working, and sometimes I forget things and I have to relearn them! And that's one of the joys and the wonders of life, actually. So, it's like the cliche, seeing your life going before you, I just see all these flashing scenes of studios and teaching rooms and students, through the ages. It's been one of the greatest privileges of my life to be at the beginning of their journeys."

At the end of the interview I understood more how Crook has developed such strong views on leadership and mentoring. I am deeply glad and honored he was my mentor giving me feedback. He changed my life (see Figure 10.2).

FIGURE 10.2 Professor Tim Crook (Photo: Marja Giejgo).

References

Almost half of job seekers lost confidence from receiving rejection letters. (2022, June 6). *Tends,* Joblist. https://www.joblist.com/trends/almost-half-of-job-seekers-lost-confidence-from-receiving-rejection-letters

Amitay, S., Moore, D. R., Molloy, K., & Halliday, L. F. (2015). Feedback valence affects auditory perceptual learning independently of feedback probability. *PLoS One, 10*(5), e0126412. 10.1371/journal.pone.0126412

Bandura, A. (1997). *Self-efficacy: The exercise of control.* W.H. Freeman.

CloudRadio. (2021, May 31). *How to make an air check as a radio host.* https://www.cloudrad.io/air-check

Fong, C. J., Schallert, D. L., Williams, K. M., Williamson, Z. H., Warner, J. R., Lin, S., & Kim, Y. W. (2018). When feedback signals failure but offers hope for improvement: A process model of constructive criticism. *Thinking Skills and Creativity, 30,* 42–53. 10.1016/j.tsc.2018.02.014

Hattie, J., & Timperley, H. (2007). The power of feedback. *Review of Educational Research, 77*(1), 81–112. 10.3102/003465430298487

Kudisch, J. (2017, March 17). Turned down for a job? You are now one rejection closer to success. *Los Angeles Times.* https://www.latimes.com/business/la-fi-career-coach-job-rejection-20170317-story.html

Lindsay, N. (2020, June 18). *Taking constructive criticism like a champ.* The Muse. https://www.themuse.com/advice/taking-constructive-criticism-like-a-champ

Lyons, M. (2022). *Job rejection doesn't have to sting.* Harvard Business Review. https://hbr.org/2022/10/job-rejection-doesnt-have-to-sting

Manson, M. (n.d.). *Screw finding your passion.* Retrieved July 2, 2023, from https://markmanson.net/screw-finding-your-passion

Olson, S. (2016, April 14). *Often overlooked, airchecking is essential to keeping public radio's audience.* Current. https://current.org/2016/04/often-overlooked-airchecking-is-essential-to-keeping-public-radios-audience/

Poulos, A., & Mahony, M. J. (2008). Effectiveness of feedback: The students' perspective. *Assessment & Evaluation in Higher Education, 33*(2), 143–154. 10.1080/02602930601127869

Weidinger, S. (2020, July 7). What are the benefits of having a workplace mentor? *The Washington Post.* https://jobs.washingtonpost.com/article/what-are-the-benefits-of-having-a-workplace-mentor-/

OUTRO

R.E.A.L. audio: A manifesto for creating compelling content

I hope in these pages you have caught something of my enthusiasm for audio and radio and you have been inspired. Pitchfork.com once wrote this about me, "Quicke exudes an adolescent excitement. To him, more than anything, college radio's most lasting influence is that it can still change someone's life." (Lozano, 2017). I believe that's true for creating all forms of audio, not just radio. I long for you to be motivated to continue the adventure of finding your voice in your experiences beyond this book. And, so importantly, for you to experience some of the joy that I have seen on the faces of students I have taught. In fact, I want to come right up to date and bookend this final chapter with a story that has just happened this past semester.

January 2023

The door opened to darkness. Stale air immediately hit me. Switching the light on I saw a small classroom, seating perhaps 20 students at most, with folded metal chairs stacked in the corner. A layer of dust covered everything. It had been years since this room had been used. Abandoned when a previous professor had left the university, it had remained locked ever since. At the furthest end of the building, utterly neglected, I now entered it with mixed emotions. Sadness because it seemed uncared for, yet also with a sense of hope. "What do you think?" said my colleague Rob Meyer. I paused, taking it all in. Yes, I saw an empty space that was once filled with activity, but I also imagined it coming back to life. "This will do!" I replied.

Over the next few days I became convinced that this abandoned classroom could be a great space for the students, and particularly for podcasting

DOI: 10.4324/9781003263739-16

production. But I would need the support of my department to use the room for that purpose. In addition, we required new equipment. At that time we were running a budget deficit, so extra money was scarce. Though I was excited about the possibilities, I was also sober about the practicalities of bringing this classroom back to life. At my university department meeting, I shared that it could be a great space for our new podcasting club, and that the students could feel at home in a space created just for podcasting production. My colleagues agreed. The vote was unanimous – we could use the classroom! But going forward, it was the students who made all the difference. They were to unlock the room and breathe life into it.

Later that week I went with a student, Vincent Civetta, and showed him the space. Vincent would be our inaugural podcasting club president. Even in its dilapidated state, he was excited. "Yes, this is great! We can record our podcasts here!" Vincent, along with his fellow student Jonny Buffa, already had a podcast up and running, called the "One Shot Movie Podcast." We all sensed that this was an ideal space to record it and where we could hold our weekly podcasting club meetings. It could serve as our headquarters. Excitement was palpable, but we needed new equipment in there or the space would be useless.

I talked with the department chair, who was positive about the project yet honest about the unlikelihood of receiving help, since this unexpected project was not in the budget. The department was technically out of money for the year. Then she sent an email telling me I would have to wait for seven months, until the new academic year. This was devastating news. I pleaded with her that I did not want the momentum and the students, now meeting weekly in a conference room, to evaporate. I really made the strongest case I could. Then, a few hours later, I received an email that *some adjustments were made* and we now had the money and to GO AHEAD and place the order for the equipment!

The end

As we come to the end of the book, let's now see how far you've come. Do you remember the self-assessment exercise you did at the beginning of the book? Now you have been on this journey of self-discovery and development, how do you view your development in the various areas of interest that you first considered in Chapter 1?

Let's now reassess your progress in exploring and developing each of these areas on a scale of 1 to 10, where 1 means you feel you have made the *least* progress, and 10 means you have made the *most*. Again, it's important that you assess each area individually, not thinking of the whole when you write your number on the line for each area. Have you:

Become a more effective communicator	Developed self-confidence	Recognized what makes me unique	Accepted myself as I am, including imperfections	Identified my unique perspectives, values, and beliefs
___	___	___	___	___
Developed my speaking voice	Identified my strengths and weaknesses as a communicator	Improved as a storyteller	Become an effective interviewer	Learned editing skills
___	___	___	___	___
Learned audio production skills	Created content for radio	Created content for podcasts	Learned from other people's audio experiences	Decided my future path
___	___	___	___	___

After you have completed this exercise, look at the numbers you have written for each area. Again, circle the top three or four highest numbers. You have now self-identified your strongest areas of progress, and you should be proud of that achievement! Also, circle the bottom three or four numbers. For these lower scores you have identified areas that you know you need to continue to work on, and that's why this is a journey that goes well beyond this book.

Now let's compare your results from this assessment to your starting assessment from Chapter 1. Did you develop the *most* in areas where you had the strongest interest? Or are you surprised that you made significant progress in areas that you initially had little interest in? If you look at both self-assessments, is there evidence to suggest that you have surprised yourself with how you have progressed? Either way, you must remember that finding your voice is an ongoing process that takes time and self-belief for your voice to develop and emerge as an authentic expression of who you are.

An important realization

As we conclude this book, let's reflect on the fact that in finding your voice in audio and radio production, it was never "lost" to begin with. You have never been speechless. From your first infant cries, you continue to verbally communicate thoughts and feelings. But hopefully this book has enabled you to take the *internal* voice, the one inside your head, that freely speaks thoughts and opinions without hesitation, and give it a more effective *external* form.

You have worked to discover your outside voice and develop confidence to create material for recording and to be heard by others. Beginning with yourself as an audience of one, this journey through *discoverer, developer, deliverer,* and *decoder* should lead you to fresh discoveries of who you are as well as how you may impact others.

This very act of creating content involves some degree of bravery. You bring to life ideas and stories that are truly yours. When you discover how best to express these thoughts, lean into the deliciousness of being free to explore and express what you feel and know. As I encouraged in the early chapters, you should do this with no audience pressure. Just for yourself, allowing for messy imperfection, as well as some surprising content which connects powerfully and personally. Beware of straining to reach perfection. Be yourself. Part of my motive in writing this book emerged from seeing how much pressure some students put on themselves.

Rather, it is my hope that you finish this book with a stronger sense of who you are, and that you feel more confident in what you have to say. It's precisely the letting go of those self-imposed standards of perfection that enables authenticity. Undeterred by what life throws at you, being willing to rise to challenges, and being true to yourself – that's the bravery of creating audio.

Throughout I have used the initials R.E.A.L. to describe the outcome of truly finding your voice. It is time to revisit each initial. I enjoy telling stories, so you will read several that underline R.E.A.L. qualities.

You'll create audio that is relatable

On Thursday, February 24, 2022, Russian tanks rolled into Ukraine. The world watched in shock and horror as the people of Ukraine scrambled to adjust to the new reality that war was upon them.

From my safe position in the United States, I immediately wondered how the students in Ukraine, and particularly those involved with their campus radio stations, were coping with this horrific event. I reached out to two stations in Ukraine that I could find online and got a response almost immediately. One station emailed me: *"The only thing left for us is to remain calm and not to panic, to pray to God, to believe in the army that protects us, to protect our health and life."* I asked if I could send them messages of support from other student radio stations around the world. The next day they responded: *"We will be happy to share your voice message with words of support ... Students of our university will be able to hear it there. In this difficult time, we really need to know that we are not alone and we have support. We hope that your words will calm people's hearts."*

I sent an email to hundreds of student radio stations around the world. Within 24 hours I had messages from Italy, Australia, England, Sweden, France, Mexico, USA, and many more countries. I edited these into a single link and sent it to the two stations in Ukraine. You can imagine their response: *"Thank you on behalf of all Ukrainian students. We have already posted this link. We want all our students to hear it. We would like to play this audio on our radio. We send the audio to all UA universities."* What happened next was remarkable.

The Ukrainian students, hearing the voices of student radio stations around the world saying "we are with you, we will never forget you," decided to record their own message. Despite the closure of the universities, and with many students in bomb shelters, they managed to record messages on their cell phones. Roman Zajac, the head of STUD Radio, was my link. When he received these different messages he asked me to produce a single audio piece bringing them together. When I listened to these clips I was speechless.

Here were students in Ukraine, speaking in English, so we could understand them. Their messages were emotional gut punches: *"My brave free country is dying, and I ask you please … don't be silent … we need your help!"* The reaction in my classes when I played the audio, as US students *their same age* heard their counterparts in Ukraine, was highly charged. When my students heard firsthand about the devastation around the Ukrainian students and their honest fear in the face of war with the death toll rising among them, some students were in tears. All were in shock. How could this happen in 2022? One student said to the class, "It's hard to believe that they were just getting on with their lives, in classes at university, *like we are right now*, when all that has suddenly changed." They were relating it to themselves, processing feelings, and asking how it would be for them if suddenly everything changed, with their university suspended indefinitely, leaving them huddled in bomb shelters. How would they respond to living with such fear, with bombs falling, and nothing secure for the future? How those voices touched them. How real the war seemed.

That audio sent from Ukraine was some of the most powerful audio I've heard students record. I was able to share it with stations around the world. Similarly moved, they played it on air to show their support.

This is a powerful, recent example of *relatable* audio or radio. As soon as an audience heard its content they couldn't help but relate to the awful situation and imagine what it would be like to be in a warzone like that. They were *in* the story. Every comment from Ukraine reinforced the need to feel the anguish and heed the plea. This was unusually powerful because the dire circumstances gave each voice impact.

Sometimes it takes effort to ensure such an audience response when the topic is less graphic, when it is harder for a listener to relate and feel they are in the story. Whenever we create relatable audio, we must always consider the place of the audience/listener. Where is their place in your story? Are you leaving room for the listener to absorb, reflect, and *feel* what you are communicating? Are you communicating clearly and effectively, so that you are ensuring maximum understanding from the listener? In your work, a listener will seek to find themself.

In your stories, they will look for a similarity to their own. In your voice, they will look for you to say what they would also like to say.

You'll create audio that is engaging

Creating *relatable* audio seeks to take audiences into identifying with the speakers and their situation, like the US students identified with the Ukrainian students in their tragic circumstances. When creating *engaging* audio the emphasis lies more with focusing on the audience's human experiences, which draws them into what they hear. From birth to death, life passes through phases of joy and tragedy and many experiences in between. Throughout, there's a human search to find meaning by processing these life events. *Engaging* audio deals with these life events by providing content that helps listeners on their journey of living and increased understanding. Providing such content is a valuable gift.

In November 2022, my father-in-law died. He suffered a bad fall at home and never recovered and slipped into the next life with his family beside him in the hospital. At his funeral, I played some audio in my eulogy of him. The last time I saw him earlier that year, I decided to interview him about his life. I like to interview members of my family, and you will remember one of my exercises encouraged you to do likewise. I had never interviewed him before, but I felt this might be significant. As I played his words back to those gathered in the church, I realized this was probably the only recorded audio we had of his voice. I could visibly see the emotional impact of hearing him talk about what he had learned in life. Later, several people told me it was a gift to hear his voice and laugh with him *one last time*. No doubt, that was the most engaging audio I have ever played to an audience.

Engaging audio creates content that truly connects with human experience. When an audience finds your content engaging they will keep listening, and will come back as you develop a reputation for consistently delivering engaging content. This type of content has value and substance. It speaks to their life condition. Engaging audio connects at a deeper level and can stay in the memory. Further, it can grow relationships with audiences that encourage participation such as joining your website, following you on social media, and attending your events.

You'll create audio that is authentic

Generally, you can detect when someone is being authentic or fake and insincere. It is instinctual. The reason why the *discoverer* stage has such importance is that it lays the foundation for self-discovery. Rather than dashing ahead it slows you down with an opportunity for you to discover who you are, which in turn leads to you figuring out what it is you want to say. This is the basis for genuine *authenticity*. Knowing who you truly are is a character issue. Staying true to your character builds personal integrity. And your integrity shows in the way you choose and voice your content.

Remember Francisco Suarez's podcast, *From Suarez's Basement,* in Chapter 6? Francisco believes that substantive content comes from being authentic. "With my students, I say, authenticity comes with maturity and comes when you reach a point in your life where you feel so secure of who you are and what you want, and what is the mark that you want to leave in this world, that you become very authentic to yourself and to others, right?" Authenticity comes from self-discovery. When you have a sense of who you are, and what you want to say, you are a powerful and persuasive communicator.

In this book, I've stressed the importance of you being *you* on air and in your audio content, so that what the audience hears is authentic and to be trusted. Indeed, gaining credibility for truthful communication so strengthens audience trust, that you may even become an influencer!

You'll create satisfying audio that is liberating

Creating radio that is *liberating* is the culmination of R.E.A.L. audio. Confidence builds through exploring what it means to deliver relatable, en-gaging, and authentic audio. This process empowers you to express yourself freely and without fear. Audiences know when you are in that zone of con-fidence, for it lifts their spirits and builds their confidence. It liberates both speaker and listener.

What is truly liberating about audio is what is happening with podcasting right now. Literally everyone can have their voice out there. People are connecting all over the globe about every topic under the sun. We have access to every expert in every field whenever we want just by searching our podcast app. If you want to use your voice, it's never been more achie-vable. By the liberating power of people using their voices, people are coming together to spark new ideas, to empower change, to create com-munities. There's never been a more exciting time to create audio. That is liberating.

I heard a fun story that also illustrates this aspect. In 2015, I founded the annual Vinylthon event, which invites radio stations to spin up to 48 hours of vinyl records to help raise money for student scholarships. Continuous play for 24 hours is a tough call, especially for small radio stations. Those stations that manage to complete the whole 24 hours win a Golden Slipmat Award – a turntable slipmat that's gold in color.

Dr. Tim Craig, a professor at Warner University in Florida, USA, is also advisor to RadioWarner, the campus radio station. He tells the story,

"We typically have a small staff at RadioWarner, but we try to make a push for events like Vinylthon. I met with the students to go over the schedule, and it just didn't look like we'd go for the whole 24 hours. I said to the group, 'I really wanted to get that Golden Slipmat.' That's when Mark Holmes, one of the seniors, looked straight at me and said, 'Oh, we'll get that slipmat, Dr. Craig. *Trust me.*'" When the day of the Vinylthon event came around, Mark was prepared to do what it took. "Mark was (and is) one of those workers who is consistent. You can count on him to get it done and on time, which, in a lot of cases, is more than half the battle." Craig describes Mark as someone with a "smooth, deep voice that is kind of quiet, but also very calm and confident."

So RadioWarner started their 24 hours and Mark opened his show from 3:00 am to 7:00 am after Dr. Craig did the first three hours. Craig remembers what happened next. "Mark took a break during the middle of the day, and then went on 15 *more* hours throughout the day – finishing at midnight!" Something inside Mark kicked in – the excitement of the moment inspired him to broadcast *hour after hour*. He found his voice and felt as if he was on an important mission!

Mark ended up doing over 18 hours of vinyl-only radio broadcasting in a single day. He won the Golden Slipmat Award for the radio station! "He was so excited to get that Golden Slipmat for the station. I think it was a highlight of his college career – and it's definitely a great memory for me," says Craig. Mark showed such determination to get to the finish line in a spirit of liberation, and the listening audience shared in his excitement and the importance of the moment.

You are a powerful, *energized* communicator when you have found your voice, and use it with freedom and energy. Whenever you are empowered to share, you invite the audience to be empowered with you. You can achieve things you didn't think were possible. Whenever you use your voice to speak into existence words of passion, truth, and reality, you are at your most persuasive.

March 2023

The new podcasting equipment has arrived and is being installed. A Rode Procaster II mixer and console, four microphones and mic arms, cabling, and headphones, with other bits and pieces. Rob Meyer has also found a huge, round table that can fit four people. It's perfect! We also have a name for our podcasting club. I was watching that classic 1989 Robin Williams film *Dead Poets Society* and was inspired when Williams's character, the larger-than-life teacher Mr. Keating, exclaims to his students, "You must strive to find your own voice. Because the longer you wait to begin, the less likely you are to find it at all!" That's it! We shall call our club The Dead Podcasters Society! I share the idea with the students, and they love the name.

Several weeks pass. We are in the middle of a Dead Podcasters Society meeting, in our new podcasting studio. I look around and take note. Twenty students fill the room discussing their podcast ideas. One will be about sports, another about board games and role playing, another about movies. Students are sharing advice and feedback. They are helping each other find their voice, as they seek to create and explore their ideas. I am moved by how supportive they are toward each other. Just as the classroom they sit in, once empty of purpose, now has new life, so they bring energy and enthusiasm in abundance. I watch them grow in confidence as they find their voices. Actually, you can hear their loud, excited voices right down the long corridor. At one point I leave the room and let the students continue working together. As I walk to the end of the corridor two students pass by, stop to listen, and ask me, "What's going on down there?" I smile and reply, "Some students are creating podcasts and you are welcome to join them." I do not know how the room will fit two more students in there, but it looks like we are going to need a bigger room. It's taking off.

What are your goals? Where do you want to go?

The biggest questions students face as they learn new skills are about their future. Students are often asked to imagine their future. *What do you see yourself doing with your life? Where will you be in ten years' time?* Only a minority who read this book will have set their hearts on professional audio, radio, or podcasting. They can picture the future more easily. But for others reading this book, it may be premature to ask where it might lead you.

Let me stress that even if this is the only book you ever read on audio production, and the only time in your life you create audio content, there are immense life lessons to be learned that can make a profound difference to your future. Particularly, developing confidence to express yourself means you possess a communication skill that opens doors for what lies ahead. The process of finding your spoken voice will never be a wasted effort. Learning how to pronounce, articulate, and accentuate a written script, for instance, are skills that you can carry for the rest of your life. They can make a huge difference to any career trajectory. Being an effective communicator is a fundamental prerequisite for many jobs and activities in life. Knowing that you have worked on your voice with a degree of intentionality gives a significant communication advantage over your colleagues who haven't.

You never know what might happen in the future. So much depends on your open-mindedness to change, and your willingness to develop a strong sense of self-identity and personality. It requires being comfortable to also experience your share of failure, setbacks, and frustrations that form an inevitable part of the process of learning and improving. The journey ahead promises so much adventure for those who dare to be changed. What are your goals? Where do you want to go? *What will you do with your voice once you have found it?*

In my experience, the final exercise in this book is either straightforward for someone, or they find themselves at a standstill. For those who know what they want to do in the future, this exercise is simply an invitation to say out loud what they hope will come to pass. But for others who genuinely have no idea of where they want to go and what they want to do and be, this is more challenging. Saying your aims and goals out loud does not commit you to them. Changing plans and goals is normal. Look at this exercise as a snapshot of where you are today, and what your current thinking is about your future. Be heartened and take heed of the words of American journalist George Matthew Adams (1878–1962), "Your success is not final – nor is your failure" (O'Toole, 2023).

The Last Exercise: Where I'm going

For this last audio exercise, you know the drill. Find a private place and keep a recording of how you answer these questions. Answer the questions honestly.

1 **Do you have a goal of where and what you want to be in life?**

2 **What will you probably need to do to reach that goal?**

3 **What is your definition of being successful?**

4 **What persons do you aspire to be like?**

5 **Where do you see yourself in ten years' time?**

The final question is a sharpening of the first and deliberately focuses on the near future while recognizing how much will change. As you play back the recording, take advantage of being an audience of one to these confidential hopes and plans. You never know, you may return to this recording a few years from now and be surprised by what you hear.

The beginning

You now approach the end of this book, but not the end of your journey. It's really a beginning. The key question is not "Did you find your voice?" but "Are you finding your voice?" Finding your voice rarely happens in a singular moment, although epiphanies do happen. After all, I have been arguing that finding your voice is also discovering more about yourself, about *who you are*. This is a path you can take for a lifetime, leading through continuous discovery and development. And that's true of the journey with audio, too. It involves a lifetime of learning through practice.

I summarized the audio journey by four stages: *discoverer, developer, deliverer,* and *decoder*. Recently a student asked me whether these stages can be applied to more than just creating audio and radio content, and I said they probably can. The famous author Bernard Malamud wrote in *The Natural*, "We have two lives ... the life we learn with and the life we live after that" (Malamud, 1952, p. 152). What we learn as a *discoverer* impacts what we will *develop* and *deliver* because of it. I guess these stages may apply to many creative and professional endeavors.

So, whatever lies ahead, I hope you will be better prepared because this journey has helped you find your voice. In the last chapter, you met Dr. Tim Crook, whose influence as a mentor shaped so much of my own career. As a renowned radio presenter, producer, and professor, I asked him whether he could identify the moment when it *starts* to come together for students. What does that look like? This was his reply:

> A key moment is when students begin to *enjoy* what they are doing more than they feel stressed and overwhelmed by the demands of the learning journey. They are flying in their thinking, writing, speaking, and doing in terms of sound editing and broadcasting. They correct themselves, they motivate themselves, and they are not only finding their own voice and identity but also their audiences. (T. Crook, personal communication, July 29, 2022)

Time seems to stand still when you enjoy what you are doing. In moments like these, you really are "flying" as Professor Crook describes. You are in the creative zone. Impediments to creativity are few and productivity is at a high. When inspiration truly strikes, you accomplish so much more in a shorter time. As you discover more of your own voice and become more confident, then the likelihood of such flying moments become increasingly possible.

Of course, along the way there will be many times of plodding through the wilderness. Mistakes and setbacks can blot out the high moments. Yet, around the corner fresh inspiration can strike again, giving freedom to express yourself confidently. It is a journey of good and bad times. Never forget though, that your voice is as valid as everybody else's. So, now that you have started the journey to *find* your voice, get out there and *share it!*

FIGURE O.1 Myself with students in the Dead Podcasters Society 2023 (Photo: Maura Perez-Hernandez).

References

Lozano, K. (2017, February 8). *Does college Radio even matter anymore?* Pitchfork. https://pitchfork.com/features/article/10018-does-college-radio-even-matter-anymore/

Malamud, B. (1952). *The natural.* Farrar, Straus and Giroux.

O'Toole, G. (2023, July 2). *Success is never final and failure never fatal. It's courage that counts.* Quote Investigator. https://quoteinvestigator.com/2013/09/03/success-final/#note-7156-6

INDEX

Note: Page numbers in *italics* refer to figures

Printed in the United States
by Baker & Taylor Publisher Services